Personal Construct Theory
in Educational Psychology
A Practitioner's View

Personal Construct Theory in Educational Psychology
A Practitioner's View

TOM RAVENETTE PhD FBPsS
Chartered Psychologist

Whurr Publishers Ltd
London

© 1999 Whurr Publishers Ltd
Whurr Publishers Ltd
19b Compton Terrace, London N1 2UN, England

Reprinted 2000, 2001, 2002 and 2006

British Library Cataloguing in Publication Data
A catalogue record for this book is available from the British Library.

ISBN-10: 1 86156 121 0 p/b
ISBN-13: 978 1 86156 121 3 p/b

Printed and bound in the UK by
Athenæum Press Ltd, Gateshead, Tyne & Wear

Contents

Chapter 17   233

Transcending the obvious and illuminating the ordinary:
personal construct psychology and consultation in the practice
of educational psychology (1993)

Chapter 18   253

What would happen if? Personal construct psychology and
psychological intervention (1996)

About the author

Born in Portsmouth in 1924, Tom Ravenette attended Woodhouse Grove School, a secondary boarding school, in Yorkshire. His higher education (University College London and Westminster Training College) was interrupted by four years' service in the Royal Air Force. After graduating in English, Geography and Pure Mathematics in 1950, he taught full time for seven years while gaining an honours degree in psychology at Birkbeck College, London in 1955. He was seconded to the Maudsley Hospital for the post graduate diploma in abnormal psychology and then became an educational psychologist in West Ham, later the London Borough of Newham. He gained a part-time PhD at Birkbeck in 1964, published *Dimensions of Reading Difficulty* in 1968, retiring from Newham as principal educational psychologist in 1988. He continues to practise, lecture, hold workshops and write for his profession and personal construct psychologists, his first selection of collected papers having been published by EPCA Publications in 1997.

Acknowledgements

I am indebted to Academic Press for permission to reprint the chapter 'Personal construct theory: an approach to the psychological investigation of children and young people' from Bannister (1977); to *AEP Journal* for permission to republish 'Everyone his own scientist, or behaviour is an experiment' (1968); 'Psychologists, teachers and children: how many ways to understand?' (1972); 'Specific developmental dyslexia: answer to Critchley' (1972); 'Specific reading difficulties: appearance and reality' (1979); and 'The recycling of maladjustment (1984); to the European Personal Construct Association's EPCA Newsletter for 'Triadic elicitation: academic exercise or key to experiencing? A mini-paper' (1993) and 'An answer to a "lifer's" three questions' (1997); to the Association for Therapeutic Education (ATE) for 'Motivation, emotional blocking, and reading failure: a unifying point of view' (1974); to *Education and Child Psychology* for 'What would happen if? Personal construct psychology and psychological intervention' (1996); to EPCA Publications for five papers published for the first time in *Tom Ravenette: Selected Papers* (1997); to Krieger, Florida for the chapter 'Transcending the obvious and illuminating the ordinary' from Leitner and Dunnett (1993); to John Wiley for permission to reprint passages from Maher (1969); and to Routledge, London, for the chapter 'Personal construct psychology in the practice of an educational psychologist' from Dunnett (1988) and a number of small quotations from Kelly (1991), *The Psychology of Personal Constructs.*

Preface

This edition of my selected papers could not have been brought about without the existence of a first (*Tom Ravenette: Selected Papers*, EPCA Publications, 1997) and I take this opportunity of acknowledging my debt to those who achieved that.

This new edition retains much of what appeared in the earlier but includes six more chapters, three from the more distant past and three from the more recent present. Looking back reflectingly on the new list of contents, arranged as they are in chronological sequence, led me to recognize the outline of what might be thought of as a professional quasi-autobiography. Each individual chapter inevitably contains a summing-up of thought and action until the point when it was written and, therefore, constitutes something of a developmental stage.

The first and last chapters, however, do not quite fit into that pattern. The first was a public statement to members of my profession of my allegiance to personal construct theory (PCT), a theory that, at that time, was probably unknown to the majority of them, as a basis for my practice as an educational psychologist. In that sense it could be described as a 'coming out'. Moreover its final paragraph points to the possibility of papers yet unwritten and hence it seemed fitting to call this chapter a prologue. The final chapter, by contrast, together with one or two those preceding it, signals my departure from the education field, and the nature of its contents points to wider areas of concern, the dimensions of which are not yet fully known. Hence it feels appropriate to call it an epilogue.

A collection of papers such as this is likely to be read as a disconnected set of accounts or stories. Yet the fact that they are written by a sole author suggests that there will be underlying themes. Over and above the dimension of time I sense three separate dimensions against which the chapters might be plotted. The first of these is 'context', the second is 'concerns' and the third, for want of a more appropriate word, I call 'awakenings'. I shall elaborate these in turn and hope that they will enable readers to construct some sense of that reality of which the book is a reflection.

'Context' might seem to be rather a strange notion for defining a dimension. Yet everything that happens takes place within a context and frequently owes much of its meaning to that context. This thought applies to each chapter in this book, especially as most of them were responses to specific invitations. I could not know how familiar the audience, or readership, would be with PCT, thus there is a degree of repetitiveness in my presentation of the theory. I might add that at various times my audience/readership were teachers, either specialists at conferences or on advanced courses, or psychologists, probably with minimum knowledge of PCT, or social workers, field or residential. Since my various presentations occurred over time, each would successively reflect something of my own reconstruction of the theory at that time together with a sense of its potential relevance, both for my audience and for myself. In this sense, each communication of the theory would bear a commonly accepted understanding of its meaning modulated by my own inevitably individual interpretations and I would like to feel this that would be recognized on reading the separate chapters. I shall refer to the theme of 'commonality' and 'individuality' again later.

In consequence of my awareness of the importance of this 'context' dimension, I have preceded each chapter with a short paragraph giving some indication of its context and the circumstances under which it was written.

Having suggested 'concerns' as my second dimension I find myself in something of a difficulty in elaborating the idea. This is because although some of titles reflect their 'concerns' others do not. They rely for their expression on the texts themselves. I have developed the idea of a 'concern' in Chapter 3, arguing that it is an issue of current importance that engages our thoughts, feelings and actions and that is central to our 'sense of professional self' – i.e. it is 'non-trivial'. Clearly there are many issues that, for me, might fit that description but I have chosen just three as especially germane to this discussion.

'Reading difficulties' and 'disturbing behaviour' might be said to be thorns in teachers' sides but they are the bread and butter of an educational psychologist's work. Not surprisingly, therefore, these two issues jointly form one of my early concerns. They appear specifically in Chapters 1, 2, 3, 6 and 10, and in these chapters I have tried to illuminate them within a broadly PCT orientation. The effectiveness of such a stance is illustrated by case material throughout the chapters of the book.

A second major 'concern' has been the effective interviewing of children. By effective I refer to the possibility of promoting change, over and above any aim of 'assessment'. This is in contrast to traditional methods of assessment, which are normative and tend, perhaps unwittingly, to treat the child metaphorically as an object to be weighed and measured. In contrast a PCT approach is very much concerned with how children make sense of themselves and their circumstances. In such an investigation a child has the chance of developing his or her self-awareness. This frequently reveals important and unresolved aspects of their own dilemmas – a matter to which I shall return later.

The various chapters illustrate my own changes over time in creating more varied forms of interviewing: verbal questioning, projective techniques for eliciting responses, use of drawings both free and structured, and mutual storytelling, all in the direction of interviewing more effectively.

My third 'concern' is the theory and practice of PCT itself. It did not take long to recognize that it was not possible to go straight from Kelly's original two volumes into a practice in schools and child guidance clinics. He did not describe the development of a person's construct system from infancy upward, nor give great enough weight to the contribution of significant adults in such a development. It was therefore necessary gradually to recreate and extend the theory in order to take that into account. (Chapter 4 provides a powerful critique of PCT.) Moreover the immediacy of response that schools expected in no way allowed the time for investigation in the style which the clinical application of the theory prescribed. There is an interesting paradox here in that Kelly's own earlier experience lay in providing a travelling school psychological service yet his subsequent formal exposition was minimally illuminating for the practice I was actually creating. By contrast his subsequent occasional papers were a constant inspiration in sustaining the attempt to turn his broad orientation into an effective practice. The various chapters form a sequence that haltingly depicts my gradual development in this task.

I now come to my third dimension. I contrast 'awakenings' with 'learnings' although the latter may sometimes fit that category. As I see it, 'learning' is the addition of skills or concepts whereas 'awakenings' means seeing things in a radically different way, in some different dimension. Awakenings give different meanings and different implications from those to which one was accustomed. And yet, paradoxically, one might in reality be awakening for the first time to what was already there.

The first of these was the simple fact that children did not refer themselves to a psychologist. Since referral by a teacher was not in any way an everyday occurrence it was pertinent to ask in what way this child was problematic to the teacher, whether or not the child had a problem. We might rephrase the issue in the following way: the behaviour of a child, which is problematic for the teacher, and the teacher's referral of that child, may each be the resolution, whether or not adequate, of underlying issues on both their parts.

This 'awakening' inevitably led to a different way of understanding, and dealing with, referrals from schools. Interviewing became a matter not just of investigating the reality of the 'problem' as presented by the referrer but also investigating the underlying sense a child made of himself or herself and their circumstances. Perhaps there were more profound issues that needed resolution. Equally, in a gentle way, the teacher was also encouraged to explore his or her ways of making sense of things. Perhaps the fact that the child did not refer himself or herself was so obvious that the importance of the implications was not recognized. Many of the chapters bear witness to the fruits of this 'awakening'.

A second 'awakening' was to the inadequacy, if not inappropriateness, of the 'diagnosis/treatment' model as the paradigm for all intervention. I call this an 'awakening' although it was, in a sense, a progressive 'becoming aware'. This became more and more obvious if we replaced 'there is something wrong with the child' with the more general 'the child has problems' and 'treatment' with 'promotion of change'.

Nonetheless the 'awakening' was certainly liberating in relation to practice. I had had the view, perhaps incorrectly, that 'proper' practice involved 'assessment', i.e. gathering all the facts, then deducing from the evidence the cause and prescribing a course of action to put things right. This is a process that puts 'assessment' in one box and 'therapeutic' action in another. Perhaps it was not expected that a psychologist should do anything different and that it was up to the teacher to take remedial action. But in relation to children and their referrers the matters were more complex. Part of the difficulty arose from the fact that if we did not take it as axiomatic that the ostensible problem was the 'real' issue, we were left not knowing what the problem was. In the course of an interview, however, as I wrote earlier, we may then uncover some important unresolved issue underlying the ostensible problem, and then find that its very discovery was also its resolution. Moreover the nature of the teacher involvement, by sharing a new understanding of the child, and by their own self-discoveries (as pointed to in the previous paragraph), was an essential part of the process. This is demonstrated in many of the chapters. There is much more that might be said around this matter but increasingly it was my experience that the 'one-off' interview could be very effective, never mind the orthodoxies of 'proper' practice. As I discovered, any intervention may sow the seeds of change. But perhaps that is in the nature of life and it is a task of the psychologist to make that intervention more effective.

A third 'awakening' was in connection with language. I had been especially interested in Basil Bernstein's work on 'elaborated' and 'restricted' codes and social class (Ravenette, 1964b) because of the dangers in a working class community of taking agreement on meaning for granted. This became even more important in that, within PCT, the elicitation of personal meanings was essential to the successful intervention enterprise. Yet at the same time there must be some commonality of meaning. It eventually dawned on me that although language is the medium for communicating meaning, its dual nature was usually ignored. In ordinary transactions this is not particularly important but in problem-centred contexts it certainly is. It was a happy invention to invoke the name of the Roman god Janus to signal the fact that at one and the same time a person's language points inwards to his or her personal meanings and outwards to the commonality or public nature of meaning. It is a matter of some satisfaction that this distinction relates also to two contrasting corollaries, 'commonality' and 'individuality' in the formal theory and that language is the medium that unites them. The acceptance of this reality not only helps reduce problems of misunderstandings but is also a powerful aid in interviewing. It can lead to the exploration of the unexpressed thoughts and feelings that may so easily be covered by a commonality that is taken for granted. Although the exploration of language had been central to my practice for many years, as many of the papers will demonstrate, it was only after I retired that I formulated it in this way (Chapter 17).

The presentation of these dimensions in a very conscious way is a verbalization of matters that, in their origins, were probably held at a low level of awareness. They might have been inferred from my actions rather than my words. It is in retrospect that they take on shape and form. At the risk of appearing didactic I suspect that the process is the same as for the eliciting of profound 'core constructs'. They too only take on this verbalized shape and form when asked for, or on reflection. The exercise is beneficial for a client as indeed it has also been for this writer and I hope it will form a framework for a 'constructive' awareness of the contents of the book.

In my opening sentence I referred to the first edition of this book and I would like here to express my indebtedness to Ingrid Lunt, Rob van Meeuwen and Anna Harskamp who were its original inspiration and compilers, and to Gwyneth Daniel who successfully brought the enterprise to fruition.

In connection with this second edition again I express my indebtedness to Gwyneth Daniel without whose monumental endeavours the enterprise would have been stillborn. I am delighted to take this opportunity of publicly expressing my thanks.

Tom Ravenette
Epsom, 1998

Prologue
Everyone his own scientist, or behaviour is an experiment (1968)

This paper had its origin on the London Underground. I was discussing my experimenting with a personal construct theory (PCT) approach to my work with the editor of the Newsletter of the Association of Educational Psychologists *and he suggested that I write about it in the* Newsletter. *This, the paper, therefore, became my first venture in communicating in print about PCT. In retrospect, I saw that its final paragraph proved prophetic in pointing to my own future development and hence to the creation of this book. In that sense I call this first contribution a prologue.*

Reading through papers and articles in the learned journals, and even in our own newsletter, one comes away with the impression that we, as psychologists, know what we are doing and why we are doing it. We seem to have reliable information about many of the problems with which we are confronted, and we seem to show a self-assurance that must, at times, be rather daunting to others. By contrast, when psychologists speak to each other about their work, an opposite impression is frequently conveyed, especially when the discussion turns on the subject of the individual child who is presented as in need of help. In this situation we often lack the assurance of knowing what we are doing and why. We sometimes look half begrudgingly at the various schools of psychotherapy, Lowenfeldian, Freudian, Kleinian or what you will, and we admire the ease with which therapists toss around the jargon of treatment and scatter interpretations so liberally that we either boggle at them or dismiss them with a derisive laugh. Nonetheless, they have a doctrine in which they can believe and which they can put into practice. At other times we may look in the direction of the behaviour therapists. They have the backing of 'solid' learning theory based on 'proper experimentation', which is 'rigidly controlled' and all the rest of it. It is true that the starting points for these theories were usually starved animals, either rats or pigeons, but we have to agree that techniques based on learning theory seem to pay off, especially when applied to adults and, not infrequently, when applied to children. On the other hand, we do not have the time and resources to apply behaviour therapy in the way that clinical psychologists in hospitals do, and we may not be entirely convinced either by the theory or by the moral implications of behaviour therapy.

I think that the unease that I have been describing is common to all of us when we are confronted with the real child who, to somebody, perhaps also to himself, presents a problem for which help is needed. This unease presents a problem to us as our own identity depends very much on what we feel able to do. We may attempt to escape by withdrawing from the clinic, but that is of no value because the problem comes up again in the school. We may retire into 'Binet bashing' but this is merely to deny the problem. We may apply projective tests on ourselves by giving projective tests to the children whom we see, but to what extent are we ever convinced that these tell us anything of practical value? We may give up being psychologists and move into other spheres where money and conditions are better.

It is unfortunate that we are never trained to do the job that presents itself. Perhaps we never could in any case. But the problem is there and we have to make some attempt to find a way round it.

It may be that we may find some resolution to this problem in the writings of George Kelly, who died in March of this year. Kelly, in his theory of personal constructs, argues that we are all of us basically scientists. We need not be good ones, and in fact we seldom are.

Children are also scientists, a fact that is recognized in the modern developments in the teaching of mathematics and science, but seldom in books on child development (Piaget excepted). Unfortunately 'science' has come to be considered a special thing in itself, something that is apart from our everyday lives, something that requires special study, special laws and special methods. But our own lives represent a venture into the unknown. We make the future knowable by living, and understandable by making predictions as to what will happen. We do not always spell out our predictions; some predictions have been validated so often that we take the outcomes for granted. We do not always make narrow predictions, and we are surprisingly tolerant, under some circumstances, about the outcomes of our ventures. Our predictions will, however, be very much related to the outcomes of previous predictions.

Viewed in this way, individuals are always experimenting with their own behaviour. Not only may behaviour be a response; it may also, and at the same time, be a question. The writing of this article arose out of a comment to the editor. His response was the question 'Could I write something on this for the newsletter?' My response to his question was a new question to myself, namely, can I put these ideas into a form which is communicable to my professional colleagues? In the actual writing I had need to experiment with the ways in which I put down the ideas in order to satisfy certain criteria that I had as to intelligibility and perhaps, aesthetic and grammatical form. I am also expecting, i.e. predicting, that there will, in turn, be a response from some of the readers, and so forth.

Every time we act or speak or keep silent we expect something to happen or not to happen. We have ideas as to the next step in the sequence of life. What makes life interesting is that some of our expectations do not come off, some of them do. If they always did we would soon be bored with life. On the other hand, if we can never make any predictions at all we shall be living as if in a fog. Under these conditions we may withdraw into a private world or commit suicide in order to create at least one uncertainty (cf. Hamlet's 'To be or not to be . . .' – but he decided against).

If we can accept the idea that behaviour is an experiment, how can this help us in our work? One thing we can do is ask what a given child's behaviour is in terms of his experimentation. What are his expectations in the situation? What is he trying to validate? Who is he using to validate his hypotheses? Does he seek the same sort of validation from everyone or does he experiment differently, i.e. behave differently with different people? How does the child experiment with his own age group? How does the child experiment with his parents? How does the child experiment with teachers? We can also ask what sorts of validation the child gets from other people. Negative invalidation plays as important a role as positive validation, and we know from a variety of sources that praise is a more effective source of validation for introverts whereas blame is a more effective invalidator for extroverts.

The problem of who validates what brings in the whole gamut of the people (adults or children) who are important in a child's life. The examination of the role of the family and the role of the school can take on a different emphasis if we ask what opportunities are provided for the child to experiment, and how teachers and parents use their own behaviour as experiments with the child. Moreover, the language of experiment is emotionally fairly neutral, and the discussion of children's and teachers' problems in this language is easier than, for example, using a psychoanalytic language.

All that I have written so far is at a rather hypothetical level. What happens in practice? A boy aged 13 years became a school refusal case. He had also attempted to commit suicide. Having helped him through the depression and anger that led to the latter, it was still necessary to help him over the problem of attending school. After a number of interviews he provided an opportunity for a series of planned experiments by telling me that he had been to school for a school medical examination. This was carried out within the school grounds but not in the school buildings proper. In imagination we traversed the route from the school gate to the head's office, where I initiated a conversation with him as though I were the head. After this exercise I said I would like him to go to see the head and asked whether he felt able, to which he replied 'when would you like me to go?' We agreed on a date and time, and on the spot I rang the school to make the appointment. Fortunately, it was possible for the boy himself to speak to the head on the telephone. He went for the agreed appointment and he was able to report what happened, and his own feelings at the time. He was, of course, extremely anxious, and this was validated. The important point, however, was that he was now able to plan further visits to the school, although still unable to attend as a pupil. He has, however, stated with conviction that he will start at the beginning of next term, and he has already started a programme of study to prepare himself for this. Between us we have used the language of experimentation and this has the added advantage for the boy of recognizing the propositional nature of the task. By propositional in this context I have in mind the question 'What would happen if. . .?' This allows for a new venture or new experiments with the patient's behaviour to be timed with maximum effectiveness. It will be noticed that ventures are imagined in the therapist's room but carried out in real life by the boy. This is his 'homework'.

Another boy aged 13 years, of bright average ability, attended the clinic on account of enuresis. After a long period of therapy, which seemed to get nowhere, I asked what the point of his coming was as it did not change his bedwetting. This was the most important experiment that he had carried out so far and it provided the basis for a change in therapeutic tactics. It was suggested to him that he might care to approach his problem as a scientist and start recording the occasions when he wet his bed, together with any other incidents that might have occurred that might make him upset, thereby affecting the workings of his own body. After many weeks of observations he remarked that he did not wet his bed when he slept in the bed of his younger brother or sister. (His parents, incidentally, saw no point in this observation.) We made sense of his findings by remarking that, although he was the oldest boy, there was a sister who was older than he was. Any demands were, in fact, made on him as the oldest boy and he frequently found this irksome. When he slept in a younger sibling's bed he was abandoning his rightful position in the family. After this discussion his bedwetting more or less stopped. Two points need to be added. This boy had decided long before to become a 'brother' in a Roman Catholic fraternity. In such a situation the authority structure would be clear to all. The other point arose in a family interview with the parents. The boy's observation was told to them, and it turned out that the father himself was younger than the mother but ostensibly carried the authority. The family had frequently laughed about this, but there was certainly some confusion in the authority structure from the boy's point of view.

This case illustrates an important consideration. The technique of making clear the scientific role that a child can consciously adopt allows the child to take a great deal of responsibility for his own behaviour. The therapist plays an important part in modulating the child's responsibility and allows the child to fail in some ventures without criticism.

A third case involved a boy who showed behaviour consistent with what we have labelled the 'big-head' syndrome. This behaviour is likely to arise in a child who has failed to learn the techniques of living with his peer group and who tends to be identified with adults. Such children frequently behave in school as though the rules did not exist; they fail to behave appropriately and to learn from their experience. They are otherwise likeable and able to talk well. Unfortunately, they tend to use language as a means of evading the troubles attendant on their misdemeanours. Therapy with such a case involves invalidating any behaviour that is 'big-headed' and validating behaviour that is consistent with his own age group. This is done in the privacy of the therapy room rather than in the school. This particular boy had come to the conclusion that his headmaster saw him solely as a troublemaker. He was invited to experiment with playing the part of a 'good' boy, but 'good' as determined solely by his own ideas, not the therapist's. He liked the idea of this, saying that he had often wanted to be an actor. The following week he was asked how his experiment had worked, and he said that he had tried the part once when he was involved in a fight. As it was not clear what he meant by this he was asked how he felt about it. His reply was 'Well, I played a pretty poor part'. This was the first time he had ever spontaneously given a response that showed him in an unfavourable light. The experiment had provided him with the opportunity of encountering new experiences and feeling things that he had not felt before. The fact of his narrating these new experiences provided the opportunity for validating his experiment with warm praise.

His subsequent progress, not, of course, dependent on this one experiment only, has been extremely satisfactory. Whereas at one time he was likely to be transferred to a secondary modern school, his work has now improved concurrently with his behaviour. The headmaster is delighted with his all-round improvement and the boy himself is now able to plot his own characteristics in company with his peer group at school along a number of dimensions. His ideal for himself has become conscious and realistic taking, as it does, something of the wisdom of his own age group. This, incidentally, was one of the aims of treatment that was suggested to him when he was referred to me after some 12 months of treatment from an orthodox therapist.

These examples give some idea of the changes that can take place in a child's behaviour when we approach him in the spirit of one who will help him in his own experimentation. It is perhaps necessary to add that the person who undertakes this sort of work also gains by experimenting with his own behaviour. The work becomes exciting and rewarding in its own right.

It is worth observing that behaviour therapy can be construed as sets of techniques whereby individuals are helped to carry out a series of experiments with their own behaviour. The therapist becomes the research adviser, although he may also be the subject of the patient's own experiments. The use of the electric blanket for enuresis is a stock technique derived from learning theory, and it would seem that no therapist is available to act as the research adviser for the patient. The blanket, however, is unlikely to be effective if the patient does not wake up. In waking up the child becomes conscious of his own behaviour in this context perhaps for the first time. Moreover, on waking up the child is faced with certain options that he or she must undertake. The child is, therefore, in the position of taking some action in the light of his new knowledge. The consequences of this we do not know in detail, but if the enuresis stops it is more likely to spring from the child's new aware-ness of himself and his behaviour than from any procedure called 'conditioning'. One of the first tasks of the scientist is controlled obser-vation. The electric blanket allows the child to undertake this. Whatever the outcome of the controlled observation that the child is forced to take if he or she wakes up, the child's own cognitive, conative and affective processes must all be involved. In this context the treatment of the child as his own scientist shows far more respect for the genius of the individual than treatment of the child construed as a human rat or human pigeon. The techniques may be the same but the orientation is different.

To adopt the view that the child is his own scientist means that we throw ourselves wide open to what the child has to tell us, either through his words or his behaviour. This may be a little daunting, but it represents a challenge that we, as psychologists, should be in a position to meet. Our undergraduate training was designed to make us scientists, even if rather self-consciously. Whether or not we accepted that aim seriously, we were given some idea of the language of experimentation – hypotheses, validation, invalidation, probability levels and so forth. It is central to Kelly's thinking that we abandon the notion that our subjects are objects. Instead, we treat them as scientists in their own right. In this sense they are not psychologically different from us, although we have the advantage of experience and training. It is the difference in levels of experience and theoretical 'know-how' that we can bring to bear when we are confronted with children and families who are distressed about what is happening or what different individuals are doing. Our aim is quite simply not some mythical cure, but the helping of these children or families to be more consistent in their experimentation on the one hand or, on the other, to undertake new experimentation on the basis of their own observations, their own expectations and their own hopes.

Our clients' problems arise as the outcome of inappropriate expectations or hypotheses. Our job is to help people out of their predicaments, and this may involve experimenting with our own behaviour as well as encouraging our clients to experiment with theirs.

I have so far talked about experiments, but not about their underlying hypotheses. If the child's behaviour is best seen as a series of experiments we need to know the nature of his hypotheses if we are to help. I would like to write about this topic in a separate article. By the time it appears, however, some readers may well have attempted to work this out for themselves. The attempt will be well worth the effort.

Chapter 1
Reading difficulties and what else? (1969)

My book Dimensions of Reading Difficulty *(1968), in which one chapter was devoted to a PCT approach to the problem, was very well received and reviewed by a member of United Kingdom Reading Association who invited me, on the Association's behalf, to address its Annual Conference. This is the paper I gave in which I offered an idiographic (e.g. Kellyan), as opposed to a traditional nomothetic approach to understanding reading difficulties. Its effectiveness was shown by two cases.*

Problems in the scientific approach

The scientific study of reading difficulties has a long history but has apparently contributed little to the understanding of those teachers who have the job of contending with problems in the classroom. The classic comment at the end of each study is that more research is needed. Some of the many variables discovered by research have been discussed elsewhere (Ravenette, 1968) and these will only be named in this paper: intelligence, social background, perceptual difficulties, neurological (real or imaginary) anomalies, family factors, and so forth. There are, however, a number of underlying issues in this scientific approach that are not fully debated, and these may be the very issues which need to be challenged in order that workers may have a better understanding of the reading difficulties of the individual child.

The classic approach used in the study of reading difficulties involves the selection of a specified group of children labelled 'retarded' and a control group in which children are 'normal'. Tests thought to be related to the learning of reading are given to each group, and the verification of hypotheses rests on establishing significant differences between the two groups. If differences are demonstrated, a variable defining 'retardates' is said to be established. The development of computers has enabled this style of research to become more sophisticated in that more tests, and hence more variables, can be introduced. The scores on tests can be intercorrelated and so-called 'factors' can be deduced whereby children in the different groups can be further defined.

One recent study (Lovell and Gorton, 1968) calls for some comment because of its comparative sophistication, and also because of its unfinished conclusions. The investigators used a number of tests that were thought to indicate impaired cortical functioning. To the investigators' surprise, they found that the spread of scores on each test were no different for the retarded children than for the non-retarded. The sophistication of the study was shown when the investigators asked if the patterns of scores for children in the two groups were different. By correlating the scores in the two groups, they found two different patterns, one for each group. On the basis of this they deduced that some 2% of the retarded children showed a pattern of test scores that was consistent with the notion of cortical impairment (specific development dyslexia). The unstated, and perhaps unrecognized, further conclusion should have been that a comparable number of children had a pattern of scores that was completely inconsistent with this notion. These children were still retarded in reading, and the research data gave no answers as to why they were retarded.

Why are such complex and detailed studies of so little help in understanding the individual child?

According to Siu (1957), the aim of science and scientific investigation is the development of concepts. The more these concepts match up with reality, the more useful they are, but there is no necessary truth value in the results of research. Frequently, the value of concepts arrived at in this way becomes apparent only in the distant future, sometimes never. The scientific investigation of reading retardation, therefore, can be reputable without the teacher deriving any practical help. The seeming irrelevance of such research, however, stems from other factors.

Individuals, unlike objects in the physical world, are complex and unique. In consequence, the research strategies devised for investigating people are aimed at discovering concepts derived from groups of individuals rather than from single individuals. But the group is not comparable to the individual and concepts relevant to the whole group are not necessarily relevant to the individual in that group. Thus, if, on average, a group of retarded readers shows lower scores on, for example, a test of visual perception than a comparable group of normal readers, this does not mean that every child in the retarded group is inferior to every child in the normal group. In fact, the overlap is usually very great, and the statistical significance of research findings need have no psychological significance.

Findings from the study of groups have actuarial, as opposed to individual, value. If it is known from such studies that, for example, working-class children are more retarded than middle-class children, then special provision should be provided for schools in working-class areas in order to meet this difficulty. But within such a school there will be retarded children for whom a different understanding may be needed. In this context the research finding has value at a planning and administrative level, but not at the level of the individual child.

A further problem highlighted by group studies is the fact that, even if a single variable is isolated, there is no one-to-one correspondence between performance on that variable and performance on the criterion (e.g. reading). Although many children who are retarded in reading may show difficulties in right/left discrimination, there are many children with the same difficulty who read perfectly well. In other words, the child's retardation is not explained away by this handicap. It might be thought possible to attempt a description of the child in terms of all the possible handicaps that are thought to lead to reading retardation, but in practice this would be quite impractical, even if all the possible variables had been discovered.

The most basic assumption underlying the study of groups, however, is at a different level and is far more important. For scientific study, individuals are treated as if they were 'objects', not as individuals. If the 'object' did not have this supposed deficit, the object would perform equally well in comparison with other 'objects' that did not have this deficit. The therapeutic task is to remove the deficit. But the individual is a living, breathing, evaluating, thinking, feeling, acting organism. He chooses, decides, acts upon his wishes, and grows. What he achieves will be related to all of these attributes. At the simplest level, when invited to undertake an activity, he can either do it with delight, see it as irrelevant, or consider it a waste of time. He can view it with active distaste or be frightened of its implications. Scientific study has not yet come to terms with the 'object' as 'subject'. But in real life, in the classroom, in front of the teacher, the child is indeed fully a subject, and he approaches the tasks he is expected to master with well-developed cognitive, affective and conative attitudes. The results of scientific enquiry lead to description, not to explanation, nor to understanding. Their certainties are probabilities, not absolute truths, and general not absolute. If, then, traditional research strategies are of little value at the individual level, what should be done?

Towards a different point of view

Koestler (1967), in connection with the development of literature, art and science, makes the following comment '. . . cumulative progress within a given "school" and technique end inevitably in stagnation, mannerism or decadence, until the crisis is resolved by a revolutionary shift in sensibility, emphasis, style.' It may not be too far removed from the present to suggest that a new sensibility is needed in the understanding of children with reading difficulties. Koestler (1967) quotes L. L. White: 'I ask the reader to remember that what is most obvious may be most worthy of analysis. Fertile vistas may open out when commonplace facets are examined from a fresh point of view.' In the case of children with reading difficulties perhaps the most obvious fact is that the child is an individual with hopes and fears, expectations and disappointments, abilities and loyalties. He brings all of these to school and to learning as a statement of himself as an individual. Is it possible to make this a new starting point for the understanding of reading difficulties?

It is unfortunately the case that theories that are developed amongst the few seldom become disseminated amongst the many. The acquisition of new ideas seems to be at best fortuitous, and at worst discouraged by the conservative inertia of existing ideas. Two basic assumptions about the nature of the individual have led to two comparatively new theoretical points of view. Kelly (1955, 1991) has suggested that the individual is basically a scientist – although not necessarily a good one – and faces the onrush of life by developing bases for making and testing hypotheses. In the light of the outcomes of his ventures he modifies his theoretical assumptions.

From a different, but related, point of view, Jackson and his associates (Watzlawick et al., 1967) suggest that an individual is always presenting a statement of himself in everything he says or does. More generally, 'Life is a partner whom we accept or reject, and by whom we feel ourselves accepted or rejected, supported or betrayed. To this existential partner man proposes his definition of himself and then finds it confirmed or disconfirmed.' Behaviour is itself a communication, a confirmation or disconfirmation of others' views of us, or a request for confirmation or disconfirmation. Learning and non-learning are each aspects of behaviour and, as such, may be seen as communications.

Both views, behaviour as communication and behaviour as experiment, imply the presence of other individuals. On the one hand, it is people who confirm or disconfirm, and on the other hand a person's behavioural experiments involve the anticipation of what others do. Thus people (parents, teachers, siblings, and peers) become important factors when the individual is seen as either experimenter or communicator, and when learning and not learning are seen as experiments or communications. The adoption of these points of views may provide starting points for that new sensibility which is needed in the understanding of reading difficulties.

Every theoretical framework leads to the development of appropriate techniques, and if this way of thinking about children and their learning difficulties is to be taken seriously, appropriate investigation procedures must be devised. The child's behavioural questions and his behavioural experiments take place in an area of life in which significant people provide the validators, i.e. those who confirm or disconfirm. It is necessary, therefore, to invent questioning techniques that encourage children to give the views of themselves and those people who are important for them – parents, teachers, siblings, and peers. Moreover, the simple answer to the simple question needs further elaboration from the child. At the same time, the child must be asked questions to embrace as wide a range of validators as possible. The interview, therefore, is comparable to a Piaget-style interview, in which reasons become important. Perhaps it is even more important for the child to be invited to indicate his wishes for things to be different, and his views on the implications of change. The style of investigation is inevitably of a different order from that of the psychometrician. There are no normative data. Comparisons are not made with others. There are no specific diagnostic signs. Instead, children are invited and encouraged, in a structured way, to explicate their views of life and in relation to people who are important for them.

The case of John

John is aged 7 and was referred by the headteacher as, although he seemed to be of above average ability, he had made no start in reading. This made him abnormal in the class because the one or two other non-readers were children of limited ability.

Investigation of his intelligence indicated that his ability was well above average, although some of his responses indicated a certain immaturity and a Piagetian egocentricism. On performance tests he worked imaginatively and efficiently. Thus, there is no reason to believe that failure to learn to read stemmed from either lack of intelligence or from deficits in specific abilities.

What happens if he is asked to describe himself in the context of his parents? He says he is not like either parent 'because we're not the same'. He would like to 'be like P.M.' (a boy in the Junior School). If he had done something he was pleased about he would not tell his parents, he would tell his mates 'because I usually go out with Mum and Dad. It's no use telling Mum and Dad, they already know, so I tell my mates.' He would like it to be different: 'I like to go out on my own.' If he wanted to attempt something new he would tell his parents first 'because they just tell me off if I try to do it first. I wish I could just walk out and do it.' He feels that neither parent understands him 'because they don't listen to me'. He would like it to be different: 'I wish they knew.'

When he is asked to elaborate his complaints about other people, he says that 'Boys like playing with dirt because it's gooder'. 'They should 'go swimming instead', then 'they would be clean instead of dirty. My mate P.M. always says "Let's go and play in the dirt."' Brothers and sisters 'like going to work'. It would be a good thing if 'they could not go to work' then 'I could play with my brothers and sisters.' Fathers 'won't let you do things' because they are 'angry'. Mothers 'are always saying shush, I'm doing the dinner'. He wished 'someone else could do the dinner, then she could play with me'.

When John is presented with a picture of a boy sitting at a desk with a book and someone standing, he can recognize what the situation is, but is unwilling to tell a story about it.

This was the evidence from one interview with the boy. The headteacher provided evidence about the family. John is the youngest of six children. The next oldest is 11 years old and is likely to go to a residential grammar school (the family is working class). Whereas the older children all came to school on their own, mother always brings John. Perhaps mother has been overprotective in the past. Mother has been co-operative and helpful to the school in practical ways, but she may have pushed John too much with reading.

In the light of John's own testimony and the headteacher's observations, what is his view of himself, of his parents, his family and his peer group? He feels an odd man out in his family, his parents don't understand him, nor do they validate his enterprises. His mother and sisters go their own way and he seeks confirmation of himself through one friend – unfortunately he has mixed views about what his friend thinks is good fun. He feels that his parents are forcing his dependence on them and that, in any case, they know everything he does but without understanding him.

Learning to read can now be seen as a refusal to experiment in one of the areas where apparently his mother is making heavy demands on him. He would seem to be rejecting their view of him and, in the process, rejecting the development of a skill that is important in his own development. He has no allies in this because the school is demanding the same thing as his parents. To opt out of the situation is the easiest solution. He may also be saying 'If you treat me as a baby still, I will be like a baby because babies can't read.'

This formulation is of no value unless it has implications for action, and the implication here is straightforward. Learning to read must be seen by the boy as unrelated to his parents, but positively related to him and to school. The evidence and the formulation were worked out with the headteacher, who agreed to advise the mother to desist completely from any concern about John's learning in school. The headteacher also made herself responsible for John's reading in her own remedial group.

The mother accepted this dictum, and within nine months John was reading at his age level and was even prepared to read to his mother. In retrospect, this action can be seen to answer some of the implicit questions that his behaviour was suggesting. His lack of independence from his mother was rectified in part by allowing his schooling to be the concern of himself and the teachers. This inevitably changed the nature of the mother–child interaction and communication patterns. The full extent of the change is not known, but it is possible that the mother might now tolerate even greater independence in John.

The case of Steven

A second case is Steven. He was referred at the age of 11 years because of failure to make reasonable school progress. The headteacher thought he might be educationally subnormal. He had been attending a remedial reading centre for some time, but he had not been able to benefit from this. He was found to have dull average ability, but his scores on different tests showed a range from an IQ equivalent of 70 (mental arithmetic) to one of 105 (two performance tests). In Piaget-type experiments his development was better than his IQ of 82 would have indicated. Moreover, he was able to give adequate verbalization of conservation of number, length and area.

In unstructured situations he was anxious and ineffectual but when he was given a model to work from he could cope in a rather restricted way. Likewise, in school, he is reported to be unable to initiate activity on his own until he has seen someone else do the activity.

Steven's view of himself in the context of his parents is interesting. He is more like Mum than Dad 'because Mum says so, Nan says so. Dad says I look like him'. If he had done something he was pleased about he would tell Mum, Dad and friends because 'I just like it'. If he wanted to do something new he would tell his parents first and his reason was 'not to do it again'. He would be more likely to make Mum cross than Dad, and would rather be found out by both parents, but in neither case does he know why. He thinks Mum and Dad both understand him because 'Mum says so, Dad says so'. On no occasion was Steven prepared to say that he would like things to be different.

When asked to elaborate his attitudes to parents and siblings, he could only refer to ideas of listening and not listening. Listening seemed to be related to being understood on the one hand, and having to keep silent on the other. To listen to what his parents said seemed to be in the nature of a moral imperative.

A picture of a boy sat at a desk with an open book and a person standing behind him was quickly drawn. Steven was invited to make up first one story, then a different one, and then a third story, to this picture.

Story 1

> A teacher came up and said 'open the book' and he said 'no', and then he has to go up to the headmaster. The headmaster said 'don't you say that again, go back and open the book and read the story'. (The boy said 'No' because he wanted to.)

Story 2

> There was a teacher sitting there. There was a boy. He read the book. The teacher said 'well done' and then he told him to sit down and he wouldn't. Then the teacher went to the headmaster and the boy got the cane.

Story 3

> Once upon a time there was this boy running about and then the headmaster told him to sit down. He said 'No'. He went to hit him but his Mum came in and then he had to go to the dentist. He had a loose tooth. That's why he said 'no', because his Mum was coming in.

The cumulative effect of this evidence points to Steven's reluctance to experiment and, in the stories, activity seems to be followed by negative outcomes. At the same time, his behaviour in the stories is tantamount to a refusal to learn. The defensive responses to questions about himself and his parents suggest that the basis for these attitudes stem from inter-actions within the family which cause him concern. Consequently he was referred to the child guidance clinic.

The impression the mother and boy conveyed to the psychiatrist is described in the following way: 'Mother was extremely dominating, non-stop talking, pushing, shoving, pressurizing the boy, plucking words out of Steven's mouth and almost preventing him from speaking. She uses verbal behaviour as a punishing technique either by nagging or by keeping silent. In her own words the boy "just refuses to read".' At a subsequent interview father was present. He is a docker and is also dominating. Surprisingly, he reads a great deal and the mother holds this against him. She nags the boy for not reading and the father for reading.

Non-reading in this case can be seen as stemming in part from the crushing by the mother of the boy's experimenting. This attitude of the mother was developed when Steven was a premature baby and she had overprotected him consistently all his life. Reading itself must be seen as problematical by Steven in view of the mother's attitude to father's reading. More generally, how could this boy view the prospect of growing up and being a man? Perhaps the low verbal IQ itself was more a function of the unsatisfactory verbal communication in the family than of genuinely limited ability.

Three family interviews in which these interactions were discussed were sufficient to allow the boy to start reading – and get pleasure from developing skill. The family interactions changed completely to everyone's satisfaction and no further appointments were made.

Conclusions and implications

These two cases illustrate the practical application of a way of thinking about child development in general and learning disorders in particular.

This way of thinking recognizes the experimental and communicational implications of behaviour and relates these to tasks in the school, and to interactions between the child and other important people.

There are clear implications for the teacher in the classroom. Is it possible for the teacher to deduce the underlying questions that a child is posing? Is it possible to deduce what learning to read means to the child in terms of what is happening between the child and others? Can the teacher be a sufficiently powerful validator for the child so that his involvement with the child will enable the child to learn?

At the simplest level, it is important that the child likes the teacher and the teacher values the child. Such statements are usually accepted as obvious but the obvious is seldom taken seriously. At a second level, the teacher needs to know the family and be prepared to ask questions about what happens in the family. The habitual family interactions may provide a clue to what the child's non-learning means. At all levels the teacher needs to pose new questions, both verbally and behaviourally, and to be sensitive to the child's questions, both verbal and behavioural.

Learning comes out of positive interactions, non-learning out of negative interactions. Whatever factors are associated with reading difficulties, reading difficulties themselves are also a reflection of the child's behavioural questions, his behavioural experiments and the interactions with life that each of those implies. Teachers are a part of a child's life.

Chapter 2
Psychologists, teachers and children: how many ways to understand? (1972)

In 1972, I was President of the Association of Educational Psychologists and this was my Presidential address at the annual conference. The theme of the conference was 'Maladjustment: Clinical Concept or Administrative Convenience', which provided an opportunity to illuminate the theme within a broadly PCT framework.

The analysis of a situation is one thing, the prescription of a remedy another. Diagnostic capacity does not prove therapeutic ability.
   In dealing with human conditions, the procedure almost always has to be specific, not generalised. (Idries Shah, *Reflections, reprinted with permission*.)

Let me state at the outset two facts that seem to be reasonably true. On the one hand there exists in the schools a large number of children whose behaviour is a serious cause for concern. On the other hand we have a professional commitment, as educational psychologists, to do something about it. Let me state further that the bridge between the children and ourselves is the school, as represented by headteachers and class teachers. This is important since it establishes our role of providing a service both to teachers and to children. I propose to take a careful look at the view on the other side of the bridge from ourselves and, in the process, I shall raise a number of issues that seem to me to call for serious examination if we are to make some positive impact there. We are all familiar, to varying degrees, with some aspects of the scene and we have all to some extent been able to invent our own maps for finding our way about. Just as, however, in the study of real landscapes, alternative maps may similarly be invented. This extended metaphor that I have used for stating my theme will be found of value in the rest of the exposition, because it runs as a thread throughout the paper. It is worth recalling that Piaget's theoretical approach is based on the child's construction of whatever might be called reality, Holt (1970), one of the most sensitive writers about children, talks of the child's several worlds,

18

and that Kelly (1955, 1991) builds his whole personality theory around the notion that the individual maps out the world in terms of his own constructions.

In essence, therefore, my concern in this exploration is the psychologists' involvement in schools, with special reference to those situations where children's behaviour is a cause for concern and where the educational psychologist is the person who is expected to do something about it.

The 'disturbed' child and the 'disturbing' child

The labels 'maladjustment' and the 'maladjusted child' have had long service and, at the time of their mintage, they probably served a useful purpose. Increasingly, however, there have been reservations as to their value except as providing a basis for deciding a child's school placement. It is an interesting feature of our language that we usually run the risk of impaling objects on our own adjectives and, in the process, we often impale ourselves at the same time. Thus, when confronted with the question 'Is this child maladjusted?' we are faced with the choice of examining him to find some way of making the label fit, or feeling decidedly uncomfortable in challenging the question. The latter choice takes some courage as it involves challenging the questioner to rethink his adjectives and elaborate the problem and, at the same time, we carry the risk of showing how stupid we are not to know what 'maladjustment' means. The dilemma is not uncommon. It arises whenever we use language in a categorical way whereby an object must be 'this' or 'that', with the probable implication that it is nothing but 'this' or 'that'. Instances can be recognized from everyday professional practice, especially where workers from different, and sometimes allied, professions are jointly involved on what seem to be common problems.

One way out of the dilemma is to use language propositionally, to talk in the 'language of hypothesis' (Kelly, 1964, in Maher, 1969). Thus, we might say, for example 'Let us assume for the moment that this child might conceivably be labelled as "maladjusted". What are the implications of this label? What else might he be? In the existing circumstances, what options does this lead to, what doors are shut?' The very style of this approach can be recognized to be scientific in the sense that to be scientific implies a willingness to entertain hypothetical alternatives, and thus it should commend itself to us as psychologists, who see ourselves as grounded in a scientific discipline. It does, however, present its own difficulties as it invites from the respondent a willingness to be open-minded and exploratory.

Turning more specifically to children whose behaviour occasions the description 'maladjusted', 'the disturbed child' and 'the disturbing child', I have in mind the fact that these children attract attention by their failure to respond positively to their teachers' overtures. As a consequence, the teachers themselves become worried and ask for help. Hence these children are, in the first instance at least, disturbing to the teachers. Whether or not they are disturbed in themselves is another matter that is open to enquiry. It may, of course, be true that there are some children whom teachers do not find disturbing but who may, in some genuine sense, be disturbed.

One of the advantages of this particular pair of alternatives is that it encourages us to look equally intensively in two opposite directions – to the child who is the subject of concern and to the person who is concerned (cf. Ravenette, 1964b, 1969). We must be careful, however, that we do not merely exchange one label for another for describing the same phenomen. I do not think this is really the case, but I would not wish, at this stage, to impale myself on the thorns of categorical discussion. It is sufficient perhaps to suggest that this distinction may open up a wider range of constructive enquiries and, at the same time, reduce the risk of a further hardening of the categories.

Nonetheless, I would be extremely timorous not to offer some suggestions as to what I would call a 'disturbed' child. If I can return to my opening metaphor of maps, I would argue that every single person develops his own personal map for making sense of his world of people and interpersonal relations. Included in this map, inferentially, is a reference point that includes some notion of himself. Most individuals modify their maps as they go along in relation to their own activities and their interactions with others, and the modifications make sense to other people. The child whom I might be tempted to think was 'disturbed' would be one who is minimally able to modify his map in the light of his experiences or, if he does, those modifications do not make much sense to other people.

In Piagetian terms this might be seen as related to a primacy of 'assimilation' over 'accommodation', whereby the individual persistently distorts experience in terms of his existing schemas at the expense of modifying his schemas in the light of what perhaps might be indigestible experience. It is perhaps significant that 'adaptation' rests on a balance of 'accommodation' and 'assimilation', and 'maladaptation' is synonymous with lack of balance. It is worth reading Mehrabian (1968) who has developed a personality theory that includes anomalies of development out of the process postulated by Piaget.

It will be noticed that this formulation, tentative though it is, contrasts markedly with descriptions based on notions of 'emotional disturbance'. This difference is real only if thoughts and cognitions are considered to be totally divorced from feelings and emotions. It seems to me that, once again, our use of language has led us to partition as real what was originally partitioned for the convenience of study. In reality, thought, feeling and action are intimately related, but our language system unfortunately hinders our perception of this unity.

There are a number of reasons why this is a useful model to use. In the first place it encourages us to look at the personal maps people have invented to make sense of their worlds. This applies equally for children, parents, teachers and psychologists. More importantly, it allows us to see behaviour as stemming from an individual's construction of his world rather than as phenomena *sui generis*. Perhaps most important of all, it allows us to see behaviour in terms of interpersonal perceptions rather than as necessarily intra-psychic.

Investigation of subjectivity

It is clear that, in advocating a model that is based on an individual's map of people and interpersonal relationships, I am also indicating the nature of enquiries that we, as psychologists, might usefully carry out. What I am suggesting in fact is the systematic investigation of an individual's subjectivity. This is not the occasion to give a detailed account of the strategies and tactics of this type of investigation but I would like to make some observations about the task and to illustrate the approach with special reference to the verbal co-ordinates that teachers develop to make sense of their pupils.

It is one of Kelly's important principles that, if you want to know a child's views, it might be worth asking him. He might possibly give an answer. Experience suggests that this is generally a useful strategy so long as the question is asked in such a way that the child is not put into an embarrassing position vis-à-vis his view of himself, and if, at the same time, the child is invited to elaborate his answers. The older the child the more likely will he be able to give some verbal account of his ways of making sense and, conversely, the younger the child the less likely he is to have a stable view of things or to give elaborate verbal answers. Nonetheless, such a child can often say a great deal through the medium of a visual representation.

What follows is part of an interview with Lewis, a six-and-a-half-year-old coloured boy referred by the headteacher because his behaviour was causing concern. We drew for him two faces, in one of which the mouth is turned upwards, the other of which is turned downwards, and ask him which would be sad and which would be happy. He responds immediately and, when asked further what a sad boy would do, he says: 'He don't like people 'cos they keep laughing at him. He's got funny clothes on. He keeps falling in the mud.' In response to the question 'Would this boy get into trouble?' said that he would because he doesn't like the happy boy. This boy would not, however, dirty himself up. (Lewis is reported to wet the bed and is frequently told off for being untidy. He doesn't mind being corrected for this.) We then turn to the happy child. What sort of a boy would he be? 'He has lots of toys. He likes his brother. A happy day, the sun comes out. He might get some sweets. He would be a good boy to get some sweets. He doesn't dirty himself up'. Already he has shown a willingness to respond to drawings that we have offered. Will he draw a picture of the boy who dirties himself up? This he does, and emphasizes the point by drawing the whole figure and scrawling in lines to indicate the dirt. 'This boy has a bath and clean clothes. He can't go out. He don't dirty himself. He likes to go out and play in the dirt.' How much further can we go? Anger is common with children. Will he draw an angry boy? He does, and this is what he says: 'He don't like his mum. He keeps doing naughty things, jumping on the bed. He keeps stealing things and hiding them.' Lewis's mother (and there are doubts about having a father) returned to the West Indies on an impulse, leaving the children with an uncle and aunt. At my request he drew one further picture, this time of the boy who gets into trouble, another situation with which most small children are familiar. Of this boy he said 'He's good, he says sorry. He doesn't have anything to say. He wishes he was a good boy like my brother.'

At this point it seems a reasonable inference that he is in fact very much identifying himself with his drawings and, indeed, giving an account of his own thoughts and feelings. We ask him which of these is most like him and, with some surprise, he says that they all are. In turn, however, he chooses first the sad one, then the angry one, then the one who gets into trouble, then the happy one and finally the one who dirties himself. Lewis did not present himself as particularly bright and, in response to formal investigations on the Stanford Binet, gave answers that did not suggest that he would respond well to verbal enquiries. Moreover, he said that he was seeing me for 'being naughty'. Yet his responses, mediated through drawings, enabled him to suggest something of his predicaments in a reasonably clear and unambiguous way. The headmistress, who sat in on the interview, felt that she was beginning to acquire some understanding of the boy.

I would like to point out that I do not see anything special about this sort of approach to the child. The techniques are simple and call for the minimum of artistic skill. What is important is the willingness to structure the interview and to attempt some systemization of the questions in a way that does not put the child in the embarrassing position of having to talk about himself in the first person.

In the same way that there is nothing out of the ordinary in exploring the children's ideas of themselves, so there is nothing out of the ordinary about exploring teachers' ideas. Any person's dimensions of appraisal, his personal constructs, are contained within his everyday speech and language. They may not be obvious, and they may be somewhat surprising in the ways in which they are expressed, but they are there for the asking.

When a teacher describes a child to us and gives an account of his behaviour she is giving us at the same time a sample of her own personal map for making sense of children. It is not always easy, however, for a teacher to select from what she knows the things she thinks we want to know. Lewis's teacher described him as obviously having ability (as shown by his drawings). 'He has a generous side to his nature. He can be very kindly. Most of his misdemeanours are probably thoughtless. Perhaps he is too generous. He shows some thought before being naughty. He is indescribably clever at being naughty when there are no grown ups. When he knows there is not much teacher control he will play up. His reading and arithmetic are not up to his ability.' At this point she did not know what else to say. How can we elicit more from her store of observations, recognizing that this store is already categorized in terms of her own personal constructs? We can ask her to give three adjectives that she feels best describe this boy. These will be a selection from her constructs. We can then ask her to document each construct with more observations. The teacher says that Lewis is 'loving', he will put an arm round you affectionately. He is very forgiving after he has been punished. If we pursue the opposite of loving, i.e. 'hating', which seems to be the equivalent of her second adjective 'aggressive', she adds that he is often cruel to little girls or anyone smaller, but not English girls. He does not hate adults, whom he respects. His foster father beats him. 'Loving' also leads to an elaboration of 'generous', which the teacher had used at the outset. He is generous all the time, with children and with adults. When a child is in trouble he will put his arm round him and comfort him. With adults he is always giving himself to them, he sidles up to them and rubs himself against them. Her third adjective was 'willing'. He will notice if you want something before you ask for it, and get it. At this point it is almost worth the generalization that Lewis is the sort of boy who desperately needs to be sensitive to the moods of adults, presumably because of the let down he had experienced from his mother.

We can, however, go further by asking the teacher to relate three ways in which Lewis has surprised her. This is an interesting question as it shows to some extent how open a teacher is in reconstructing her image of the child and, therefore, to what extent she may be able to respond to a child in a different way. In this case the teacher gives three examples, each of which seems to justify her view that Lewis is quite an able boy. He made a very detailed drawing of a boat after a lot of scribbles. He makes deductions from graphs and is often the quickest to grasp the principle and put it into lucid English. During number games in the hall he is often the quickest at abstract calculations. In some way her surprise is related to schoolwork, not to Lewis as a person. Perhaps in this area she is relatively closed.

I have deliberately left the complaints about the boy until I have been able to give the detailed picture presented in the two interviews. The headteacher describes him as 'dangerous: throwing bricks around, very aggressive to other children, as a result of which he is scapegoated. He throws books around the library but he is intelligent enough to know that it is wrong. He does this to try to find out "how far the teacher will go".' Of the teacher she says that she is very patient but, when Lewis goes on and on, she has to slap him. She then gives the usual moral chat and a cuddle. She appeals to the class: 'How can we help him to be good?' but then he goes out and causes more trouble. Lewis is 'nice as pie after a slapping'.

I want to make it clear that both the headteacher and the class teacher would be considered as outstandingly good teachers. The school, which has a difficult population, is well run on liberal lines. What they have said and how they have acted would seem to me to fall within the ordinary limits of infant school practice. Nonetheless, Lewis is a 'disturbing' boy. There is no gainsaying that his behaviour causes concern, and this shows through the verbal maps that are used to describe him. He may, indeed, become a 'disturbed' boy unless ways are found of helping him, experimentally, to reconstrue his world of children and adults.

Hostility in the classroom

At this point I want to introduce the concept of hostility in the formulation suggested by Kelly (Kelly, 1957, in Maher, 1969). Kelly bases his elaboration on the Procrustes myth. Procrustes, you will remember, lived in a house at the end of a valley leading to a pass, and would invite travellers to spend the night under his roof. He was a very sociable person and entertained his travellers well. Unfortunately, he was very concerned that everything should be exactly right for his guests and, to make sure that the bed fitted, he chopped off the guest's legs if they were too long, or stretched them if they were too short. This action illustrates the hostile choice, the choice to constrain people within one's own particular dimensions.

Kelly suggests that the hostile choice arises in people who are socially aware, who are anxious that social situations should be right, who are, in fact, aware that the outcomes owe something to themselves, but at the same time, who are rather rigid. Stated most simply, hostility is the attempt by one person to force another person to conform to his own constructs and to confirm his expectations. Hostility does not necessarily imply wilful damage to others, nor does it necessarily lead to delinquency, aggression (in its usual sense) or maladjustment. It is interesting, in fact, that Kelly sees some resolution of hostility in aggressive social experimentation.

If we apply the notion of hostility in the sense in which I have described it to the case of Lewis, it seems reasonable to suggest that both teacher and child are striving to constrain each other within their own personal constructs. If it is the case that Lewis sees himself primarily as sad and angry, but the teacher is appraising him in terms of love-hate, aggressiveness, intelligence and moral rectitude, then each is responding to a false image of the other. Lewis actively seeks to extort support for his views and perhaps to be slapped provides a welcome confirmation that he, after all, is right. The teacher looks for signs of loving and finds confirmation when he snuggles up to her and is affectionate. But perhaps each is mistaken as the battle has gone on for some time.

I have a suspicion that hostility must be an occupational risk for all teachers in their relationships with children. For children who have endured serious anomalies in their lives at home, and have thus developed rather brittle and idiosyncratic views of themselves and others, the risk of hostility must be even greater.

Understanding, feeling and action

Having related the details of this small investigation of child and teacher subjectivity, it is necessary to look at the issues surrounding the next stage of the process. It is an unstated, and sometimes, I feel, unrecognized fact that, if we are to carry out our task with any effectiveness, we must be concerned with change. Yet it is so frequently the case that our attention is directed very firmly to ideas of assessment and putative cause/effect relationships rather than towards theories that are concerned primarily with ways of instigating psychological change.

It has occurred to me that we need a minimum of two theories, one of which is concerned with understanding, the other of which is concerned with the pragmatics of change. Freud, Piaget and Kelly (to some extent) provide examples of the former; Skinner et al. Watzlawick et al. (1967), Haley (1963) and again Kelly provide examples of the latter. This would be an interesting theme to develop in its own right, but to do so would go too far afield. It seems to me that we are frequently asked by teachers "what to do" and we offer "this is how we understand" (perhaps an example of teacher/psychologist hostility), and this is an issue that needs to be resolved.

It is possible to indicate three basic approaches to ways of initiating change, and also two different foci in which change needs to take place. The first of these two is personal change, or change of the individual, the second is change in the interpersonal situation. They are not, of course, completely independent.

It is generally true that, for a given individual, there is some integrity underlying his thoughts, his feelings and his actions, and it is an interesting observation that, over the centuries, personal change has been sought through these three different channels. Stated most simply it can be said that, if a person arrives at a new understanding of a situation, or a new set of feelings about a situation, or does something different in a situation, he can effect a change in himself that might have consequences for those with whom he comes in contact. Insight theories of psychotherapy and casework provide examples of the first two, the third tends to have gone by default, although Kelly reports how people on his waiting lists for treatment were advised to find out how other people were coping. A number of these subsequently reported that their problems were no longer of any importance.

It seems to be important to spell out these three approaches as different people can be effective in different ways and, in the case of teachers, different people are differentially responsive. Perhaps we have to be prepared to try all three approaches to see what works. All of these methods, however, are basically related to the inner change of one person and only indirectly to a change in the interpersonal relationship. In this particular area the only well-documented approach is provided by operant conditioning techniques. This is somewhat paradoxical as the intent behind a Skinnerian approach is to modify the behaviour of one person. When, however, this is attempted within a family or within a school, the manipulandum is, in fact, the interpersonal relationship existing between child and adult. It may well be that attempts to lead to a change directly in interpersonal relationships involves a recognition that ethical issues may be involved that have not yet been worked out. The basic process that is involved in any intervention is one of communication, verbal and non-verbal, digital and analogic, report and command (Watzlawick et al., op.cit). The question then is 'what do we communicate to the teacher?' followed by 'what difference might this communication make?' In the light of what I have said, there is quite clearly a need to broaden the teacher's understanding of the child using the ideas we have formulated from talking with the child. We might, more directly, elaborate the teacher's own understanding of the child and include in this our awareness of her feelings. If these are to be effective they must lead the teacher to adopt a different standpoint, a difficult and delicate enterprise. Yet again we can invite the teacher to undertake some different action in relation to the child, and this need not depend on a full understanding of either the child's difficulties or her own. By taking a different action she may require an alternative viewpoint within which her own feelings and actions may change. This can be illustrated by a specific case. A teacher reported that a 10-year-old boy was now a completely different person. He was no longer resistant to learning and was making good progress. She was asked what difference my intervention had made to her. She said that I had suggested that this boy showed some originality but, more importantly, that I had asked her to keep a detailed record of what he did during the day. She produced her book of recordings, which was in itself a fascinating document, and she went on to say that it had made her stand back and observe the boy much more carefully. In some way this had helped her to take some of her own pressure off. There is nothing special about this illustration, but it shows one way in which an invitation to do something differently enabled the teacher to view things from an alternative point of view. In the process the interpersonal relationships were changed. The point I would like to stress is simply this. That the easement of the teacher–child problems can only be based on a change in interpersonal relationships and, in order to achieve this, we need to develop the skilful means of communication.

Conclusion

My title deliberately included psychologists, teachers and children and, in the early part of this paper, offered the draft of a model that, I argued, had universal application. It follows, therefore, that everything that I have said about teachers and children applies equally well to psychologists and children and psychologists and teachers. Let me summarize some of these issues. We too have invented our own maps to enable us to make sense of people and relationships, but we have to go one step further in developing maps to subsume both teachers and children and their interrelationships. What, in fact, I have offered in this paper is my own provisional map, which has developed over the past and which I hope will develop in the future.

By virtue of the private ways we have of making sense, we are blind to some phenomena and issues and alert to others. Our language conveys the dimensions that we find useful. Bowlby, in an early work, talked of five instinctual reactions that typified the mother–infant relationship. Significantly, resting in the mother's arms was omitted. St Augustine, some few hundred years earlier, specifically mentioned resting in this context. What would a Bowlby research psychologist student see and what would an Augustinian research psychologist see (Leman, 1970)?

Just as hostility, as I have described it above, is endemic in many interpersonal contexts, so it is between children and us, between teachers and children and between teachers and us. How often do we identify with the child against the teacher or the teacher against the child? How seldom can we identify with each in turn? How easy it is to escape into non-identification with either by restricting ourselves to objective tests and written reports? Just as we would like teachers to have skilful means of communication with children, we need skilful means of communication with both children and teachers. Just as we hope that teachers and children will be open to new understandings, feeling and actions, so should we be open in the same way.

The problems surrounding the 'maladjusted' child can thus be seen to be a mirror that reflects some of the problems that arise when we are invited to intervene in a professional capacity.

Psychologists, teachers and children. How many ways to understand? How many ways to intervene?

Chapter 3
Motivation, emotional blocking, and reading failure: a unifying point of view (1974)

I was invited by the Association for Therapeutic Education to write a paper on children with reading difficulties for their journal. Although the paper does not refer explicitly to PCT, it was formulated within that orientation. It represents, therefore, an extension to my thoughts about the subject by introducing 'concern' as a unifying concept. Evidence from the literature is produced to support the notion.

Introduction

It is probably true to say that the use of the expressions 'lack of motivation' and 'emotional blocking' as explanations for reading retardation assume that a child is primarily a processor of information, a 'knowing machine'. The first term implies that there is no energy to activate the machine, the second that something is impeding the flow of information. Each explanation, whilst ostensibly placing the problem within the child, has a secondary usefulness in accounting for our own failures in getting children to meet our expectations. 'Motivation' as an explanation is especially interesting since casual observation suggests that we use the term only when people (including children) fail to do what we want or, occasionally, do something that takes us completely unawares. In this paper I want to attempt an integrative approach to those cases of reading retardation that are usually attributed to 'lack of motivation' or 'emotional blockage'. At the heart of this approach is the view that the child is far more than an information processor, and that the teacher is far more than an imparter of knowledge. I shall quote two cases of reading failure and then explore some theoretical ideas that may provide an understanding of children within which reading failure makes sense. Following that I shall produce some evidence that may not be well known but which supports my arguments. Finally I shall relate this to an alternative view of the teacher's role, together with further evidence that seems to justify the approach.

Case study: Mark

Mark (aged 9 years) is the youngest child of rather old parents and comes 10 years after the rest of the family. He has failed to learn to read despite the provision of a very good remedial programme within his primary school. When a teacher developed techniques that might especially help him he became awkward and hostile. In many ways he might be called a 'reading refuser'. After a number of interviews designed to undercut his reading refusal he told a story about the uselessness of getting a good education since it did not help to get you a better job. Moreover you would have to look after the old people, and there was all the trouble about money, insurance and mortgages. When Mark was asked if he was talking about himself he said quite simply that be was.

Case study: Perry

Perry (aged 11 years) has been attending a remedial reading centre for three years and has still made no progress in reading. He is very keen on boxing, like an older brother, and has boxed for his school. When he was interviewed in connection with reading he was singularly uncommunicative. One day he ran away from school and was brought back by his father, a docker. He said nothing in his own defence but his father said that Perry had told him that he was expected to make a cake with the other children in the class. When it was put to him that making cake was women's work he immediately replied that he wasn't going to be no 'pansy'. (It might be added that in this part of London, even to speak well is considered by many children to be 'pansy'.) Neither of these two boys is unintelligent and each had been labelled as suffering from 'lack of motivation' or an 'emotional blockage'. Neither label has led to any ameliorative action. Is it possible to develop an alternative form of explanation which may have implications for helping children to make something out of what a school has to offer and to develop a skill that has at least a utilitarian value?

Concern

I want to make two rather simple observations. In the first place it is the child who learns to read, not the teacher who teaches the child to read. It is true that the child may learn out of what the teacher offers but the child's involvement in learning is his own. In the second place, a child is very active in making a working sense out of himself and his environment (which includes of course the world of persons as well as the world of things) and this working sense involves the head and the heart, actions and speech. In other words, knowing is not only head knowledge but feeling knowledge also: feelings of doubt and certainty, hope and fear, love and hate, meaning and nonsense, triviality and importance.

Central to all of these feelings lies a child's concern for his own deep sense of himself as an individual, and his adequacies as reflected in those things that he can do. This concern arises within the context of the approval and disapproval of people who are important to him and his own approval and disapproval of himself.

I wish to take the word 'concern' and give it rather special import-ance. If we have a concern about some issue, we are committed to it in a rather total way and this shows itself in thought, word, feeling and action. Moreover, so long as this concern remains at the centre of our lives it inhibits our involvement in other issues. If someone is to under-stand us in any meaningful way he will need to have some under-standing of those concerns that engage us intimately. He will not make much sense out of our choices unless he makes this effort, and may in fact say that we are unmotivated in those issues that are important to him but which fall at the periphery of our own concerns. To state this even more simply is to say that our concerns are based on issues that are important to us.

I need now to elaborate the concept more fully. In a way, a person becomes concerned about the business of life, and of himself, which he considers to be in some sense incompletely finished. It is a part of living that some business will remain unfinished until we die, and life is concerned with trying to work through that business. Other business is quite clearly related to successive events in life; the birth of siblings, separations, the beginnings of things (e.g. school), the reactions and actions of other people, leaving school, marriage and so forth. Moreover, every event in life represents business, which remains in various stages of completion, satisfactorily or otherwise. Concern, therefore, as I am using the term, arises out of business that is unfinished, and presents therefore transactions that leave us with some unease.

I might seem to be saying that concern is something that is conscious and verbalizable, but this is not necessarily the case, as underneath an obvious concern there may exist a less obvious concern, and below that a still less obvious concern. Although the focus of a person's concern may appear to be centred on external matters, at the heart of every concern will be some notion of a person's sense of himself, in relation to his own and other's view of himself, or his own and other's views of his actions. We can also recognize that a person's concerns may range from a mild interest to a deep and overwhelming preoccupation, and that they may be transient or long enduring. A person's feelings are not directly open to examination but may be inferred from what he says and does. They are likely to be most powerfully engaged the nearer his concerns are to his sense of his identity, the longer they endure and the extent to which they become deep preoccupations.

A further aspect has to be considered. Just as a person has many and varied transactions with the world, so he may have many ongoing concerns at the same time. It is a mark of some maturity that different concerns can be dealt with in sequence or can be isolated to the appropriate contexts. It may well happen, however, that a person's concerns may be mutually antagonistic. When this happens, the effect is a form of paralysis. Imagine a child who is desperately concerned to be like his mates, who are not particularly good at reading, but at the same time desperately needs the approval of his teacher. He is faced with an impossible situation and may present as his solution a failure to read accompanied by protestations that he wants to learn but somehow cannot remember the words. The solution is doubly inappropriate since he fails to develop a useful skill but at the same time has added the further problem of trying to serve two different masters at the same time. This now becomes a further issue about which he is unavoidably concerned and the observer's view of the situation might well be that the child has an 'emotional blockage' or is 'unmotivated'. It is fortunately the case that the concerns of most children are congruent with the learning ethos of the school.

Concern and learning

Learning proceeds most easily and efficiently if our attention is directed to the task itself. Where, however, we have deep concerns that are not related to the task our attention and energy is placed elsewhere. What we centre our attention on looms far more largely than any other activity and these other activities become peripheral. At times they may be antagonistic or alternatively merely irrelevant. Moreover, in order to learn a skill we need to be relatively detached in order to isolate what is important and what is not important in the material to be mastered. This detachment is impossible when powerful and perhaps conflicting feelings force themselves into our awareness. It is the very nature of our concerns that they command our attention and at the same time generate feelings. Thus the existence of concerns as I have described them is likely to inhibit any learning that is unconnected with those concerns. Where the reading task is antithetical to the child's concerns we can expect reading resistance and reading refusal. This might be called 'emotional blockage'. Where the reading task is peripheral to the child's concerns his reading failure might be described as 'lack of motivation'.

Let us return to Mark and Perry. Mark has been the baby amongst much older siblings and rather old parents. It is a guess, therefore, that his transactions with people have been at a much more adult level than was justified but, at the same time, his dependency as a small child will have been obvious. Dependence and independence therefore may well be an issue of deep concern to Mark. At the same time, if we accept the validity of the story he told, the independence of adulthood is not something to look forward to. To accept help is to confirm his dependence despite the fact that this would be the way to independence. But independence itself is seen as a chimera as it is yet another form of dependence from which he cannot escape. In the outcome he insists he wants to read, refuses the help which might further this and then asserts that he cannot read.

Perry, the boxing boy, seems to have the issue of his own masculinity as a matter of major concern, where masculinity is determined by the psychological attributes of toughness and aggressiveness. In this sense learning to read is irrelevant to the solution of this problem and Perry can then be described as 'unmotivated'. In a deeper sense, however, he may see reading as antithetical to his main concern so that his non-learning is a reading refusal.

It is clear that to persist in trying to teach these boys reading is likely to be unproductive as this would ignore the underlying bases for the initial failure. For each, the prescription should be to explore the boy's concerns, and expose them, so the boy may become free to learn to read out of the resources that the school offers.

Supporting evidence

The ideas that I have so far elaborated stem from my own concern (in the way I have used the concept) about children who fail to learn to read despite adequate intelligence and adequate resources within the school, and they represent an extension of ideas I have put forward elsewhere (Ravenette, 1968). They have received support, however, from some work which previously had been rather puzzling but which, in the light of these ideas, seem to carry a great deal of meaning.

Maxwell (1960, 1972) analysed the subtest intercorrelations for children who had been tested on the Wechsler Intelligence Scale for Children and the Wechsler Pre-school Intelligence Scale. The first report describes children tested at the Maudsley Hospital consequent to referral to the Children's Department and these are compared with children tested as part of a research project. There were surprising differences between the two correlation matrices and Maxwell's conclusion was that the hospital children showed a pattern of inefficient functioning in contrast with a relatively efficient style of functioning for the research sample. In his second report he found that children tested on the W.P.P.S.L. could be subdivided into two groups according to their level of reading eighteen months later. The above-average reading group showed a pattern of functioning similar to the research sample in the first study and the below-average group showed a pattern similar to the hospital sample.

It seems to me that a generalization can be made in terms of the concerns of the children who were tested. The children in the hospital sample were, almost by definition, singled out as problems. They were taken to a special place and subjected to detailed investigation. Despite the best intentions of the testers, the probability would be that a large number of these children would be as much concerned about themselves as children as with the task itself. Under the circumstances their attentions and energies would be dominated by a concern about themselves, and their performance on an intelligence scale would thus seem to be inefficient. If we now carry the argument to the children in their second study we would say that there exists within an apparently normal sample a large number of children who are likely to feel that they are under inspection as individuals and would see any formal test situation as a threat to themselves. These children would again appear to function inefficiently in a formal test situation but, moreover, would function inefficiently in school as they would be carrying their concern about themselves through every situation in school. It is not surprising that these children would be below average in reading attainment towards the end of their infant stage of education.

The second research to be reported is by Singer (1973). He argued that a major feature of people who were neurotic was their excessive self-concern. One implication of this for the children would be the existence of a pattern of communication that could best be described as hypocritical, as ostensible references to children's interests would in reality be the self-interest of the parents. He then argued that reading retardation itself might be seen as neurotic – as a function of self-concern rather than a concern for learning. He was able to demonstrate that retarded readers were, in fact, much more sensitive to hypocrisy in contrast to what was genuine and that this was also true for the parents of retarded readers. Singer is careful to make the point that some hypocrisy, both from parents and within institutions is unavoidable, and that most children can cope with it without too much unease. Where, however, the family pattern lacks authenticity, the children are likely to be very sensitive to the lack of sincerity in the outside world, and this will hamper their readiness to learn from the resources that the world has to offer.

Implications for education

At this point it is necessary to restate the argument of this paper. I am suggesting that many children who are retarded in reading are like this because their major concerns are unrelated to, or antithetical to, reading. Because of this they function inadequately in the learning situation and give the impression of being unmotivated or suffering from an emotional block. It follows from this that, for such children, a direct attack on reading is unlikely to be of much value as it leaves their basic concerns untouched. It would seem more useful to become involved with children at the level of their own dilemmas, their unfinished business, thereby working to a resolution of their concerns, and at the same time validating them as persons in their own right. If this is successful these children might become free to learn in school those skills that will be important to them in the long run.

Such an approach has, in fact, been carried out. Lawrence (1971) isolated four groups of retarded readers and allocated each child to one of four groups. One group was given nothing extra. A second group was given remedial teaching. A third group was given remedial teaching and counselling and the fourth group was given counselling only. The improvement in reading was exactly the reverse order to that which I have given. As I understand Lawrence's report, counselling was provided by a firm but sympathetic adult who discussed with the children, in an open way, their day-to-day problems in relation to their families and their peer groups thereby helping them with their everyday transactions. In other words, the counsellor was fulfilling the prescription that seems to follow from the analysis of the problem that I have suggested. Moreover it was not necessary for this to be done by a professional psychotherapist but could become part of the professional skill of a sympathetic and realistic teacher.

Conclusion

'Emotional blockage' has had a value in protecting children against the charges of stupidity and laziness. 'Motivation' has had a value in sensitizing teachers to the children's own interests. In my view, however, these terms have outlived their usefulness as they inhibit the development of a unified theoretical framework for understanding children, which itself can provide a better guide for the teacher's own actions. I am aware, however, that in talking about a child's concerns I have presented 'concerns' in too negative a way and I have ignored their positive value. It is very relevant to say that our concerns sensitize us to a range of notions that might otherwise seem unrelated, and that they provide a dynamic for growth and change. In other words, appropriate concerns are central to learning itself. After all, this paper could not have been written without my own unfinished business of trying to understand children who are failing to learn to read.

Chapter 4
Personal construct theory: an approach to the psychological investigation of children and young people (1977)

This is the first account given to workers within personal construct theory (PCT) of how I had developed the practice of PCT in schools and child guidance. It does two important things. The first is to give a powerful critique of theory and practice in the light of my own developments, and the second is to offer a range of ideas and techniques appropriate in that area of work. The opportunity arose from the late Don Bannister's invitation to contribute to a forthcoming volume.

This essay presents an opportunity to put into writing some of the thoughts and experiences that have arisen out of the application of personal construct theory to the problems associated with children and with the people who work with children. Inevitably the essay will be personal in the sense that it will reflect something of my own development as a professional psychologist, and implicitly it will reflect something of my own personal prejudices and biases. I shall not, however, make this an occasion for the confessional nor for excessive self-examination, although personal construct theory might sanction both of these activities as basically growth promoting.

As a professional psychologist my concern is practical rather than theoretical and pragmatic rather than academic. This needs to be said in order to give a general direction to the reader. Having said that, however, I must also say that theory and practice should go hand in hand and that the detachment and involvement that each implies may be seen as a rhythmic redirection of energies as part of a growth process. A practitioner must be prepared to act, and therefore to err. He cannot wait until the niceties of theoretical ambiguities are resolved, nor can he wait for the findings of academic research. He is involved jointly with his clients in the ambiguities and dilemmas of life itself, and this is the context within which personal resolutions and personal research findings are created. Nonetheless, out of the dynamic of successive engagements between psychologist and client, ideas emerge that may lead to revised ways of working and these, in turn, may provide material that can enrich the basic formulations of theory, both as theory and as practice. Although my own involvement is with adults as complainants about children, and with the children who are complained about, there may be some original notions in this essay that are relevant in other therapeutic contexts. In the light of the very nature of personal construct theory it would be surprising if this were not so.

This essay will first explore something of the historical perspective leading up to my own present thinking and practice. This perspective will provide the basis for presenting some ideas that have not previously been made clear – ideas that I think may have important implications for practice. I shall then work out these implications by describing a number of techniques, each of which illustrates one facet of a single theme. Illustrative data will be drawn from children either having problems or presented as problems. I shall not offer an exhaustive account of interviewing techniques – that would be well beyond the scope of this particular essay – nor is the presentation concerned directly with developments in grid methodology, which has itself now become an independent field of study (Bannister and Mair, 1968; Bannister, 1970; Landfield, 1971; Bannister and Fransella, 1971; Fransella, 1972). I shall, however, refer to them as necessary stages in the development of interviewing techniques. The sequence of the essay therefore runs from practice to theory and back again, a rhythmic pattern that is embedded in personal construct theory itself, and which seems to reflect some of those universal rhythms that underlie development and growth.

Historical perspectives

In this part of the essay I propose to elaborate two themes that, although quite separate, are linked in an interesting way. The first theme is that of my own developmental steps in the use of personal construct theory. The second is the queries and difficulties of research students anxious to use grid techniques in the planning of their research, together with the difficulties that trainee psychologists experienced in adopting a personal construct theory approach to their work.

The decision to embark on a personal construct theory approach to children stemmed from dissatisfaction with the irrelevance of traditional psychometric approaches and with a distrust of the framework of assumptions underlying the use of projective techniques. Neither provided me with a basis either for understanding the troubles that children presented, or for helping teachers make a more useful sense of those very children who were causing them anxiety. Personal construct theory, on the other hand, immediately offered the promise both of purpose and relevance. There were of course no guidelines to show how the theory could be made to work with children. Kelly (1955, 1991) himself says little or nothing about his own work with children although he describes in graphic terms some aspects of his involvement with people who did deal with them. Under the circumstances it was natural to make a start with the techniques that Kelly devised to elicit constructs and to elucidate their organization (i.e. grids). After all, these techniques were easily understandable and were easily assimilated within a conceptual framework of numerical description and statistical analysis. Needless to say, however, this direct transposition of grid techniques from adults to children did not work (Ravenette, 1964a). The reason is clear. The population for which Kelly invented his construct elicitation procedures and his grid techniques was made up of university students, not children, and what was within the grasp of students certainly far exceeded the understanding of children. The world in which Kelly moved was manifestly not the world of working-class children within which I moved.

Bannister's work (Bannister and Mair, 1968) provided a key for the first development of grids with which children could cope, i.e. by using photographs in association with ranking techniques. It was a long time, however, before the question of children's constructs and their elicitation was resolved. The issue was dealt with in practice by providing constructs that were concerned with what significant people might expect and what these people might feel about children (Ravenette, 1975, gives a résumé and an illustration of this).

When I started developing a grid methodology that worked with children I was convinced that this was personal construct theory. Fortunately the falsity of this belief did not matter and it was possible to elaborate a variety of different grids with which it was possible to explore some of the ways in which children were able to make sense of things. All the time, it was clear, however, that the child himself was given little scope for providing his own observations within a grid framework. This weakness was resolved when situational pictures were used as the elements for a grid. Under this condition, the ways in which constructs clustered together made no real sense unless the child described what was happening in different situations. In this way the grid procedure provided a means whereby the psychologist's prescribed constructs acted as keys to unlock the doors of the child's own world. The formal use of a grid that prescribed constructs therefore now becomes a technique where the child's own construction of his world can be investigated. Clearly we can use the same procedure when the elements are photographs of children, and the first description of those elements can therefore provide a knowledge of some of the child's store of words whereby he discriminates his peer group, and perhaps himself. Where, for Kelly, the personal construct was essential to the grid itself, the use of the prescribed constructs within a grid structure provide a powerful means for eliciting the child's constructs and constructions. The procedure is illustrated by the following case, using a two-way analysis of an 8×8 grid.

The case of JB

JB was aged 15 years and 10 months. He was of bright average intelligence and was seen in a remand home. He had a history of school refusal and had recently left a succession of jobs. As a result he had been labelled 'work shy'. His father had killed JB's older brother, probably whilst drunk, and it was known that there had been tension between husband and wife. Father had been in gaol for manslaughter. There was trouble between mother and son. Recently his mother had turned JB out of the house. Previously JB had been in a children's home in the hope that he would attend school from there.

The prescribed constructs were derived from an awareness of the family relationships and also from a knowledge of the boy's behaviour in the remand home. They were:

A. Least likely to have friends.
B. Most likely to get on well with mother.
C. Least likely to get on well with father.
D. Most likely to understand other boys.
E. Frightened of what he sees in the family.
F. Feels he must keep away from other boys.
G. Most likely to be the same sort of boy as himself.
H. Most likely to be the sort of boy his mother would not like him to be.

Constructs A, C and H were presented in the opposite direction. The spontaneous constructs, i.e. his descriptions of the boys in the photographs, were:

1. Fairly quiet and reserved. Probably more interested in staying home than going out.
2. Probably very shy. Probably very good in school. Very interested in his work.
3. A little bit shy, not very much. Not particularly interested in school-work.
4. Probably like to go out. A little bit quiet. Very tactful.
5. Likely to go out with his friends all the time. Very outgoing. Probably untactful.
6. Likes to go out some of the time but helps at home. Probably quite interested in schoolwork.
7. Very outgoing. Fairly tactful. Probably likes to stay in quite often. Prefers friends to come to him.

8. Not very bright. Probably stays in quite a lot. Probably sees a few friends regularly.

The analysis of the correlational data indicated two construct clusters and these are reproduced with rearranged rank order in Table 4.1.

Table 4.1: Rearrangement of basic rank order data in relation to construct clusters for the case of JB

		Elements								
		2	3	5	4	8	1	6	7	
Least likely to have friends	A	1	2	3	5	6	4	7	8	Most likely to have friends
Mother would not choose him to be like	H	2	3	1	6	5	4	7	8	Mother would choose him to be like
Frightened of what he sees in the family	E	2	3	1	5	4	8	6	7	Not frightened of what he sees in the family

		Elements								
		2	3	1	4	8	6	7	5	
Most like himself	G	1	2	3	6	5	4	7	8	Least like himself
Understands other boys	F	2	1	3	5	4	6	7	8	Least likely to understand other boys
Feels he must keep away from other boys	D	1	3	2	5	4	6	7	8	Least likely to feel he must keep away from other boys

Construct cluster (A, H, E)

This cluster brings together the following ideas: boys who are 'least likely to have friends' are boys whom 'mother would not choose him to be like' and who 'would be most likely to be frightened by what they see in the family'. The opposite pole of the cluster would be defined as the opposite of this statement.

Construct clusters for JB

The corresponding element clusters for the two poles are (2, 3, 5) and (6, 7). An examination of the boy's spontaneous constructs for these two sets of elements reveals a lot of differences that cut across the two sets but one clearly defined pair of opposites, namely 'untactful–tactful'. If we broaden cluster (6, 7) to include element 4 (which is more like it than it is like (2, 3, 5)), 'tactful' again appears and this lends some support to the idea that 'untactful–tactful' is a central theme for the definition of this particular construct cluster.

It is interesting that, during the interview, the boy himself introduced the importance to him of being tactful in the presence of at least one member of his family. Psychologically, therefore, the construct seems particularly meaningful for this boy and within the context of his family.

Construct clusters (G, F, D)

This cluster brings together the following ideas. Boys who 'are most like the sort of boy he is' are also 'most likely to understand other boys' and 'would be most likely to feel that he must keep away from other boys'. The opposite pole of the cluster would be defined as the opposite of this statement.

The corresponding element clusters are (2, 3, 1) and (7, 5). Examination of the spontaneous constructs related to these elements shows a fairly clear contrast between 'shy, quiet and reserved' and 'very outgoing'. This might be labelled a form of social introversion–extroversion. His behaviour in the remand home suggests that the boy was, in fact, beginning to experiment along such lines, and his previous history of school refusal and not staying long in the outer world of work is consistent with self-characterization along this dimension.

Useful as grid procedures may be, it is also necessary to develop other questioning methods in order to explore the child's construction of his world. One specific technique involved elaborating with the child such causes of complaint that he might have with other people. Kelly (1955, 1991) provides a set of questions (originally formulated by Maher) whereby the child can state what he sees to be the trouble with boys, girls, teachers etc., how he understands why they are like that, what he would wish to happen, and how such changes might make a difference. Later I shall present this technique in more detail, but at the moment it is sufficient to say that even 6- and 7-year-old children are able to respond to such enquiries in a meaningful manner. Other sets of questions were invented to sound out a child's identifications within the family and his expectations of school.

These developments lead to the formulation of certain principles that seem to me to derive from, and be extensions of, personal construct theory as a means of working psychologically with children and young people. The basic tool of the psychologist is the question, and a part of his professional skill lies in his ability to invent better and better questions. Better in this context means facilitative for the child and penetrating for the interviewer. The investigation itself can be seen as a process in which elicitation of constructs comes first, and the operationalization, or use, of constructs comes second. The grid is one way in which this second phase is carried out, but it is possible to invent different ways and later in this essay I shall present one such alternative.

The second of the two themes in this historical account is concerned with my contacts with students. These students were of two kinds, the first kind was research psychologists aiming to acquire higher degrees, the second kind was trainee professional psychologists who were trying to broaden their interviewing techniques by using grids in particular, and perhaps a personal construct theory approach in general. The research psychologists had two questions: how could they use grid techniques in their research and how could they elicit children's constructs.

As my own experience increased I found it more and more difficult to help research psychologists with their questions since, in order to do so, I had to challenge some of their fundamental assumptions about children and personal construct theory. Quite correctly, they were seeking test instruments that fitted in with the methodological canons of academic research, but they also seemed to have an implicit notion that measures should or could be simple. At the same time they seldom saw the possibility of involving children themselves in resolving some of the researcher's own difficulties almost as though it must be the psychologist who knows best. I cannot go into all the issues that these questions pose but I would like to raise just a few.

The first of these is in relation to grids and their interpretation. Clearly a grid that is completed without any spontaneous involvement of the child other than in the rank ordering of elements will be restricted by the sensitivities of the psychologist. It will not say much about the child and his psychological processes. Any statement about reliability and validity can only refer to the extent to which the child fitted himself to the task and intentions of the experimenter. If we invite the child himself to contribute to the grid we are faced on the one hand with the difficulty of standardizing the procedures and on the other arriving at general observations. These remarks are about grids in relation to meaning. Other remarks are about grids in relation to statistics.

It is, of course, easy to refer basic grid data to a computer and then abstract out what we want. I must confess, however, to a feeling of unease when confronted with printout from the computer of one child's eight-element grid. The amount of material thus presented hardly seems justified by the basic data. More importantly, however, the use of a computer removes the psychologist from his data and this may cut him off from the possibility of making important discoveries for which the computer was not programmed. As an example of this I would mention a phenomenon that I call the 'joker in the pack'. If the reader will return to Table 4.1 he will find that element 5 is responded to somewhat anomalously. If this element is removed from the grid the two construct clusters will be positively correlated. Its presence, however, at opposite poles in the two clusters leads to correlations in the original matrix which are nearly zero. This element is the 'joker in the pack' because its presence throws awry an interpretation based on assumptions of linearity. In psychological terms this element presumably has a special significance for the client but in statistical terms its presence might well suggest some form of non-linear relationship (rather than no relationship). A perfect curvilinear relationship provides a zero linear correlation, but this will be revealed only by an examination of the basic data.

Many more reservations might be made about the use of simple grids as research instruments, but perhaps they are best summarized in a more general form. Academic research seems to demand abstractions based on populations of individuals. The grid, however, when carried out as a joint investigation between a psychologist and child, may reveal truths only at an individual level. To find truth requires looking at the fine detail of what happened whereas traditional research demands that the fine detail be ignored, in favour of high-order generalizations. In many ways the best use that can be made of the generalizations that statistics provide is in re-ordering the basic data in the light of those generalizations. This may well be true both for formal research as well as for the study of the individual.

When we turn to the research student's enquiries about children's actual constructs the problem becomes much more difficult. At the heart of this question is the issue of what a construct is. I shall present my clarification of this issue in the next section, and make only a few remarks here. The most obvious difficulty stems from the fact that the students seemed to be committed to the notion that constructs were words and, moreover, that there might exist, or might be invented, lists of words that were children's constructs. When, however, we took their questions seriously and suggested they asked children for themselves it became clear that this presented even more difficulties. On some occasions, when they did this, a transcript of the conversation read rather like a lesson in school carried out in the style that the student himself had suffered as a pupil. In other words, the students needed to learn how to interview children before they could elicit the material they wanted.

This particular difficulty enables me to bring in my second kind of student – the trainee psychologist learning a way of interviewing. He invariably showed exactly the same difficulty in questioning children as the research students, almost as though the whole of his training and experience so far had acted against the idea that if he asked good questions he could trust the child to come up with some worthwhile answers. Even when children had produced a wide range of attributes that might be usable in some form of grid, these students seemed to feel that there were rules whereby they, the psychologists, choose the most important ones, rather than the children themselves. It is as though, somehow, the child was not to be entrusted with the task of making his own choices. This was the psychologist's prerogative, although he may need help and guidance in order to do it correctly. Such a stance is, of course, in flat contradiction to the stance of the personal construct psychologist. Hopefully we do have some expertise that we can make available to children, but this may be more in the direction of helping them to communicate about themselves and their difficulties, and how to envisage alternative ways of thinking and acting.

The point of this historical perspective is twofold. In the first place I think it is clear that my own progress in personal construct theory was in some way measured by the increasing difficulty in giving answers to those research students who, year after year, came up with the same questions. In the second place, by trying to implement a personal construct theory approach it became apparent that I was progressively learning what it was. It is possible that learning the theory from other people's existing practice may have been quicker, but it may not have had the same personal validity. Thirdly, this résumé provides a frame of reference in which I can develop some thoughts about theoretical issues that stem directly from this learning process.

From practice to theory

Kelly did not write a developmental theory. Although he was clearly concerned with the problems surrounding children, he wrote in greater detail abut the work of people who had to deal with children than about the development of children themselves. When he was asked his views about the development of constructs in children he suggested that the earliest constructs were states of the organism. At a later stage people who were important in a child's life acted as constructs, and later still they became represented by verbal symbols. My own experience suggests that he omitted one very powerful basis for children's expectations, namely children's own actions and the actions of others in relation to children.[1]

It was perhaps inevitable that this area of personal construct theory elaboration should be missing from Kelly's work. He was, after all, primarily involved with a university population and drew some of his inspiration from the similarities he saw between clients with personal problems and students with research problems. When, therefore, he illustrates constructs and construct systems his samples are drawn from relatively articulate students and consequently appear as rather abstract verbalizations. It is true that he frequently points to the fact that many of our actions are based on anticipations that were developed before we had verbal means of labelling, and he also warns against the dangers of equating constructs with verbalism or literalisms. Nonetheless, the very fact of writing about these things puts a premium on verbalisms and the impact of this on students coming to grips with the theory for the first time seems to be in the direction of their equating real constructs with their verbal representation.

There are, of course, a number of important differences between adults and children, and these need to be pointed out. To a great extent the adult is already relatively mature and any psychological change that takes place is on a base of reasonably stable expectations. The years of childhood represent a time during which this relatively stable base is being developed. They are years of transition. Moreover, with children, even if their bases for anticipating acquire some stability, the verbal representation of these anticipations is likely to be itself unstable and ephemeral. It is part of the growth process that the child is able to make progressively finer levels of discrimination and to develop a greater hierarchy of abstractions, both of which, over time, lead to richer and more complex construct systems. It follows from this that the elicitation of children's constructs is a far-from-simple affair, especially when children are young. The words they use should not be taken for the constructs, nor should it be assumed that a child's constructs could be couched at a high level of abstraction. In many ways the constructs which are important behaviourally may be just those that defy easy verbalization and that in fact exist at a rather low level of awareness.

I think that some of the difficulties and ambiguities that these last observations imply stem from a single failure in semantic discrimination. We need to recognize a distinction between 'scientific' and 'spontaneous' or ordinary language. When Kelly talks of constructs and construct systems he is offering a 'scientific' language in which the terms have very precise meanings within an articulated theory. Sadly, however, we so easily use scientific expressions as a part of ordinary discourse and frequently it is not at all clear, when these expressions appear, whether they are to be taken in their 'scientific' sense or as ordinary words. The expressions 'construe', 'construct' and 'construct system' all share this double usage. I think that Kelly himself sometimes fails to discriminate between these different usages, or at least he fails to point out the nature of the trap. Before presenting my own resolution of the problem I would like to say a little more about what I think constructs are meant to be or to do.

We can go along comfortably with Kelly in seeing the construct as a two-ended affair whereby we have a basis for discriminating the phenomenal world or people, of objects, or internal states and of all their manifold interrelationships. Discriminating in this sense also carries something of the meaning of anticipations or expectations. It is also easy to go along with the idea of hierarchical arrangements of constructs and a progressive development of system complexity over time. These statements are all, of course, couched in unscientific language within personal construct theory. When, however, I have worked with children and young people trying specifically to elicit constructs, both they and I have found the work extremely difficult. We have struggled hard, frequently ending up with 'one-ended' constructs and on occasions I have had the suspicion that the client has merely gone in for 'word-spinning' in order to finish the ordeal. It has not been unusual for the client to challenge the whole enterprise as boring and irrelevant.

Gradually it dawned on me that when I was asking my clients to produce constructs I was inviting them to do something they had never done before. That being the case they were committed to finding expressions for abstractions that they had never before verbalized, or they had to generate abstractions where previously their experiences, their thoughts and feelings had been relatively fluid. Under these circumstances it is not surprising that they found the task very difficult and exhausting. If, for a moment, we forget the scientific language of personal construct theory and revert to everyday language the interview begins to flow. I say to them that I am interested in how they make sense of things, and ask questions to that end. They are then able to respond fluently, meaningfully and often with considerable perspicacity. I cannot say that, at that stage, they had produced constructs. They have talked of what they saw, what they did, what they felt, what they said, what other people said and so forth. They did, in fact, produce material out of which constructs might eventually be fashioned, and, if they were invited to reflect back over all they had said and done, they were sometimes able to produce abstractions that were novel and meaningful and that might indeed be called constructs in their own right. The transition from scientific terminology to an ordinary terminology therefore enabled interviewing to become a live possibility instead of an arid exercise. Clearly I am advocating a further level of description in addition to those that Kelly formulated in the theory of personal constructs. The justification for this is that it loosens up the whole process of interviewing by allowing the invention of questions that enable clients to talk about themselves. This, of course, is but the first step in the resolution of their dilemmas. There is, however, an implication from this argument that is both theoretically important and clinically useful.

I would like to put forward the view that the knowledge of a person's constructs is, of necessity, inferential, both for the client and for the psychologist. This follows from the argument that the client does not 'know' his constructs until we provide a situation in which he is asked to produce them, and when he does produce them, he produces them for the first time. Although we may have a personal hope for fact rather than inference, there are certain advantages in this formulation. The very speculative nature of inference forces us to go back to the client for his observations on the validity of our thinking. Further, the acceptance of inference allows us to think and think again if our first inferences seem unproductive. The retreat from a factual basis for asserting what a person's constructs are to an inferential judgement about what a person's constructs might be offers a far greater range of therapeutic options whilst at the same time reducing the risks of wasted time and energy on discussions of what the truth of things might be.

None of this is, of course, out of line with Kelly's own practice. His extended chapter on self-characterization (Kelly 1955, 1991, Chapter 7) seems to me to be an essay in inferential analysis. In this task the client is not invited to produce his constructs but rather to write a self-characterization sketch as by someone who knows him intimately and sympathetically. Under these circumstances a knowledge of his constructs can only be inferential, based on a study of the ways in which the material is composed, the interrelationships between its various parts and the internal consistencies and inconsistencies of the whole work.

I now want to extend the argument to construct systems as such. I have already said that people do not know what their constructs are, and indeed are frequently puzzled when asked formally to produce them. The notion of a construct system must therefore be of the same order. People do not appeal to their construct systems in order to act. They are their construct systems and always have been. Life goes on reasonably smoothly for most people without such conscious deliberation, and problems are usually taken in their stride. That being the case it follows that construct systems as such are built up and maintained at a low level of awareness. If conscious choices are made that lead to a proliferation or simplification of construct systems, the choices, once made, cease to be matters for conscious concern. Our construct systems therefore are an essential part of ourselves that we, perforce, take for granted, do not need to formulate and to which we seldom, if ever, need to refer.

This formulation has certain implications, the most obvious of which is that in order to discover something of a person's construct system we have to invite him to explore and communicate that which he is already taking for granted. It also means that we, as interviewers, must be careful not to take for granted those things that are self-evident to the client, but not perhaps to us. If we fail to do this we are likely to fail in understanding what he has to say. I can illustrate this best with an example taken from an interview with a mother. She described an incident where her son was 'showing off', an expression which to me (and to most people whom I asked) meant boasting or unnecessarily drawing attention to oneself. This meaning, however, did not make sense in the context of the mother's report so she was asked to say what her son actually did. She reported the following sequence of events: he pulled a face, ran over to the door, threw it open, ran out slamming it behind him, and ran down the stairs into the street. The description, seemed to me more likely an expression of anger (which did fit the context) and the mother agreed that this was indeed the case.[2]

In this particular case we chose not to take the mother's abstraction for granted and invited her instead to elaborate the concrete referents underlying that abstraction. As one outcome, we were able to agree a different abstraction to cover the concrete data, an abstraction that had important implications in relation to the mother's relationship with her son. The same principle also applies to the reporting of events by a client. The events that clients report have meaning only in relation to their own construct systems. Just as we take our constructs for granted, so many events in a sequence will go unreported because they also are taken for granted. What is reported in relation to what is left unsaid is comparable to the relationship between figure and ground. When a client gives us the salient facts as he sees them we tend to provide our own 'ground' in order to understand what he is telling us. This may be good enough in ordinary conversation, but in psychological work with clients we frequently need to investigate the ground against which the client's own report has meaning. In other words, when we are offered the spoken events in a sequence, we must ask for the unspoken events. I can illustrate this with a small part of an interview with John who is aged 15. John was seeing me because he had been threatening to commit suicide. He was having violent angry outbursts at home. He had not been able to go to school. His father had died in an accident some five months previously. John himself had complained of his bouts of violent anger and as a therapeutic task I had asked him to observe and report one of them to me in detail. In this particular interview I asked him to report back on the last outburst. He said that he had asked his friend to join him so that they could do something together. Everything John suggested his friend turned down. This made John very angry and he stormed out. This was his report. Whilst the sequence does indeed carry a consistent logic it says very little about the detail of the events. So he was asked to close his eyes and recreate the whole sequence from the time he went to knock up his friend to the final angry outburst. He was to report what he said, did, felt and thought, what other people did, what noises he heard and so forth.

The very ordinariness of the task made it difficult and John needed considerable prompting in order to do it. What did come out, however, was extremely important for an understanding of many aspects of John and his place in the family. The revised account now included many more events: his friend was not ready to go out and would not be for 30 minutes. John spent that time with his mother and with Paul (an adult) who, as John said, would marry his mother when he, John, was 'straightened out'. Between them they discussed the possible things that John might do with his friend, but it was John's mother who made most of the suggestions. In fact the suggestions that John's friend turned down were very much those that John's mother had put forward in his absence. It seems to me very clear that this elaboration now includes a number of issues that are important in understanding John's relationship to his family and the bases for his anger. One might specify his mother's intention to remarry so quickly, the onus placed on John to 'straighten himself out' and the conflict in loyalties his friend inevitably imposed in unwittingly turning down the various suggestions for joint activity which the mother had offered.

I have been stressing in this section the view that people are, by and large, ignorant of their constructs and construct systems, and in this sense their construct systems are part of that large aspect of living and experience that is taken for granted. At the most general level of practice, therefore, I would suggest that when things in a person's life, or in a family's life, go so wrong as to call for outside help, the problems are likely to be located in just those areas that the person takes for granted rather than on the outside events with which the client claims to be failing. People usually cope remarkably well with new tensions and new demands. When they fail it is my guess that the existing constructions that a person is using must be looked into rather than the events that the person presents. To do this, of course, is rather daunting as it requires the psychologist to question what is taken for granted and to look again at the obvious. This is daunting too for the client, who may well prefer to explore the dramatic rather than the commonplace.

From theory back to practice

As I said at the outset of this essay, my main concern is a continued involvement with children and young people and with those adults who are worried about them. Thus my excursion into theory (which stems directly from work with children) becomes important if it leads to improvements and changes in interviewing techniques and therapeutic strategies. Before illustrating this, however, it is necessary to present a framework within which interviewing techniques can be described.

We are unlikely to make much progress in understanding our clients unless we can induce them to talk about themselves. Thus a prime function of interviewing techniques is that they make it easy for a child to respond. It needs to be remembered that children do not present themselves as having problems for which they require help. It is rather the case that they are presented as the focus of complaints by adults. Under these circumstances there is no reason why a child should see a psychological interview as other than meaningless and irrelevant.

One of the greatest inhibitors of communication about oneself is that we do not know what the enquirer wants, nor what he will do with it if he gets it. This is even more likely to be true for children. It becomes important therefore that children know why they are being interviewed, and what the purpose of the psychologist's questions are. If, therefore, we specify the topic of the enquiry and the nature of the questions that will be asked, the child is given freedom, within limits, to communicate his understanding of himself and others. An enquiry that is contained within a systematic structure allows a wide range of thoughts and feelings to be explored with relative safety for the child and with a considerable economy of time for the investigator.

A second principle indicates that if we want to know someone well we should explore the areas in which he is expert. In relation to children, granted a state of trust, we should be prepared to investigate the child in relation to school and in relation to his family, and with delinquents their expertise in delinquency.

A third principle suggests that we must be wary of assuming that we know what a child means by his descriptive labels. We do not necessarily share common ground with children, nor is the recollection of our own childhood a guarantee that what he says matches our own experiences. Thus we must be prepared to ask and ask again. If, for instance, a child says that he is upset when he is involved in a fight we need to ask if this is because of the possibility of physical pain, or because of psychological embarrassment in case he loses, or because the edicts of his parents are being flouted, thereby testing his loyalties and so forth. He takes for granted that we know which aspect of the situation is upsetting, but, of course, we do not know unless we ask.

In summary, therefore, I am suggesting that if we are to maximize our chances of helping a child to talk to us we must take him into our confidence about the issues we might both be interested in, ask questions in a systematic manner and enquire in areas in which the child feels relatively safe in his own expertise. At any point we can choose to question the basis for the child's response and we may need to help him in this by offering a number of possible answers from which he alone can pick the one that is personally relevant. Structure frequently enables the verbally inhibited to talk and can also be used to constrain the garrulous. Within this framework the point of my theoretical exposition becomes clear. We do not, in the first place, seek for constructs; instead we try to find out how a child makes sense of himself, and people and their interrelationships. This is the overall aim of the interview. We shall arrive at a child's constructs as a result of inference, and hopefully this will be a shared activity. In the second place we shall be concerned with exploring those aspects of a child's perception and awareness that he takes for granted, that part that operates at a low level of awareness. In a way we can call this an exploration of ordinariness because it is in the everyday experiences that we seek a child's construct system, not in fantasy or in the dramatic incidents of life. It must be conceded that to talk about the ordinary, and the part of ourselves that we take for granted, is not easy.

There is, however, a way around this difficulty. Those aspects of life that, in one way or another, we label 'trouble' represent ways in which our expectations are invalidated. In fact, the variety of troubles we experience may be valuable pointers to expectations that we take for granted. If, therefore, we invite a person to talk about troubles we are automatically exploring his unverbalized expectations of life. Troubles are, in fact, a rich source of enquiries. Individuals themselves may represent troubles, as in delinquency. Individuals may complain of the ways other people are a trouble to them. Troubles may be those inner feelings, as when we are ourselves troubled or upset. We can use these different aspects of 'troubles', which will form the last part of this essay.

Delinquency implications matrix and polygon

This technique was developed in work with delinquent boys and its use assumes that the boys are to some extent already fairly conversant with delinquency. 'Trouble' in this context is the fact that boys brought before the court are already 'in trouble'. A boy is invited to give his knowledge of eight common delinquent activities, and only if he does this satisfactorily is the implications grid given. The eight activities are recorded on separate pieces of numbered paper (an activity that the boy shares). The main task is for the boy to consider each delinquent activity with every other, and say if, in his view, boys who commit the one are likely, by and large, to commit the other. His responses are recorded in a matrix and when that part of the task is completed they are analysed through the implications polygon. Every step of the task and the analysis is explained so that he sees the pattern of his own thoughts reproduced in diagrammatic form. It is usually difficult to see the pattern of clusters that is implicit in the polygon until the linkages are teased or 'shaken out'. When this is done, clusters of delinquent activities emerge that can then provide the basis for further elaborative questioning.

The following example was worked out with a 15-year-old boy (Joseph) who had been in trouble with the police for 'going equipped to steal' and 'housebreaking'. He had also been pupil at a residential school for maladjusted children from which he had frequently played truant. The eight delinquent activities appear at the left of Table 4.2 and the symbol '0' in the body of the grid means that the boys who commit delinquent activity numbered on that row are likely also to commit the activity numbered by the column.

The implicative links in the body of the grid are represented in Figure 4.1. A dotted arrow shows one-way linkages and a solid line shows a reciprocal linkage. The pattern emerges much more clearly in the 'shaken out' diagram in Figure 4.2.

Three possible forms of interpretative analysis are possible in terms of hierarchies (cf. Hinkle, 1965) in terms of mutual exclusiveness, or (and this is the simplest form of analysis) through reciprocal implications.

The reciprocal implications for Joseph's responses appear in Figure 2 and it can be seen at a glance that 'housebreaking' (4), 'going equipped to steal' (5) and 'receiving stolen goods' (6) form one cluster, and 'truancy' (8), 'GBH' (2) and 'vandalism' (7) form a second. These two

Table 4.2: Delinquency implications matrix for Joseph

		1	2	3	4	5	6	7	8	
1. TDA (Taking and driving away)	1				0	0		0	0	1
2. GBH (Grievous bodily harm)	2			0				0	0	2
3. Mugging	3		0		0	0	0		0	3
4. Housebreaking	4					0	0	0	0	4
5. Going equipped to steal	5	0			0		0	0	0	5
6. Receiving stolen goods	6	0			0	0			0	6
7. Vandalism	7		0	0					0	7
8. Truancy	8	0	0					0		8
		1	2	3	4	5	6	7	8	

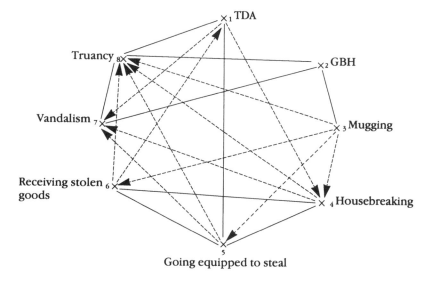

Dotted lines indicate one-way implications
Solid lines indicate reciprocal implications

Figure 4.1: Implications polygon for data in Table 4.2

clusters are linked by 'TDA' (1) and 'GBH' (2) also has reciprocal implications with 'mugging' (3). We can now ask more questions to elaborate
the bases for these clusters. He says that the (2, 8, 7) cluster is made up
of boys who would be hard nuts whereas the (4, 5, 6) cluster is made up
of boys who would be crafty. In response to my question about who
would be criminals for life he says the (4, 5, 6) boys but of those at the
opposite end (2, 8, 7) he says as they grow older they will grow out of it,
they realize what they are doing. His attention was then drawn to the
other axis represented by 'vandalism' at one end and 'mugging' at the

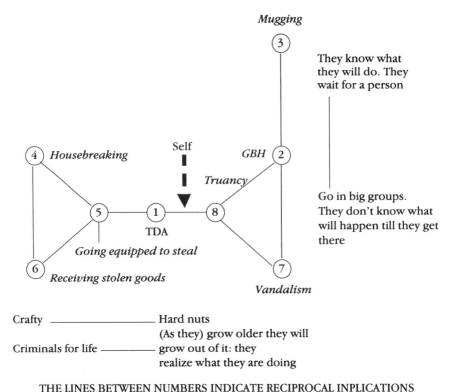

THE LINES BETWEEN NUMBERS INDICATE RECIPROCAL INPLICATIONS

Figure 4.2: Delinquency implications for Joseph ('shaken out' version)

other. Of boys who do 'mugging' he says they know what they will do, they wait for a person. Of boys who commit vandalism he says they go in big groups, they don't know what will happen until they get somewhere. He was finally asked where, in this pattern of delinquency activities he would place himself. His answer was unequivocally as the 'TDA'/'truant'.

If we wish to infer constructs underlying Joseph's conceptualization of delinquency and delinquent boys it would seem that two should be sufficient to encompass the data. The first would have reference to aggressive, unthinking adolescent delinquency as opposed to craft, near professional delinquency. Included in this construct would be correlated ideas of delinquency as a stage of development as opposed to delinquency as a final stage of development. The second construct would be concerned with violence and sets criminal intent together with a degree of social isolation against spontaneous delinquency as an aspect of group membership. 'TDA'/'truant' forms a linking concept and, as this is where Joseph places himself, it seems to imply for him a choice point between a growing out of delinquency on the one hand and a life of professional delinquency on the other. The more important question of whether or not Joseph can abandon the delinquent choice goes beyond this presentation.

The elaboration of complaints

The focus of this technique is, quite simply, the complaints that an individual voices against people who might be important in his life. I quoted the technique earlier in the essay but present it here in greater detail as part of the theoretical stance based on the investigation of troubles.

The pattern of the enquiry runs:

1. The trouble with most . . . is . . .
2. They are like that because . . .
3. Another reason they are like that is . . .
4. It would be better if . . .
5. What difference would that make?
6. What difference would that make to you?

(The people presented in (1) include boys, girls, teachers, brothers, sisters, fathers, mothers and self.)

In order to present the child with an orientation to the task, he is reminded of the way in which for instance teachers will say 'the trouble with that boy is . . . ' or a mother will say 'The trouble with that boy is . . . ' or a mother will say 'The trouble with that family is . . . ' He is then invited to say what he considers, from his own point of view, the trouble with different people might be. Some children, of course, immediately offer adult complaints, but this can be challenged. If for instance a boy says that the trouble with most boys is that they fight, we need to know if he is echoing parents and teachers or if this is a real complaint of his own. Other children will deny that they have any trouble with some of the persons, and this is perfectly acceptable as a response. Some children fail to answer each part of an enquiry about an individual person. This, too, is acceptable. Omissions are as informative, in their own way, as answers.

To illustrate this technique I shall use the responses of a 16-year-old West Indian boy who had been remanded for the two apparently unrelated crimes of indecent assault and receiving stolen goods. (In connection with the charge of indecent assault we do not know the details so we cannot establish either the extent to which there was provocation or the seriousness of the assault. As frequently happens, the technical language of the law obscures rather than reveals the behaviour of the delinquent.)

In reporting James's responses I shall reduce them to consecutive prose by omitting the number of each question in the sequence, and italicizing his actual words. I shall also insert an interpretative comment where I feel it appropriate.

1. The trouble with most BOYS is they most likely want to go round with each other in a gang. They are like that because they have nothing to do, they follow each other, and because they like to have friends. James could give no way in which things might be better.

2. The trouble with most GIRLS is they also like to go round in gangs. They are like that because they like to follow the way of the boys, and boys and girls have to get together sometimes, that's when it begins, when they start liking each other. James could give no way in which things might be better.

James is here pointing out a contrast between solitariness, which he seems to find painful, and being in a gang, which by definition is a trouble. A sense of the emptiness of life permeates these answers, yet the resolution of this emptiness implies trouble. It is noteworthy that James can give reasons but he can give no implication for how things might be better.

3. The trouble with most BROTHERS is the old brothers and sisters like to put the young ones down. They are like that because they have to stick together and because there might be some disagreement. It would be better if they stuck together and tried to work together. If this happened and they worked together they would really understand each other's feelings, and if they understood my feelings they might be able to help me.

James here points to disharmony with his older siblings and the barriers that he feels are put in the way of understanding. He points to the need for solidarity, presumably against a hostile world, amongst siblings as opposed to group membership, which merely fills an emptiness of life. In the end, however, he points to the primacy of his feelings and a need for these to be understood – a need that could be met by working together, rather than talking together, with his siblings.

4. The trouble with most FATHERS is they most likely favour the girls more than the boys. James could give no reasons. *It would be better if they not only liked the girls but liked the boys as well. If this happened they would be able to help the boy in his feelings and if this happened to him if my father showed me that he really liked me he would help me not to get in such trouble.*

5. The trouble with most MOTHERS is they most like the boys. James could give no reasons. *It would be better if they liked girls as well as boys, if girls got on with them as well as the boys.* James could not say what difference this would make.

James describes a family system in which the alliances are across the sexes rather than within the sexes. This can obviously create problems for an adolescent boy, especially if he sees the outside world as hostile. It is perhaps not surprising that he documents the case against his father more fully than the case against the mother. This is in line with his complaint that his brothers have also failed him.

6. The trouble with JAMES himself. *I like my way too much and don't get it.* He is like that because *I suppose my mother likes me more than my dad (does), and because I was brought up that way. It would be better if I was liked by both mum and dad, then my dad would understand my feelings.*

Although James puts forward the issue as one of having his own way, almost inevitably he points back to his feelings and the failure of his father to understand him as the real problem. With the family constellation as James describes it, perhaps homosexuality might be one logical next step for this boy. We do not know what happened.

I shall illustrate the remaining two 'troubles' techniques with material from one case. The boy in question is Mark, aged 10 years. He presents a serious problem in school, both to teachers and to other children, because of his behaviour. He is said to have been difficult from the time of starting school. He alternates between being 'good, hard working and conforming' and being a 'troublemaker'. Other boys are suspicious of him because of his unpredictability and the instability of his interpersonal relationships. He is said to have acquaintances rather than friends. It is known that there are considerable tensions within the family and between the parents and school. Mother is dominating and unpredictable; father tends to be self-effacing. In the first part of the interview (not reported here) Mark showed an awareness of many tensions at home. He indicated that he was closely identified with his mother but seemed to regret a lack of involvement with father. A younger brother, in fact, was closely identified with father, and, as a boy, was aggressively masculine, assertive and daring.

Perceptions of troubles in school

In this technique the child is offered eight pictures of ordinary situations in school, drawn with some ambiguity as to detail, but otherwise quite straightforward. He is then invited, within a sequence of questions, to isolate and describe the child who might be troubled or upset. If the child says that no one is troubled, he is invited to consider 'if someone is troubled, who would it be?' If the child gives an adult as the one who is troubled this is accepted but the child is then invited to give an alternative version in which it is a child who is upset. The sequence of questions runs thus:

1. What do you think is happening?
2. Who might be troubled and why?
3. How did this come about?
4. If you were there what would you do and why?
5. What difference would that make?
6. What kind of boy is the one picked out in Q.2?

From the responses to this sequence it is possible to gain some idea of how a child actually perceives various situations in school and how he understands some of the interactions that take place there, how willingly he identifies himself with these situations and the extent of his understanding of different ways of coping. The final question in each sequence presses the child to a level of abstraction that summarizes the troubled character whom he has presented.

This sequence represents a complete technique in itself and, as will be seen from the data obtained from Mark, the information is extensive. We can, if we so wish, proceed to some method of systematizing the data. The therapeutic value of this rests on the fact that the child is thereby committed to a serious review of his own understanding of things. At the same time the possibility arises that he might make some important personal discoveries that could influence his future behaviour. With Mark we used the formulations arising from his answer to question 6 as the material for an implications matrix (as previously described).

Before giving the details of Mark's responses I should make some comments on the differences between the aims of this technique and the more commonly known projective techniques, e.g. TAT and CAT (cf. Ravenette, 1972a). In the first place the child's imagination is turned to the reconstruction of ordinary things rather than to the creation of 'fantasy' stories. The telling of stories would, in fact, be a disadvantage as it avoids the questions that are posed, and uses up a great deal of time in doing so. In the second place, the investigations take the form of an active dialogue, not only in setting the structure, but also in collaboratively clarifying the meaning of a child's responses. In the third place, we invite the child to be an observer and reporter on incidents that he shares, and also to take some responsibility in imagination for his own involvement in school. Fourthly, at the interpretative level, a premium is put on the mapping of conscious awareness, rather than the deliberate exploration of lower levels of awareness. That aspect of a child's functioning is taken up either inferentially as in analysis of the data, or as a basis for feedback and further exploration with the child himself during the interview. Mark's responses to the eight pictures are given in Table 4.3.

The amount of information provided by the questions in Table 4.3 is very great – so great as to make interpretation itself very difficult even if such an analysis were necessarily called for. (Should we wish to undertake such a task, Kelly's suggestions for analysing self-characterization sketches might well be relevant. In this he assumes that the client seldom moves far from his starting point, and when he does it is usually by means either of contrasts or through the elaboration of what he has already presented.) At a very simple level of analysis we can take all the descriptions given in response to Question 6 and see in them the characterization of at least one boy who would find school a difficult place in which to exist. We should not assume, of course, that this characterization is Mark himself, although it might be one version of him. The version he, in fact, offers must be inferred from his answers to Question 4, and his view of his effectiveness from the answers to Question 5.

In practice we used seven of the characterizations given in response to Question 6 as the material for an implication grid matrix (as previously described). The graphical analysis was carried out with Mark and the 'shaken out' version appears in Figure 4.3. The elaborative choice after this graphical analysis was simply to ask Mark to indicate where he fitted in the diagram, where his parents and his teacher would put him, and, if he could be different, where he would choose to be.

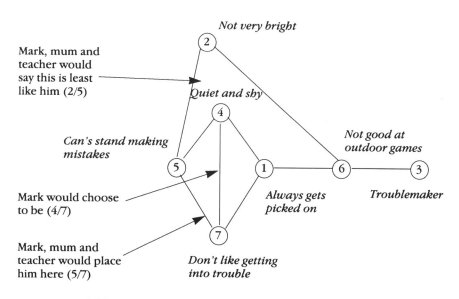

A SOLID LINE STANDS FOR RECIPROCAL IMPLICATIONS

Figure 4.3: Personal attributes implications for Mark ('shaken out' version)

A study of the content of the clusters suggests that three dimensions (or, inferentially, constructs) may be necessary to understand the pattern of implications. The first dimension could be intellectual brightness with only the 'not-very-bright' pole named. Mark confirmed this himself. A second dimension would be concerned with trouble, with the two extremes labelled 'not liking to get into trouble' and 'troublemaker'. The third dimension is defined by only one end, 'quiet and shy'. Later in the interview Mark does in fact define a boy who is rough, able to beat people up and not scared. Presumably this could be the missing pole, in which case this dimension would have important implications for the style of interpersonal relationships open to him. The use of an implica-

Table 4.3: Mark's responses to perception of trouble in schools

What do you think is happening?	Who do you think is upset and why?	How did it come about?	If you were there, what would you be doing and why?	What difference would that make?	What sort of person is the one who is troubled?
1. Playing a game	The 2nd from left would be upset because he is always getting picked on.	This is a game when they are fighting. The weak one is upset.	If Paul were there he would not mix, as they would pick on him.	This would probably lead to trouble.	The central figure is the boy who *always gets picked on*.
2a. They are coming out of school, mother is waiting for them.	The mothers are upset. They did not realize the time. Housework not done.	Probably they did not start their housework until late.	Paul would do nothing. He cannot do the work.		
2b. The boy had a bad day at school. His sums were wrong, and he was told off.		He probably got up late. He was still tired.	Paul would say to the boy 'it is not your fault'. He would do this to please him.	The central character here would be *not very bright*.	
3. A lesson in school – arithmetic.	Boy at blackboard is upset trying to do a sum. He may be unable to do it.	He does not like doing sums, he does not listen.	If Paul were there he would say 'don't worry', nothing he can do.	This would make no difference.	The central character here would be a *troublemaker*.*
4. They are playing on some apparatus.	The boy does not like the apparatus, he is scared of heights.	He had been up a hill before and fallen down.	If Paul were there he would say, 'have another go'.	It might make some difference to the boy.	This boy would be a *quiet and shy boy*.

5. A lesson.	One of the boys does not like the lesson. He is not doing it.	He does not like the lesson.	Paul would tell him to have a go at it. He may get it right.	The boy might like the lesson if he gets a few right.	The boy does not like the lesson, *cannot stand making errors.*
6. A game of football.	The boy who cannot play, they won't let him play.	They do not like him.	He would ask the boys whether I could play and maybe he could.	It is worth asking.	This boy would be *no good at football* (or outdoor games generally).
7. This is a presentation.	The boy who gets nothing is upset. He was not in to pass the things.		Paul would say to him 'you can have another go next year maybe'.	The difference is the boy would think I will try and not get colds.	The boy is *untidy*, he hasn't a Dad. He would be a good. sportsman.**
8. Two boys getting the cane	They were not in the wrong, but were getting punished.	The boy who picked on him gets in trouble and retaliated.	Paul would say it was not his fault.	He may not get the cane.	This *boy does not like getting into trouble.*

* Did not like doing work.

** This sequence is extremely puzzling because it seems to bring together very contradictory ideas, probably indicating extreme anxiety.

tions grid procedure provides a way in which the ideas generated by the 'perception of troubles in school' technique can be reduced to manageable proportions.

The exploration of personal troubles

The fourth technique explores a child's personal troubles as expressed through the medium of his drawings. He is reminded that (all people) boys, girls, men and women, have times when they are troubled inside themselves. They feel hurt, angry, ashamed, embarrassed, worried and so forth. We would like him to draw pictures to show five occasions in which he would be troubled or upset. While the invitation is being made a sheet of paper is folded into six rectangles and a mark is put into five of them. It is pointed out to him that these marks are merely to help him get started on his drawings and he does not have to use them. He is given the pencil and invited to carry on. If he says he does not understand what he has to do, an example is given of what another boy has done. This is usually sufficient for him to understand. Some children produce fewer than five drawings and this is acceptable. In the sixth space the child is invited to draw a situation in which everything would be fine, he would feel good, and people would seem good. When he has finished drawing he is asked to say what is happening in each picture. This completes the basic task. He is then invited to respond to a rather challenging elaboration. He is asked to think of a child who, in all of these troubling situations, would not in fact be troubled. Specifically he is asked to give three descriptions of such a boy. Two more questions are asked: when would this new character be troubled or upset, and when did this new character accurately describe the child himself? The answers to these two questions frequently show a depth of understanding and an originality that is surprising both to the interviewer and to the people who are familiar with the child. In many ways this particular enquiry forms a dramatic high point in an interview.

The material that illustrates this technique is drawn from the last part of the interview with Mark. He was able to give only four occasions on which he would be troubled or upset.

In the first picture boys are kicking footballs into his face. The physical hurt and possible nosebleed would be the upsetting aspect. The second picture shows a boy spitting at him. The spit would go down his clothes and his mother would tell him off. In the third picture a boy is throwing stones at him and it would cut his head open. The fourth picture shows a boy ducking him in the swimming baths, pushing his head under. The fifth picture now shows the occasion in which everything would be fine. Mark would be winning a game of table tennis against another club.

The pictures illustrate the theme of personal inferiority as opposed to personal superiority in relation to the peer group. In essence, when Mark can demonstrate superior skills and when interpersonal relations are governed by clear rules, he will feel good. When he lacks skills and situations are unstructured he will expect to be in trouble.

Mark's description of the boy who would not be troubled in these situations is of someone who is (1) rough, (2) could beat people up, and (3) is not scared of anything. Implicitly, therefore, Mark seeks himself as troubled or upset when he is not rough, when he feels physically inferior and when he is scared. This newly invented character would himself be troubled when someone older was doing these things to him (i.e. the events in his pictures) and this character would best describe him when younger children get on to him. Mark's age status therefore becomes an issue against which his own behaviour needs to be understood.

It is tempting to see these alternatives as having some relationship to acceptable masculine and feminine roles, a formulation that also fits the cluster of attributes already described in the previous section. Such a formulation also receives support from the father's relative inaccessibility at home, from Mark's identification with his mother and feminine activities at home, and his brother's aggressive masculinity. It is probably of some significance that both Mark and his parents set great store by his imminent transfer to a secondary school, and have specifically requested a place in an all-boys' school.

And what difference does all of this make?

I have presented the illustrative material in a rather detached, if not academic, manner but it can be of little value unless its practical utility and therapeutic potential is indicated. I shall conclude by showing two ways in which this kind of investigation has the possibility for generating change. The first way relates to the client himself. The second way relates to the people with whom the child or young person is interacting and to whom the child presents a problem.

When a child is confronted with this style of interview he is, perhaps for the first time, invited to think seriously about himself and his ways of making sense of things. We could call this a stocktaking, or a mapping exercise. Either analogy is useful. Out of this exercise he may develop alternative ways of making sense, or, at the very least, become aware of the sense he has traditionally been making of people and things. Whilst neither of these experiences is necessarily therapeutic, each contains the possibility of generating some change of view when the old events reappear.

A new awareness of habitual choices at least opens up the possibility of a new response. The interview itself presents the child with an opportunity of being treated with seriousness, and not being given pat responses to what he himself offers. In many ways Kelly's sociality corollary is relevant here: *to the extent that one person construes the construction processes of another, he may play a role in a social process involving the other person.*

The techniques and strategies, of which those in this essay are examples, are implicit communications to the child of the possibility that at least one person might be capable of understanding him. If he can be understood, perhaps he can pose his behavioural questions in ways that generate less distress. This is one aspect of therapeutic change.

The second practical value rests on the fact that the complaints that lead to our involvement with children are those of the adults rather than the children themselves. In this sense the problems reflect a failure in mutual understanding between adult and child. But adults bear the greater responsibility, and if the communication between them bears no relationship to the child's construction of himself and others, then misunderstandings and problems arise. It is sadly the case that when the adult, in his communication with a child, does not understand the child's construction of himself, the relationship between adult and child will probably generate friction. A small example will illustrate this. A very disturbed boy raised a fist to a teacher. The headteacher took the boy away to his office and playfully smacked his bottom. He then asked the boy if the treatment was fair. The boy immediately said that it wasn't. Rather puzzled by this the headteacher asked why, and the boy replied that he wasn't a baby, and that to smack him on the bottom with his hand was to treat him as a baby. It would have been fair if the teacher had used a cane. In this way the boy himself was given an opportunity of communicating his own construction of himself, thereby reducing the risks of further interpersonal failure.

A personal construct approach to interviewing children should, by definition, lead to the finding of those constructions whereby the child makes sense of himself and others. The communication of this to teachers, and others who are involved with children, improves the chances that the child's outlooks are taken into account by those significant others who so often complain of difficulties. The sociality corollary is again very relevant here together with the concepts of hostility as defined by Kelly: 'Hostility is the continued effort to extort validational evidence in favour of a type of social prediction which has already proved itself a failure.'

When children and teachers continue to maintain their own constructions of each other in the face of continued interpersonal difficulties, we see this as hostility in the classroom. When a teacher can abandon his existing constructions of his problem children (if only for a limited time) he may provide room for growth for each of them, and for himself. When a child, if only for a limited time, can become aware of his own constructions of himself and others, he too may enjoy a breathing space in which more harmonious relationships can develop. Kelly, through personal construct theory, invites the psychologist to reconstruct his role in such a way as to help him to promote just those kinds of change.

Notes

1. It would also be my view that this sequence, if it is genuinely developmental, is not restricted to the chronological development of
   children into adults, but may also be continually recreated at all ages
   when an individual is confronted with new contexts within which to
   operate.
2. Subsequently, I have always asked my clients (all of whom might
   loosely be described as 'working class') what they have meant when
   they said 'showing off' and more often than not they do in fact mean
   being angry. This observation has of course considerable implications
   for a proper sensitivity to language in cross-cultural researches.

Chapter 5
The exploration of consciousness: personal construct theory and change (1978)

I presented this paper to an annual conference of workers in Child Guidance. In general they would tend to be of a psychodynamic orientation, especially interested in 'unconscious processes'. Hence the focus and content of the paper was directed to less favoured 'conscious processes'. Subsequently, when Al Landfield asked me for a contribution to his next book, I offered this paper. In the process, the title suffered a change. In the context of the book the expression 'and change' was replaced by 'with children'.

By way of introduction, let me present an excerpt from an interview with Jane. Jane is a 13-year-old girl, living with a family that is well known to the Social Services Department because of her mother who is chronically depressed. Jane herself attends school spasmodically and with considerable reluctance and it is for this reason that she was referred to the Child Guidance Clinic. In the process of systematically exploring some of her ways of making sense of school, it became apparent that Jane felt she was the kind of girl whose thoughts, feelings and actions made no difference to anyone at all. As such a state suggests a denial of effective social interaction I decided to explore it more fully. She agreed that she was the kind of girl who felt she made no difference to anyone but would prefer to be the opposite. In other words, there was an indication of some need for change. As, however, the solution was to some extent in her own hands there was the possibility of some advantage in remaining isolated. I asked her, therefore, to tell me what was 'bad' and 'good', 'good' and 'bad' about each of these two states.

To make no difference to anyone is *bad* because 'that makes you a child of air'. To make no difference is *good* because 'then they don't treat me bigger than everybody else. I just like to be like everybody else'. To make a difference is *good* because 'everyone knows I'm there'. To make a difference is *bad* because 'they might think I'm like somebody I'm really not. They might think I'm big.'

I would like you to consider for a moment the complexity, and scope and poetry of Jane's answers to these very simple questions. If you can catch hold of the quality contained in this extract and retain a memory of it throughout the paper, you will have a key to what I am trying to say.

I have started with a specific instance from practice and shall follow with an extended theoretical discussion about my twin themes of consciousness and theory. In the second part of the paper I shall reverse the balance by giving a detailed account of an interview followed by a very short restatement by way of quotation of my two generalities. The paper will show the relationship between the personal construct theory of George Kelly and both theory and practice.

Consciousness

> When I once told a friend that it was my intention to explain consciousness he exclaimed 'But consciousness is everything!' After thinking about it, I agreed with him. (Deikman, 1973)

It is my suspicion that if any one concept has underwritten the theory and practice of psychotherapy in child guidance (and therefore the prescriptive rights as to who should or should not practise psychotherapy) that concept would be 'the unconscious' together with its elaboration, 'unconscious motivation'. Doubtless, at the time Freud formulated the concept it was both a necessary and appropriate reaction to an excessive reliance on rationality (which is not its opposite). Unfortunately the consequent overvaluation led it to be used as a key explanatory concept both for the height of man's creativity and the depths of his iniquity. With the passage of time such explanatory excursions have been found wanting, but the corresponding revaluing of consciousness has been late in developing.

My immediate concern is to look at the 'conscious–unconscious' dichotomy insofar as it has practical rather than conceptual implications. The underlying theme in this pair of opposites is 'knowing' and 'being aware', 'not knowing' and 'not being aware'. Although these expressions refer to psychological processes the adjective 'unconscious' has, by way of the metaphor 'unconscious mind', been changed into a noun, 'the unconscious'. It is instructive that although the expression 'the unconscious' has passed into common language, no comparable metamorphosis has taken place for the expression 'conscious'.

I would hold it to be axiomatic that no person can ever be fully *conscious* of all of his psychological or physical processes. Nor can he ever be fully aware of all that he knows. He is therefore always *unconscious* of many things. It does not follow however that there is some entity in reality that can be labelled 'the unconscious' and to infer that such an entity exists is one of the tricks into which language often betrays us. Unfortunately, its usage as a noun leads to a distortion in thinking through the concretization of what are, in fact, hypotheses. That of which we are unconscious is not experienceable, and as Govinda (1977) says: 'A reality that is not experienceable is only an abstract concept, a product of our speculation, a hypothesis.'

This semantic confusion, although very serious in its own right, is of less importance than the lack of balance when the notion 'consciousness' is relegated to the background because of the corresponding over-emphasis and over-reliance on 'the unconscious'.

In the first place, consciousness itself is undervalued. What a person knows, and the sense he makes of things, takes second place to what some other person, such as the therapist, knows, namely unconscious contents and unconscious processes. Invariably, however, these unconscious contents and processes are based on theory in the mind of the therapist, not experientially based in the client – they cannot be if they are unconscious. I might put this more aphoristically: 'If I wholeheartedly and deeply adhere to the notion and power of "the unconscious" then the contents of my "unconscious" are to be found in the "conscious" mind of my therapist. Unfortunately he won't keep quiet about it.' If, in fact, we give primacy to unconscious factors for explanation, interpretation and treatment, it is patently of little relevance to carry out deep and systematic enquiries into a person's consciousness.

In the second place, and perhaps surprisingly, the complexity of the client tends to be ignored. Descriptions of a person that are given in terms of unconscious processes are indeed often very complex. The complexity, however, is complexity of theory, not of the person. Moreover, since any theory reflects a simplified version of reality, explanations in terms of theory are basically in relation to a simplified version of the client. The client, in his own reality, is too easily replaced by theoretical abstractions.

Thirdly, there is a serious danger, for theoretical rather than experiential reasons, of distrusting the client's use of his own intellect and the veridicality of his own perceptions, especially when these are manifested in his reports of himself and others and the events in his life. If it is the influence of the unconscious that is all-important, then what figures in consciousness must inevitably be distorted either for self-defence or self-delusion.

In essence, the use of 'the unconscious' and 'unconscious motivation' places the user at risk, either at best in playing 'one-up' with his client, or at worst invalidating the client's sense of self as a knowing person. In my view these criticisms arise from the overvaluing of the unconscious pole of the conscious–unconscious dichotomy, not from the dichotomy itself, and my observations on consciousness which follow represent an attempt to redress the balance between the two poles.

- Consciousness includes being aware, and being aware means being aware of something.
- Consciousness includes knowing, and knowing also implies an organization of what is known.
- Consciousness serves a purpose. It is the means whereby the individual adapts (in a Piagetian) sense to the phenomenal world of people, and objects, and their interrelationships.

It is easy to be misled about the depth and quality of a person's consciousness. In the ordinary give-and-take of social interchange we expose these depths only to those whom we know well. With casual acquaintances and colleagues we will, as likely as not, keep our thoughts to ourselves. And we will give as little as we can get away with to the person who seeks to intrude on our thoughts and feelings without a recognized right. On this basis it is easy to assume that consciousness is shallow and superficial, is made up of the trivia of communicational habits or the banalities of second-hand attitudes and opinions. If, however, we turn our attention to ourselves we would need to note that our consciousness includes a vast range of thoughts and feelings, actions and aspirations, hope and fears, questions and moral judgements. What is true of each of us is no whit less true for everyone else. We should not assume that a ready verbalization is the hallmark of consciousness, nor that because a thing is not expressed we are not aware of it. Nor should we assume that what is asserted is identical to that of which we are conscious. We know from self-experience that consciousness has many levels, and not all are mutually consistent. The relation between what is asserted and what is known is a function of the relationship between speaker and listener. Indeed, I have heard it said that the only two occasions when a person tells the truth is when he trusts and when he wishes to hurt.

Knowledge is also organized. It develops out of the interplay and elaboration of similarities and differences, and the complementarity of opposites. Out of these contrasts arise associations, implications, the awareness of regularities and contingencies and hence the ability to understand, to anticipate and to predict. In this sense, consciousness, seen as the organization of knowledge, is also meaning.

Consciousness is also dynamic. Its scope broadens to include new events and deepens to illuminate more fully old ones. Its organization changes as an outcome of experience. Just as the organization of knowledge is shaped out of the interplay of opposites, so the organization itself changes out of the interplay between the individual and his environment. The environment here includes all that is felt to be other than self: objects, persons and their interrelationships. The person also is a part of that network of relationships, as also are the contents of knowledge he has of himself: his own thoughts, feelings, actions and processes.

When we look at consciousness from this standpoint we can see it as a source of great psychological wealth, hidden perhaps by the dross of superficiality that is frequently all that is apparent. We should be prepared to go below the outer appearances and explore the depths of consciousness. We should ask: 'what does he know? How is his knowledge organized? What is the sense he makes of things?' We may then have some understanding of the problems with which he is confronted. Moreover, we should recognize that the very posing of questions of this nature includes the possibility of influencing both the contents and the organization of consciousness itself.

Theory

I shall now turn to a discussion of theory, the second of my two themes, and in the development of the argument it will become apparent that there are important parallels between theory and consciousness.

Any theory is made up of axioms (statements that are not provable, but which have a self-evident quality), categories (which are the verbal labels by which we record our discrimination between things), and laws (which are statements of the ways in which categories are related). To know a theory is to know the axioms, the categories and the laws. A theory arises out of the attempt to produce order out of chaos: it gives organization to knowledge: it offers an understanding of the past and the hope of anticipating what is to come.

It is implicit in what I have just said that there are two different aspects to theory – its construction and its use. These two aspects are related to the academic search for knowledge on the one hand, and the pragmatic application of theory to do a job of work on the other. From the academic standpoint, theories are to be constructed, preferably in ways that are disprovable through the dynamic of research activity, with the aim of producing in public and linguistic terms a verbalized version of how the universe in question works. By contrast, from the pragmatic standpoint, theory, whatever its shortcomings, is there to be used for dealing with problems. When we are committed in this way to action, theory gives salience to some information at the expense of other. It simplifies, at a price, the true complexity of reality in order to make provisional understanding possible. It opens up certain lines of action whilst sealing off others. Thus some form of theory, implicit if not explicit, is crucial if we are to cope with the problems with which we are presented. Theory, however, should not be mistaken for truth.

Whilst it is certainly the case that the pragmatic use of theory may lead to its modification, it is important that the academic approach should not be confused with the pragmatic. The essential activity of each is necessarily different. That there is a relationship between the academic and the pragmatic is obvious, but its ramifications go beyond the scope of this paper.

There is a component of theory that I have so far deliberately omitted. Every theory is based on metaphor (cf. Mehrabian, 1968). The metaphor is an assertion by analogy that some aspects of what is relatively well known can give meaning to what is relatively less well known. The metaphor is not derived logically; it seems to arise of its own accord out of the theorist's perception of situations. In this way it may well carry meanings, thoughts and feelings that are sensed at a very low level of awareness and which may have been derived from the very roots of consciousness. (May I point out that I have just used as a metaphor for consciousness the growth of a tree or plant? The word 'roots' gives the key to the analogy.) Theorists seldom state their metaphors and it is not always easy to spot them. Nonetheless, they represent unverbalized and unacknowledged aspects both of the assumptive framework of the theorist, and perhaps also of the times themselves. Much of psychoanalytic theory, in its concern with the flow of energy, is derived from the metaphor of nineteenth-century hydraulics. Other aspects use biological metaphors involving the separation of compartments of an organism by its membranes. Some aspects involve metaphors from topology. The key metaphor, however, is conflict between the individual's own wishes and those of society – between various parts of the individual's own psychological makeup and metaphysically between life (or love) and death. The acceptability of a theory is a matter of both a head reaction through reason and a gut reaction through feelings. A theory's comprehensiveness, its apparent validity, its logical consistency decide the former. The latter is determined by the way an individual senses the underlying metaphors.

Just as in my general discussion of theory I distinguished between two approaches, so, in discussing the pragmatic approach I propose to make a further distinction. This distinction is not commonly made, but is in fact somewhat revolutionary, so I shall come to it gently.

We are familiar with the great public theories, or accounts of 'Man': Freud and Jung, the behaviourists, Allport, Rogers and so forth, each of whom offers answers to the question 'what is Man?' The pursuit of answers to this question is, of course, an essential component of the academic approach to theory. We seem to take it as axiomatic, however, that having arrived at generalized answers for the generalized 'Man', these answers are also true for each individual man. I would suggest, however, that if we really apply these answers to ourselves we do not readily say of any of them 'yes, this is me'. How could we, if they are to some extent mutually contradictory? Moreover the fact that we can stand outside any theory means that the theory is not big enough to account for ourselves. Despite these obvious comments we do not easily see that each of us, in fact, makes his own sense of things, of people, of events, of himself. Each of us creates his own theory about people, not in the academic sense of formal theory construction, but at the pragmatic level of getting along in the world. Thus my distinctions between theories at the pragmatic level is between the great public theories on the one hand and the personal, private theories that each one of us constructs out of the raw material of his experiences.

From the distinctions I have now drawn it can be seen that there are close parallels and similarities between consciousness on the one hand and theory on the other. Each involves the structure, categorization, and organization of knowledge. Each is a tool for coping with problems. Each represents a means of adapting to phenomena. Each is purposive. When we now take the step of fitting ideas of consciousness on to the idea of a personal personality theory, we have arrived at George Kelly's personal construct theory (Kelly, 1991, 1955; Maher, 1969) to which I can now, at last, turn.

Personal construct theory

Everything I have said up to now points to personal construct theory and everything that follows is based on it. I shall not attempt a formal exposition, however, but instead I shall use some of the themes I have already developed in relation to consciousness and theory to reflect some of the essential features of personal construct theory. In particular, I have chosen metaphor, categories, organization, function and dynamics, but there will be resonances of other themes as well.

Kelly developed his theory in the double context of academic learning and psychotherapy. From these two contexts he recognized a similarity between the activities he followed with his research students and his activities with his therapy clients. He would invite each to define the issues with clarity, to undertake careful observation, to formulate and test hypotheses and to modify them in the light of their outcomes. At the same time, he made an interesting observation from psychology textbooks. He noticed that when, in the introduction, the writer described the activities of the psychologist, he presented the image of the scientific enterprise. When, however, the writer came to the chapter on personality, he described man using rather different terms, such as motivation, needs, unconscious forces and motives. Kelly saw no reason at all why the creative theory about man that the psychologist applied to himself should not also apply to the man in the street. Thus: 'Let us, then, instead of occupying ourselves with *man the biological organism* or *man the lucky guy* have a look at *man the scientist*' (Kelly, 1991).

The metaphor for man, therefore, is *man the scientist* and from this certain implications follow. The theory does not distinguish between the formulator of theory and the people about whom the theory is invented. Moreover, although Kelly has written a theory in public terms about Man in general, the theory is built round the idea of each individual man himself as a theory builder – it is couched in terms that include the idea of a personal or private theory. Just as the research psychologist carries out his own research programme to elaborate and exemplify his theories, so the man in the street carries out his research programme, which is the business of everyday living.

Kelly states this formally, together with a statement about organization, in the following way: '*Organisation Corollary:* Each person characteristically evolves, for his own convenience in anticipating events, a construction system embracing ordinal relations between constructs.'

More generally, and in less precise language, he says:

> Man looks at his world through transparent patterns or templates which he creates and then attempts to fit over the realities of which the world is composed. The fit is not always very good. Yet without such patterns the world appears to be an undifferentiated homogeneity that man is unable to make sense out of at all.
>
> Let us give the name *constructs* to these patterns that are tried on for size. They are ways for construing the world. They are what enable a man, and lower animals too, to chart a course of behaviour, explicitly formulated or implicitly acted out, verbally expressed or utterly inarticulate, consistent with other courses of action or inconsistent with them, intellectually reasoned or vegetably sensed.

The expression *construct* is important within the theory as it represents Kelly's formulation of the categories whereby the world is discriminated. He expresses it formally in the following way: '*Dichotomy Corollary:* A person's construction system is made up of a finite number of dichotomous constructs.'

The essence of a construct is that it is two ended: it is made up not of simple attributes but of pairs of attributes that are opposite, not necessarily in a logical or semantic sense, but in terms of the individual's own terminology. The construct is the means whereby an individual categorizes and discriminates the event with which he comes in contact. It is not merely an intellectualism, but involves thoughts, feelings and moral judgements. It also offers the choice of alternative courses of action. Kelly also makes the point that the construct has a limited range of applicability – it is not equally relevant over the whole range of a person's experience. Let me illustrate the nature of a construct with an example. An adolescent boy describes some of his acquaintances as 'rough'. The opposite, in his language, is 'queer', meaning, in his terminology, 'effeminate and potentially homosexual'. The construct 'rough–queer' is applicable only to boys of about his own age, not to girls, nor to adults. In relation to action, if the boy has no other means of discriminating among boys he is likely to have difficulties in his definition of himself. If he does not wish to be 'rough', which has the implication of trouble with the police, his only other choice might be 'queer', with equally disastrous implications.

Personal construct theory is also dynamic. It postulates that man is always active in his affairs and does not wait to be stimulated or motivated. Further, his personal construct system is itself also open to change as the outcome of experience. Kelly states these two issues in his 'fundamental postulate' and in his 'experience corollary':

Fundamental Postulate: A person's processes are psychologically channelized by the way he anticipates events.

Experience Corollary: A person's construct system varies as he successively construes the replication of events.

The presentation of these corollaries shows how closely consciousness and theory come together in personal construct theory. They are not the same, but if theory, implicit or explicit, is not the whole of consciousness it is indeed a large part, not in formally stated terms, but as the personal construct system whereby an individual is able to relate to, and make something meaningful out of, oncoming events.

Pragmatics: personal construct theory and change

The practical application of a personal construct theory approach must inevitably be shaped by the nature of our involvement in our professional work. It needs to be clearly recognized that we become engaged in work with children only because others have complained about them – a child's actions, the expression of his thoughts and feelings, his interactions with others, are such as to cause parents, teachers, social workers and others to be worried. The adults then seek help, usually saying that something is wrong with the child, and asking us to put it right. When the adults are troubled, it is a reasonable inference that the child is troubled too. It is seldom, however, that the troubles the child complains of are the same as those that upset the adults. The overriding generalization from these observations is that a referral to child guidance means that things are somehow going wrong in relation to the child. It is our commitment to do something about it, either with the child on his own, or with the adults who are part of his life, or with their interactions.

Kelly's presentation of personal construct theory is given in technical language with precise meanings. In practice we can use a broader formulation. A person's behaviour depends on how he makes sense of things and on his viewpoint. When troubles arise it is likely either that his ways of making sense are inadequate, or that he has adopted a point of view that leads to false perceptions. If we construe trouble as interactionist rather than intrapsychic we would say that the sense that individuals make of each other does not match the sense that these same individuals make of themselves. Thus the first step to be taken in order to bring about some difference is to find out just what sense people are making of their circumstances or of each other. The aim of therapeutic intervention, then, is to generate a change in behaviour by initiating a change in their ways of making sense or in their point of view.

The metaphor, *man the scientist,* that lies behind the theory, immediately suggests lines of action whereby change might be initiated. The scientific process involves skilled and dispassionate observation, and this itself implies a modification or enlargement of consciousness. In a clinical setting a child might be asked to report in detail the experiences that he has when he wets the bed or has a temper tantrum. Sensations and feelings can be located in the body and information required as to how these change. He can be invited to describe the psychological, temporal or situational sequences within which the troubling behaviour arises and to develop guesses or hypotheses to account for this behaviour. These tasks involve the extension and elaboration of a child's knowledge. They may also show up gaps or inconsistencies in his ways of making sense (cf. Raimy, 1975). Out of all these activities a change of viewpoint or consciousness can become possible. More important, however, is that underlying all this work is the expectation that the child can become responsibly active in the enlargement of his consciousness and in the solving of his own problems.

These are some of the general strategies that arise from the theory. My special aim, however, is to advocate the exploration of consciousness since this is fundamental, especially if we see misperceptions of identity as the central issue.

The contents of consciousness do not stand up in line ready for inspection. They are available only when deliberately looked for, and then only if the child knows where the interviewer is going and the nature of the information he requires. The means whereby these ends are achieved is the question and in some ways the exploration of consciousness could be rewritten as the art of questioning. If we use as a metaphor the notion of the map, we can say that the child, out of his experience of life, has developed maps whereby he can plot his way through everyday events. Our task is, then, one of finding out the nature of his maps. Any map is created as a projection from a round surface to a flat one and maps are described by their projection as well as by their content. Kelly described personal construct theory also as a theory of projection (cf. Ravenette, 1972a).

We need to specify those areas of experience where troubles arise and then question systematically. This process will include the child's awareness of internal as well as external events. Consciousness, as I described earlier, includes thoughts, feelings, potential actions and moral judgements and we must make reference to these in our questions. Out of such an investigation a number of things may happen. The child himself frequently shows a sense of personal responsibility for his dilemmas and a serious involvement in the interview. He is frequently surprised at the amount and quality of his own knowledge and this enhances his feelings of self-worth. He is usually able to give a coherent sense of his own identity, and hint at the unspoken metaphors that colour many of his actions.

Knowledge of this nature is crucial if we wish to bring about some change in the interactions between adult and child and Kelly gives this a theoretical basis in his sociality corollary: '*Sociality Corollary:* To the extent that one person construes the construction process of another, he may play a role in a social process involving the other person.'

Very simply, without some understanding of the other, the inter-actions are likely to be tangential. But the understanding must be of his understanding not of him. This is a subtle distinction.

I can now illustrate this approach with a case in point.

A case in point

Graham is a 10-year-old boy about whom the headteacher is worried. He presents no behavioural or learning problems in school but had frequent absences because of illnesses, which had involved hospitalization. Despite many investigations, however, nothing abnormal had been found. For a period of time, Graham was exhausted in school by midday and the headteacher had allowed him to go home. The parents were worried and the family might equally well have been referred to the Child Guidance Clinic. The head knew, however, that he would have the oppor-tunity of sharing the interview and in that way would acquire at first hand an understanding of the boy out of what he said. The interview lasted for a full hour but I shall restrict my account to those interviewing techniques that will not be well known, and to responses from Graham that reflect more directly on himself than on his construction of the rest of the world.

The interview

Graham could not tell me why I had been asked to interview him, but agreed that people might be worried about his frequently being ill. He said that he himself was not worried by his illness but that his parents and relatives were. I asked him where he had his pains: he showed me his right side. He said that his legs would ache round the ankles and the pains would move up his legs. He had stomach aches and headaches.

When I asked him to describe boys, not himself, who might have the same pains as himself, he was at a loss to say anything. Yet he could not readily accept that he was therefore different from all other boys. All he could say of boys who never had pains was that they were fit. They could not become boys who had pains unless there was some difference to their bodies, for example their blood.

I want to make the point here that to ask Graham questions about what he knows is already to force him into thinking carefully about himself and others, and to stretch him to the limits of his own consciousness. He is not a static entity giving information without undergoing any change, but a boy operating a personal theory. Perforce the interview will itself draw his attention to gaps and inadequacies in his theory (cf. Raimy, 1975). The evidence so far suggests that Graham's identity is firmly rooted in an awareness of his physical body rather than in some psychological sense of self.

Graham's family drawing showed him in contact with his dog but isolated from his two bothers who are six and eight years older. Mother and father appear to one side of the picture, facing each other, mother with a garden hoe in her hand, father eating his dinner. According to the headteacher, mother is aggressively the boss in the family and is also involved in running a troop of Girl Guides. He could say nothing of the father.

Troubles in school

The technique that follows is concerned with a child's awareness of situations in school, with a special emphasis on troubles and upsets. I have described earlier versions elsewhere (Ravenette, 1977b) and the current practice is complex.

The child is invited to choose three out of eight drawings of situations in school. Each situation is used as the focus for a detailed enquiry and the child is told in advance what the questions are:

1. What do you think is happening?
2. Who do you think is troubled or upset, and why?
3. How do you think this came about?

These questions tap the ways in which a child makes sense of troubled situations in school. He is directed to reality, and is asked to show his awareness of psychological, situational or interactional sequences:

4. If this child were you, what would you think? What would you feel? What would you do? What difference would that make to anyone? As a result of all of this, would you feel good or bad? and why?

These questions put the child fairly and squarely into familiar situations and demand of him an awareness of his own thoughts, feelings and potential actions. Perhaps the most important of these questions is about the difference he make to others since this issue is at the heart of a child's sense of potency in the world.

5. If the child were not him, what sort of a boy would you say he was?

This question allows a child to entertain the possibility of alternative identities, and therefore the possibility of change (Ravenette, 1977a). By implication, he will also be giving some idea of the kind of boy he is not, as well as the kind of boy he feels that he is.

Let us follow Graham's responses:

Picture 1
1. The children are coming home from school and meeting their mothers.
2. Three are upset, but eventually he settles on just one of them. He had done something wrong in school, he had not done his work.
3. He looks sad, he did his work wrong, he wasn't trying.
4. If this boy were Graham, he would feel miserable. He would go home and tell his mum. He would think 'I wasn't trying.' After a long pause he said this would make no difference to anyone. He would feel bad; he would feel ashamed.
5. If the boy was not Graham, he would be lazy, not trying hard enough.

Picture 2
1. This is in assembly.
2. The boy at the wall is upset.
3. The other boy started it; he joined in.
4. If this boy were Graham, he would feel stupid. He would sulk. He would think 'You are stupid.' He said this would make no difference to anyone. As a result of his action he would feel bad because he had messed up someone else's assembly.
5. If this boy were not Graham, he would be a boy who mucks about, who does a lot of wasting his time and other people's time.

Picture 3:
1. They are having a lesson.
2. The boy at the front is upset.
3. He has not been doing his work properly.
4. If this boy were Graham he would feel unhappy. He would sulk. He would think 'I am stupid'. This action would make no difference to anyone. As a result he would feel bad.
5. If this boy were not Graham it would be a boy who mucks about a lot and doesn't do as he is told.

A sixth question was also asked for each of these situations. Was the boy who, in question 5, was not Graham, the kind of boy who could have the same aches and pains. Each time he said 'no'.

From these responses, Graham appears as a boy who is open to very negative thoughts and feelings about himself, but for whom the expression of these thoughts and feelings makes no difference to anybody. Even sulking is a compromise between admitting, and acting on, bad feelings. He draws a moral implication from all of this that he is bad: he mucks about, doesn't work and wastes people's time. This boy, the alternative identity, could not have the same physical badness that plagues Graham. Is it the case that a moral link between sin and suffering is already being forged in Graham? Or is it simply that his proper and ordinary bad feelings are not allowed to exist unless channelled into a physical rather than a psychological form?

Portrait gallery

Whereas the previous technique aims to explore Graham's sense of self within the school setting, the portrait gallery (Ravenette, 1972b) is concerned with the elaboration of feelings. Two schematic faces are drawn, one to stand for a sad boy and one for a happy boy. The child is asked to distinguish which is which and to say three things about each. He is then presented with blank faces and asked to fill in each of them in turn to represent other feeling states, and say three things about each of them. Graham's responses were as follows:

Sad
1. Naughty, he gets told off.
2. Doesn't get what he wants.
3. Doesn't do as he's told, therefore he gets smacked, therefore he is sad.

Happy
1. He doesn't get told off all the time.
2. He is good: mum asks him to do something: he does it, he sets the table.
3. He doesn't want things straight away, he waits, he knows he will get it later.

Angry
1. He gets angry when he doesn't get what he wants, he wants it straight away.
2. He gets angry if he is talking to somebody and they don't talk to him back.
3. Someone calls him names, he gets angry, he starts fighting.

Worried
1. If he has hit someone, his mother is after him with the slipper, he knows the slipper hurts.
2. Like his brother has got 10p. If he takes it without telling, if his brother comes round and says 'you took my 10p'.
3. He stole something off a shop. The shopkeeper knows who took it and goes to the parent.

Things go wrong with his body, like aches and pains
1. He feels worried, he is afraid he might have an operation.
2. He feels horrible inside.
3. He loses colour in his face.

Despite the simplicity of the technique, there is a wealth of personal content in Graham's responses. Sadness goes with badness and having to be patient for needs to be met. Happiness seems not to exist in its own right, but only as a consequence of meeting the demands and values of the parents, or in the absence of sadness. Graham's sense of his family suggests that they preach, if not practice, a puritan morality within which bad thoughts and feelings are also immoral and which may well be at variance with the values of the neighbourhood. Inadvertently he gives the lie to happiness when he admits to anger for not getting what he wants. When we also see that he gets angry at being ignored, do we recognize shades of the isolation that he so graphically portrayed in his family drawing and might we not hazard the guess that he is frequently angry there, but to no purpose.

The good and the bad of it

The final technique uses the basic idea that in any state which is held to be good there is the possibility of something disadvantageous, and in any state that is considered to be bad there is the potentiality of something that is to a person's good (Tschudi, 1977). We obtain agreement with the child of what is bad for him at the moment, or what stands in the ways of his being all right. We then ask what he would prefer it to be. This gives two contrasting states, and we ask of him what is 'bad' and 'good', 'good' and 'bad' about each. It will be remembered that it was through this technique that Jane, with whom I introduced this paper, showed something of the quality of her awareness.

Graham conceded that what was wrong with him was: 'he has aches and pains that people do not understand. The *bad* thing about this is that it really hurts the body. The good thing about this is . . .'

After a pause Graham said, 'experiments'. When I asked him for whom this was good, he said, 'the pathologists'. This would be good because it helps the body. And after a long pause he added 'to help my blood'. By contrast, he would prefer: 'To be fitter. The good thing about this is you run around a lot and take part in things. The *bad* thing about this is it makes you get tired, your muscles all tie up, you can't walk.'

These questions push Graham to the limits of his awareness of the implications of his condition, forcing him to verbalize links that previously he can hardly have considered. As at the beginning of the interview, Graham, as someone who is ill, is a body that can attract the attention of people who are important to him. He is also an object that can be used, ostensibly for his own good but, as he sees it, for the benefit of the pathologists. The contrasting pole to that of the body is not, as might be expected, a soul, or a mind of a person, but a social interaction, 'taking part in things'. Where, one is forced to ask, is the psychological self that seems somehow to have been lost, or perhaps has never existed? Hopefully, we shall find some answer when we meet the parents.

It seemed necessary to offer Graham a contribution that might bring together some of the themes which appeared in response to my questions. Such a contribution does not have to be absolute truth, but it should say something meaningful to the situation. It should also contain a psychological understanding that Graham can be free to accept or reject, but which he would find it difficult to ignore. To this end my remarks ran something like this:

> I know a boy who is like you but who is not you. Whenever this boy feels, thinks and does things which are bad, he knows it doesn't make any difference to anyone. Because this also makes him feel bad inside himself the only way he should show it is by having a lot of aches and pains. This means that people take notice of him. This does not have to be true of you, but perhaps a little bit of it is.

I thanked him and sent him back to his classroom.

Résumé of 'a case in point'

It needs to be pointed out that the problem for which Graham's behaviour was a solution was not the problem for which the headteacher sought help. Nor, incidentally, was Graham's behaviour in itself a problem. The problem for the headteacher was that he could not understand or have an effect on that behaviour. As will be seen, some resolution of the headteacher's problem seemed to have arisen out of his sharing the interview.

Graham's own difficulties were of a different order and what follows is an inferential reconstruction. In terms of Graham's own sense of things, he lived in a family where morality was important and where at the same time he felt isolated (part of which is to make no difference to anybody). Moreover, the acknowledgement or expression of bad thoughts and feelings was unacceptable. What the family did accept was badness of the body as expressed in physical illness or disorder (aches and pains, and bad blood). Physical illness therefore provided a channel for expressing 'badness' and at the same time it provided a means both of making some impact on people and of being acknowledged in return. The price, however, may have been the atrophy of his sense of self as a 'person' in favour of a more limited vision of himself as a 'body'. The exhaustion that was manifested in school may well have provided a means of escaping from a world in which demands were made on him as a person.

The construction that I gave back to Graham at the end of the interview contained some of these ideas.

The sequel

I was discussing the implications of the interview with the head, who was present throughout. After about 10 minutes there was a knock on the door. It was Graham, who wished to ask the headteacher a question. This might seem to be a small and apparently trivial incident until the headteacher turns to me beaming and says that the boy has never before been to the office to ask for anything. Perhaps, he continues, the boy feels good that for the first time someone has understood him.

Conclusion

This brings my formal exposition to an end, but I want to bring it to a completion very simply with two quotations, which, as I indicated at the beginning would represent a synthesis of much that I have been trying to express. I do not see our work as curing peripheral psychological ills, but rather as intervening in the very fabric of life itself. Thus our frame of reference should extend beyond the circumscribed ambit of child guidance and link with broad streams of thought which have universal implications.

My first quotation comes from the Eastern metaphysical traditions, through the words of the Lama Anagarika Govinda (whom I have already quoted):

> Thus all reality is built upon polarity, the polarity of part and whole, of individuality and universality, of matter and energy, differentiation and oneness etc. [to which I would add conscious and unconscious]: and there can be no question of 'higher' and 'lower' values between these polar, mutually complementary qualities. The concept of value depends on the merits of the momentary situation, the particular circumstances. Wherever there is an imbalance between the two poles, the one that is in danger of being outweighed represents the greater value.

My second quotation comes from a Western poetic source. TS Eliot, in *Little Gidding*, the last of the Four Quartets (1944), wrote these lines:

> And the end of all exploring
> Will be to arrive where we started
> And know the place for the first time.

Chapter 6
Specific reading difficulties: appearance and reality (1979)

This paper stemmed from an invitation to contribute to a DES course for teachers of children with learning difficulties, in particular 'specific reading difficulties'. As the title indicates, I put forward alternative ways of thinking about the topic. In particular I was concerned to demonstrate the need to recognize that children with reading difficulties also grow up within family interactional contexts. This was in contrast to the neurological dimension as implied by the 'dyslexic' label. To that end, I illustrated the issue with two cases, one putatively so labelled and the other having carried the label for some six years, each interviewed with a PCT approach.

Introduction

Dyslexia, both as a concept and as a diagnosis for incipient or prolonged failure to learn to read, has now, through the agencies of television and the national press, become the common property of all people regardless of social class. And when an eminent actress is given a programme on TV to expatiate on her life as a dyslexic child, the label takes on an almost talismanic quality.

The expression 'specific reading difficulty' was created in an attempt to obviate the medical, and rather controversial, overtones of the label dyslexia. It has no explanatory value and no specific implications for treatment. Neither has it captured the imagination of the media or the public. It is therefore innocuous. By contrast, the use of the label 'dyslexia' has generated serious and lasting hostilities between all kinds of people: doctors of medicine and psychologists, neurologists and local authorities, teachers and parents, parents and local authorities. At times the matter has even been taken to the courts of law. It is difficult to recall any other concept that has generated so much hostility despite the fact that the concept was developed in an attempt to help rather than hinder, and to promote educational provision rather than set the providers against each other.

Most of these hostilities hinge on the assumption that there is an answer to the question 'does dyslexia exist?' So long as the protagonists are caught at this level of enquiry, so long will the hostilities continue. By putting the matter in this way, I am saying implicitly that the formulation of dyslexia, and the way the label is used, reflect important oversimplifications in the ways we make sense of things and in the epistemological assumptions that underlie our knowledge of people and processes. It is my intention in this paper to broaden the argument beyond the question of the existence or non-existence of dyslexia by setting the issue into a more comprehensive context. In the process, I shall comment on some of the problems that are associated with the use of dyslexia as a diagnosis. At the heart of the matter is my own concern both to add something of value to the understanding of children who, over long periods of time, persist in not learning to read, and to give something of practical consequence to those professional workers, especially teachers and psychologists, who have to deal with such children and their families.

A title and its relevance

The subtitle of my paper 'Appearance and reality' is taken directly from a book of the same name by Ichheiser (1970). Ichheiser's own subtitle was 'Misunderstandings in human relationships' and it follows from this train of thought that I am interested in the human relationship aspect of children who fail to learn. The choice of title is an acknowledgement of my debt to Ichheiser. One of his most telling insights appears in a story he recounts of someone who has fallen into water and is close to drowning.

The man's plight is, of course, obvious to anyone who is close enough to see and get to him and he can indeed be rescued if he shouts loud enough for help. If, though, someone who is unemployed feels he is sinking under the pressure, he is unlikely to cry out because 'it is not done'. If he does so he might be told he is making a fuss or that he has brought it all upon himself. After all, history shows that competent people can and do find work. This is how invisible pressures of many kinds can be harder to cope with than obvious ones such as drowning. The victims are just as threatened, but others do not see the threat and assume that the victims have the same freedom as themselves.

I shall argue that we need to look for the invisible chains which hold children back from learning, and, following Ichheiser, I shall point out that these invisible chains may be discovered in aspects of children's lives which we take for granted.

The problem of realities

In the field of theory, the question of reality is academic, because it does not need to make any difference to anyone. In the field of action it is crucial since it determines what people are expected to do. Let me present four propositions:

1. It is a reality that some people believe dyslexia to be an entity, and that a diagnosis of dyslexia entitles a child to special educational provision.
2. To those people who believe in dyslexia, dyslexia is a reality.
3. The construction of reality is personal, subjective and not easily transferable to another. The communication of reality is even more personal and subjective.

My third proposition may seem surprising and to fly in the face of common sense. I should therefore elaborate the matter more fully before proceeding to my fourth proposition.

Reality, as it affects our everyday lives, is a relatively stable sense of the orderliness of things and their tendency to remain the same or to change in more or less predictable ways. Although we must indeed recognize some absolute reality, which is beyond ourselves and which is approached through metaphysics, religion and perhaps science, the everyday realities, I suggest, are our own construction. Although they owe something to what is 'out there' they do in fact inhere within ourselves and not in external things (c.f. Piaget – for an understanding of the child's construction of the phenomenal world, and Kelly (1955, 1991) for an understanding of the person seen as pre-eminently a constructor of reality). Without elaborating further, we should also recognize the reality of the apparently self-evident and the reality that is an inference of that which underlies appearances. But as Ichheiser says, 'The appearance is also a reality'.

We arrive at our realities, our sense of the stability of things, out of our life experiences, our interpersonal interactions, our worlds of thought and feeling, the judgements of people and groups of people who are important to us. Our realities are a part of the stuff of coping with life and because of this we are likely to take them for granted. Indeed, they need to be called into question only when things go wrong. In some ways, just because of their usefulness, they may also be *invisible chains* that prevent us from constructing alternative, and perhaps more useful realities. Although some realities may seem to be the common property of all, we would probably find that what was common was language, whereas what was personal was the feelings, associations and experiences that lie behind the language. Indeed, it might well be the case that mutual understanding can arise only from spelling out and defining the differences rather than the identities between apparently similar realities (Kursh, 1971).

My fourth proposition now follows:

4. The assumption that realities, and their associated prescriptions for action, are unilaterally transferable is a major source of interpersonal and interprofessional hostility.

This proposition, following on from the other three, is the nub of the difficulties associated with the use of dyslexia as a diagnosis and as a prescription for action. The argument about the existence or non-existence is basically an argument about the nature of reality, not about children and not about reading failure. It is also an argument about the use of power and the locus of control. At a very fundamental level the division may also reflect basically different personality dynamics but to explore that would be to stray too far. Instead I must turn to the more prosaic task of looking carefully some of the inadequacies that surround the use of dyslexia when we use it as an explanatory model rather than a circumscribed entity.

The dyslexic model and an alternative

As I intimated at the beginning of the paper, the formulation of dyslexia as a diagnosis raises certain assumptions that need to be questioned. I want to comment on some of these and then develop a more far-reaching model that is built on realities other than those that have traditionally been used.

If there is any truth in the label, the child diagnosed as 'dyslexic' suffers from two very separate handicaps, not one. The first is physical. A failure in the neurophysiological system is inferred, if not actually demonstrated or proven. The second handicap is an inability to learn to read. This distinction needs to be made as there is no evidence to show that all children with the adduced physical handicap also suffer from an inability to learn to read. Thus, to assert a causal relationship between the two may not be justified. Dyslexia, therefore, is a portmanteau word in that different meanings are carried in the one verbal container. A number of interesting consequences follow. One would expect little by way of reading attainment from a 5 or 6 year-old child. If then he is labelled dyslexic, is the reference to the reading handicap or the physical handicap? If a 15-year-old is labelled dyslexic, which handicap is being signalled? How young must a child be before he can be diagnosed as dyslexic, how old before he ceases to be called dyslexic – if ever?

What, therefore, is in appearance a unitary notion, is in reality two separate notions. What in appearance is a diagnosis, is in reality an assumption about cause and effect. Thus the label presents a fine example of the shifting sands in communication that a portmanteau word like dyslexia provides.

A second feature of the dyslexic model is that, in an old-fashioned way, it is mechanistic. The child is seen as a learning machine in which some of the parts are either defective or inefficient. Even when human feelings are acknowledged it is rather as though they were bits of extraneous matter clogging the works (cf. the expression 'emotional blockage'). It is of course true that in relation to vegetative processes individuals operate like machines, and in relation to skills it is the expectation that they will take on a machine-like quality. At the point, however, when an individual is confronted with the task of learning new skills, he manifests involvement, alertness, and the ability to use error constructively in mastering a task, rather than be defeated by it. More importantly, because the child is human, any new task becomes an option to be taken up according to his loyalties, his interests, his concerns and his notion of what is fitting to his sense of self. Thus, a mechanistic model scans too narrow a range of phenomena to account for children who chronically fail to learn to read.

The third feature is related to the second: a preoccupation with the modalities and cross-modalities through which a child takes in information. A relative failure in any of these is taken both as evidence of neurophysiological impairment or developmental lag and as the cause of learning failure. The choice of these features as a focus for understanding reading failure, stems from the occupational and historical interests of those ophthalmologists and neurologists who first formulated the concept 'word-blindness' and from psychologists and educators who found the greatest security in psychometric and psychosensory assessments. Within that historical context, the change of emphasis to the physical was valuable, in that intelligent children who did not learn to rend were saved the opprobrium of being called stupid, or lazy or neurotic. To keep the focus in order to preserve the protective value of the label is not enough. Without denying the reality of these psychosensory failures a case might now be made for seeing them as peripheral rather than central issues. After all, we do not know the extent to which practice in reading, writing and spelling sharpens and enhances the very psychosensory skills, the absence of which is held to be the main handicap of the non-learner.

The fourth feature of the model is the assumption that learning to read is intrinsically an extremely difficult task for intelligent young children to master. Allied to this is the expectation that the child is entirely dependent on outside agencies and resources for help and guidance rather than the view that *the child* is the learner who turns to outside agencies only when the need arises. I must confess to being on rather shaky ground in my comments on this issue, but I am reminded that most children do in fact learn to read fairly easily, and the more intelligent they are the easier it comes. Frequently they are not dependent on formal schemes of instruction and are able to resolve many of their difficulties in reading by themselves, using adults as validators of their solutions. It needs to be asked, therefore, of children who become chronic learning failures, what factors stand in the way of developing their own learning initiatives and what lies behind their reluctance to use the adults as guarantors of success.

In general, therefore, the implication of these comments is that the current models that are used for making sense out of learning failure, set the problem within too small a frame of reference. The constraints against learning are too narrowly conceived and the view that the child is human and full of initiatives is replaced by the view of the child as machine, dependent on outside stimulation in order to set it in motion. To become aware of these limitations already contains the possibility of developing a broader perspective within which to see an understanding of chronic, and perhaps more importantly, incipient learning failure in children. In doing this I hope I shall be able to go beyond the confusions implicit in the dyslexic diagnosis and beyond the aseptic sterility of 'specific reading difficulty'.

We need to start with the rather simple observation that a child is born into a family, and that a family is an established interactive system. (I should say in passing that because something is simple it is usually taken for granted. And once it is taken for granted, it tends to become invisible.)

The essential point in this observation is that a family is a system. It is a property of all systems that in their existence they manifest certain functions. I mention functions rather than the rules because although these functions are fairly standard, the rules that different families create may be very different. The first function of a family system is self-maintenance and this is measured by its stability in time and its cohesiveness. In a sense the family system seeks to maintain something of a status quo. At the same time, however, when children are born it is a requirement of the system that it should foster and encourage growth in the children. This, of course, is to go counter to the first function of maintaining the status quo. Moreover, because a family does not exist in a vacuum it is also necessary for it to be open to systems outside, e.g. work, school, the neighbourhood and so forth. But this again opens the family system to change through the interaction of its members with the outside world. Thus there is a further dynamic tension based around the family's relative openness to outside influences. Yet a further tension arises around the question of the autonomy and conformity allowed to or demanded of each member. This is loosely related to the question of dependence and independence, which inevitably is one of the core issues within any family. Independence and autonomy, almost by definition, can be seen as implicit criticisms of the family system, either when practised by a parent or by a child. It is a part of the child's task in growing up to achieve a degree of autonomy and independence, but if this is also seen as a threat to the family stability, his power to withstand their sanctions is limited. This is a further dimension of difficulty for the child to master.

Before moving to a consideration of how this affects the child growing up in his family, it is necessary to say something about communication, the process whereby meanings, messages and values are transmitted within the system. I want to make it clear that communication is not just spoken messages, and not just the obvious content of messages. All behaviour is a communication and all communication is at two levels (Watzlawick et al., 1967). At one level there is the obvious content, such as a verbal message (request, command, information), or a physical action (a look, a gesture, a caress, a blow). At a more subtle level, each message is also a statement about how a person sees himself, and how he sees others, and who, at that moment, has authority to define the situation. The totality of behaviour within a family interactive system is, therefore, a web of communication about identity, about control, about the manifest world and about relationships.

The task for a child growing up in a family is very complex. Progressively he must construct and reconstruct for himself the reality that his family represents, and learn that his construction is not the same as that of any other member. Just because he is growing, his very being represents a challenge or threat to the stability and status quo, the openness or closedness of the family to the outside world. He will need to recognize and resolve this. He must also gradually become familiar with the obvious and the concealed messages about relationships within the family, and, because those relationships already existed before he did, he must at worst come to terms with and at best help to shape them.

In the light of these observations I would like to posit the following formulation as an alternative framework for understanding children: *the child's thoughts, words and deeds represent his ongoing attempts to find an accommodation with the tensions and conflicts that the family system inevitably generates without at the same time violating his growing sense of personal autonomy. This behaviour itself is a communication of how he defines himself and the family system. Its acceptability or non-acceptability will then be signalled back by other family members. The same process then operates in the outer world when the child meets the extended family and eventually enters school.*

The process that this formulation describes is, as I see it, a construction that does justice to the fact that a child is unavoidably part of, and grows up in, a family. It is a construction of normality and, as such, implies no value judgement. There is only the invitation to see if it makes sense psychologically and is experientially satisfying. The model takes on practical value when problems arise, as in marital discord, difficulties between generations (and this can include three as well as two generations) and anomalies in a child's development. When these problems occur we should expect them to reflect threats of breakdown or weaknesses in the family system. These can come to light through the observation of the family in its interactions, or through the individual constructions that family members have of themselves and the system. We would also expect serious failures in the communications between members as shown by messages with double meanings, ambiguities and misunderstandings of individuals, and, for the growing child, messages that lead him to doubt the validity of his own perceptions and self-knowledge.

Within this framework I can offer a short list of messages or meanings that might well be associated with a child in the family who is labelled dyslexic.

> I am an intelligent child and I cannot read. Am I stupid? But I know I am not.

This message stems from the child's sense of self in the face of contradictory information.

> Because I am/he is an intelligent child and I/he cannot read, I/he deserves to be treated as special. If I learn to read, what becomes of my special status? If I haven't got that what have I got?

This message stems from a consideration of self within the family system.

> If I remain a non-reader, I maintain my status quo within the family as a person requiring special provision, but I lose my status quo with my peer group because I do not keep up with them. If I maintain my status quo with my peer group by matching their attainment, do I lose my special niche at home which my parents have made such a dance about?

This message relates self, family system and systems outside the family. All three messages, however, follow logically from the fact that the child is committed to growing within this complex set of systems, which represent his self, his family and the outside world.

If we now return to my formulation of the growing-up process of a child within a system we might put the diagnostic implications of such a model in the form of a simple question: *for what problem, or dilemma or difficulty within the child's construction of himself and his family system is his failure to learn to read an accommodation?*

There are some important implications that stem from this question. We need to distinguish between, on the one hand, the earliest checks on the child's natural learning initiatives together with his failure to use adults as validators for his solutions, and, on the other hand, the perpetuation of non-learning as a chronic condition.

In some families, whether a child shows some minor developmental anomaly or not, the parents will create a handicap out of a child's failure to match the image of growth which they hold in their own minds, i.e. the expectations of normality or even superiority that they feel is appropriate for their child. As their own contribution to the handicap is invisible they are committed to looking for an explanation within the child, either as stupidity, or laziness or in physical terms. In a family where physical causation is acceptable the parents will seek for confirmation for a physical cause by insisting on the reality of the imagined handicap. This is a difficult matter for a doctor to refuse as any normality is a short fall from perfection and in this sense normality in relation to perfection can be considered to be a handicap. Thus, everybody is trapped: the doctor in his inability to challenge wholeheartedly the inappropriate expectations of the parents, the parents by their demands for a perfection, which are unrealistic, the child by being imprisoned in the parents' delusion. To be normal in his normality is to discredit his parents' hopes. To collude with them is to perpetuate his state of non-growth, despite the knowledge of his own senses that he is not stupid.

Where developmental anomaly exists in a child, either genuine or arising as an accommodation to the family system, and it is not recognized, or not recognized as having meaning, the family system continues unchanged and the anomaly is taken for granted, even though the accommodation, for which the anomaly is a signal, is painful. The involvement of the child and parents within the wider system represented by school, leads to misunderstandings between school and parents. The child is accepted in good faith by the school as he is, but as soon as his parents start to make comparisons with children from other families or wake up to a continuing relative failure in their child, they become dissatisfied with his progress. Since their own involvement in his growth and development is unrecognized, they seek for explanations through the inadequacies of school or through factors within the child – laziness, stupidity or physical factors. The realities experienced by the school and by the parents are now of such a different order that hostilities and antagonisms are likely to follow. It is not surprising that the failure of these children to learn is difficult to understand. The original dilemmas to which the child had to accommodate by not developing remain undisclosed. By this time the family has already stabilized around the special status of the child as a non-learner and around the rectitude and goodness of the family. By contrast, school and local authority are firmly fixed in a category of badness. Paradoxically for the child to learn to read now is a challenge to the stability of the system as it will cast doubts on the parent's version of reality in favour of the school's version. He is bound hand and foot by these discrepant loyalties (c.f. Ravenette, 1968) and the bonds are strengthened by each attempt of the parents to prove their point. Thus the condition of non-learning is perpetuated.

The implication of this kind of reasoning is that, in order to arrive at an understanding of a child's incipient non-learning or chronic failure to learn, we need to explore the sense the child makes of himself and his circumstances. At the same time we need to explore the interactions between him and his family, the family's construction of him, and the interactions between the family and the outside world. If the word 'cure' has any meaning, then cure will reside in the attempt to create alternative realities for the child, the family and the school so that the problems for which non-reading is an accommodation are changed. The effect of such a change is to free the child to use his own learning initiatives and to accept the adults as trustworthy validators of his own learning.

Thus, after a long theoretical journey, I have arrived at the change of focus and perspective that I indicated at the beginning of the paper that I would try to develop. Even if what I have said is intellectually and experientially meaningful, it is still, however, just so such theory until it is shown to have practical relevance with real cases. In the rest of the paper I shall try to demonstrate this through the information that came from my investigations of two cases.

Two cases

In each of these cases it is a reality that the mother insists that her daughter is dyslexic, and therefore for each mother dyslexia is also a reality. The source of the label was the same in each case, directly in the case of Susan, the second case; indirectly via a nephew in the case of Sadie.

There is a gentle irony in this. The person who was the source of the diagnosis was a very valued medical colleague of mine with whom I disagreed on this issue. Subsequently she lost faith in the value of the diagnosis and doubted its validity. Susan's mother, however, was still clinging to the label six years later when her daughter was 15 years old, and was still demanding action in terms of the label. Sadie's mother, however, was under the false impression that I had said her nephew was dyslexic and that I had been the one who had put him right. She was delighted therefore to find that I was to be the psychologist who would be involved with her daughter.

Sadie

Sadie was nearly 7 years old. Her mother is worried that Sadie is like her cousin who had himself been labelled dyslexic, but now was doing well. She had communicated her anxiety to the head teacher who, quite correctly, asked for an outside view. Her teacher, who was very experienced in teaching reading and in diagnosing children's reading difficulties, recognized that Sadie was a little behind the other children but not enough to raise anyone's anxieties. She was aware that the mother was applying a great deal of pressure on Sadie, and, as she told me later, Sadie was able to put on or put off her reading ability at her own pleasure.

The purpose of the interview is to find out the sense that Sadie makes of herself, her family and her circumstances. She presents a picture of pleasant, cheerful co-operation, but her behaviour shows that she is skilled in giving contradictory messages at the same time, as will be seen later in the interview.

She conceded that her mother would be worried about her not learning to read, but teachers would be worried, not about that, but in case she ran out into the street. She denied that she herself was worried, and she accompanied her answers with a knowing smile, almost as though she was aware of the game-playing possibilities that these questions suggested.

We asked her to draw her family and herself – everyone doing something. She drew mother first, cooking a meal, and the heat of the cooker is perhaps over-elaborated. She next drew her sister Diane (9) passing the plates. Father is drawn next playing word games with his mate. Finally, she drew herself passing round biscuits, having first interposed a huge table between herself and the rest of the family.

Every member of the family is given a full complement of facial details except father, for whom nose and mouth are missing. Moreover, the theme of his activity, word games, is shared, not with the family but in a relationship outside, almost as though within the family he has no voice on what, in relation to Sadie, is an important matter. Sadie draws herself clearly separated from the rest of her family and her activity, even though of the same order as that of her mother, passing food, is inappropriate for the meal that her mother is preparing.

We next ask Sadie to say of each member of her family who they find it easy and difficult to get on well with. Her answers indicate that mother is the person who no one finds it easy to get on with. By contrast, father is hardly mentioned, and for the children might be non-existent. By way of justification, about her mother Sadie elaborates 'She has a bad back, her leg plays her up. Doctor gives her tablets. She has to lie down.' Since this is the justification for mother being so difficult, it must mean that she uses physical complaints as a means of controlling and influencing some of the family interactions. Both daughters find it difficult to get on well with mother, but they do get on well with each other. Sadie's presentation of this material was more akin to that of an adult than a 7-year-old girl.

On this evidence, Sadie sees her family as a system of crossed communication, contradictory messages, confused identities and loyalties, and little mutual understanding. Mother is the effective power and can use physical complaints to control and influence others, possibly even to avoid physical contact. Father's involvement is limited, he finds satisfactory relationships outside the family, and within the family is silent.

We move now to an exploration of Sadie's knowledge and understanding of feelings and the circumstances that are associated with different feelings. We draw a 'happy' face and a 'sad' face and ask her to say which is which. We then ask her to say three things about such girls.

Next we ask her to draw faces for 'angry' and 'lonely' and also for a feeling of her own choice. For each of these she is required to give three descriptions. For the last she chose 'cross'.

> HAPPY: She will like playing out, and mum wouldn't know. She would have ice-cream and get money from her mum.

> SAD: She wouldn't have everything she wanted. She would have to go to bed early because mum and dad say so. Mum wouldn't let her have clothes she would like to have.

These replies repeat the hostility to mother that was apparent in the account of her family. They also reflect a greater involvement with parents than with children.

> ANGRY: She would be shouting. She would not let people go near her she doesn't like so she would hit them in the face. She would kick her dad. Her dad doesn't want her to be near him.

This is a powerful expression of anger and violence, and leads to the thought that she may have either had experience of this form of physical involvement, or possibly been a witness to this either in fact or in verbal threats. She also gives expression to a potential feeling of hostility to her father.

> LONELY: She has no one to play with her, no one likes to play. Her sister wouldn't play, she doesn't want her. Her cousin won't play with her.

> CROSS: Angry would be cross. Children would be naughty to her, they won't eat their dinner. The wife said 'don't have children on their own.'

In this response Sadie identifies with the adult rather than with being a child, and repeats the theme of parent child hostility. In fact if there is one theme running through all of these responses, it is children's hostility to parents, with the associated feelings of anger and potential violence.

We now wish to explore Sadie's construction of herself in the context of people who are important to her. To this end we draw a straight line and add a sloping extension at one end. We ask her to make this into a picture and to include in the picture herself and four people who are important to her.

She makes the line into her Nan's caravan. She draws herself, a policeman, a doctor, a sergeant policeman and a fire brigade man. She said that someone had got knocked over and these people had been sent for. In terms of the situation that she had drawn it is certainly correct to include these people as most important. The situation, however, is a perpetuation of the theme of violence rather than those I had asked for, namely, people who were important to her. In an attempt to bring her back to the task, I set it again, but asked her to draw her own picture. The themes were continued, but this time she said her father had been knocked over. She had come to watch.

In a further attempt to free her from the theme of violence, I asked her if she dreamed and then asked her to draw one. She drew a church and two people, a man and a woman. I asked her what it was, to which she replied, 'mum and dad getting married'.

(In a speculative way we might see contradictory meanings to this. Does she wish they would 'marry' in the sense of 'living happy ever after', or is she equating marriage with interpersonal violence – or the interpretation of physical interaction as violence?)

At the first interview with the parents, it was clear that they were communicating mixed values about education and serious differences between themselves about Sadie. Her mother stresses reading as important yet she herself had abandoned an interest in education because her younger brother was extremely bright. She came from a favoured part of Surrey, her husband from a working class community. There is little contact between herself and her family of origin. Her husband, as a child, attended remedial reading classes and had needed speech therapy. Mother insisted that it was something in Sadie's head that stopped her from learning to read. Father said that Sadie could 'turn it off' or 'turn it on'. Perhaps I should point out that at no time had anyone said that this family was in any way other than nice, pleasant and normal. They certainly conveyed that message in the interview. Nonetheless, Sadie's picture may also be true. No family presents, in public issues that they wish to keep private and the interview was about Sadie's reading, not about the family.

We interview the family, not merely to understand what is going on, but also to intervene in a way that will make some difference. Out of the many issues revealed by our investigations we single out just one cluster. Reading is closely tied in with mother's demands and anxieties about Sadie. It is also a matter of contention between herself and her husband. There is the appearance of hostility from child to mother. Sadie's skill in manipulation is manifest in relation to whether or not she reads. Thus, it would be useful to dislodge reading from its active association with mother and place it fairly and squarely in school. If mother does become involved it must be at the invitation of Sadie, and even then only to validate and approve. This instruction was given and accepted in a good spirit and the interview was terminated.

The class teacher provided confirmation of some of these issues. Following our detailed discussion of my interview with Sadie she made the interesting discovery that although Sadie was apparently unable to read the books in the formal reading scheme, she could easily cope with the associated workbooks. In other words, Sadie 'turned it off' when approached directly to read, and 'turned it on' when the approach was indirect. The discovery opened a door whereby the teacher could more powerfully influence Sadie's learning.

At the second family interview, with Sadie present, it became clear that mother was unable to honour the instruction. If Sadie did approach mother with a book, she felt impelled to test and to teach rather than validate and approve. It also became apparent in the interview that Sadie was fully aware of the serious differences between her parents about her abilities and showed illicit pleasure when these differences were publicly expressed.

Sadie was due to transfer to the junior school after the summer holidays and it was recognized that something needed to be attempted to consolidate her gains. Since father's view of Sadie was similar to that of the teacher and father had little voice in the family on this issue, we decided that it might be helpful, therefore, for Sadie to use her father as an educational adviser for her reading, but not as a teacher. Hopefully this would also have some effect in modifying the family system by involving father more directly, albeit in a controlled capacity, with his daughter, and, at the same time, removing Sadie's reading from the negative involvement with her mother.

By way of summarizing the case of Sadie, we can make a number of points. Mother, father and teacher have constructed conflicting realities about Sadie and her ability or non-ability to learn to read. Sadie is aware of these differences and is able to use them in a manipulative manner. My own understanding of the case runs along the following lines. The most important feature of Sadie's behaviour is her ability to communi-cate in complex and manipulative ways. This is the reality behind the discrepant views of her ability to read, and represents her ongoing accommodation to the tensions, conflicts and mixed messages of which she is aware in her family. Through this behaviour she is able to create some sense of stability for herself within her family without losing her sense of personal autonomy. Since reading and learning to read are secondary to the manipulative communication, they are likely to become and remain impaired. Without some such intervention as we have offered, she might indeed become an apparent non-learner.

Susan

Susan represents the opposite end of the age spectrum. She is already 15 years old and is a 'confirmed dyslexic'. The diagnosis had been made when she was 9 and she had attended a dyslexic centre every afternoon for two years before transferring to a comprehensive school. Her attendance at the centre stopped when the teacher retired, but she has been given the best that a good remedial department can offer in a secondary school. For the last year she has been attending a hospital dyslexic centre for one afternoon a week. Despite this continued help, Susan was still extremely retarded and mother was applying pressure on the headmaster for 'something to be done'. I had been involved earlier on the periphery of the case and therefore suggested that we convene a meeting between the parents, the headmaster, the head of the remedial department and myself in order to take stock of the present position and see what kind of help might be made available.

At the first meeting, Susan's mother complained that the authority was not providing enough for her daughter, nobody was really concerned about her and she would leave school illiterate. Even when it was pointed out how much the authority had made available in the past, she still would not desist. It seemed more important for her to demand extra help than to understand why Susan did not learn. After all, she had been told Susan was dyslexic and that was enough of an explanation. It was pointed out that the real issue might well be why Susan had successfully withstood the proffered help, especially as the teacher at the dyslexic centre had been outstandingly experienced and profoundly sympathetic.

Gradually more issues emerged. Mother was very much opposed to Susan going out without her. She could not tell the time, she would not find her way about, she would not be able to read the numbers on the buses. The reality that mother presents is of a rather young subnormal child, not of an adolescent of at least dull average ability. I offered to give Susan three interviews in which I would try to help her to take advantage of the resources that were being put at her disposal. Mother was extremely sceptical about this, but I asked her to accept that I did know a thing or two about the matter and, as a courtesy at least, to listen to anything I might say by way of understanding. For the first time father took the lead by accepting my offer as reasonable and he almost chided his wife for not matching his reasonableness with her own. I also said that what happened in the interviews was between Susan and myself unless she herself offered to tell her parents about them. We agreed to the possibility of meeting again after Susan's interviews.

In my interviews with Susan I wanted to attempt two things: to find out how Susan made sense of herself and her circumstances and to ask questions or make comments that would challenge her current realities. I must confess to having had a great pessimism about the task. At this point in her educational career, and after so many had tried to help her and failed, how could I hope to make any difference? Although, in my interview, there is nothing that does not have some importance, I shall restrict my account to those parts that seemed to have special significance, either in providing an understanding, or in challenging her view of things.

The first interview was concerned with exploring some of Susan's ways of making sense of herself and things. We focused on girls who could and could not read, the family interactions, her perception of troubling situations in school, and, finally, the good and bad implications of being either a non-reader or a reader. I shall present aspects of each of these in turn.

In describing girls who could and could not read, the central theme reflected a concern with the difficulty or ease of carrying on interpersonal relationships with her peer group. In the light of mother's reluctance to let Susan out on her own, this would certainly seem to be important. Interestingly, non-readers could change into readers by stopping being shy.

Susan was less informative about her family. When faced with the question of members finding it easy or difficult to get on, she said that they all got on well with each other. When I put this back to her – 'everything is sweetness and light in your family' – she said, 'yes'. In my experience this is always a defensive response, and under further questioning she conceded that there would be trouble if she disturbed mother's peace by fighting with her brother or teasing the dog.

Arising out of the ways in which she attributed thoughts, feelings and actions to girls in troubling situations in school, a number of inferences were put for her to accept or reject. 'Other girls are important to you?' This was fully endorsed. 'Susan can never see herself as bad.' Again this was fully endorsed. 'The only time when you really make a difference to anybody is when you are not as good as the rest' and 'if you are just as good, or even better, it doesn't make any difference to anyone.' Each of these was half agreed.

Her answers to the questions 'what is bad and good about not being a good reader?' and 'what is good and bad about being a good reader?' are highly instructive. The bad things about being a bad reader were exclusively that *other* children did things better. There was no reference at all to herself in this. The good thing about being a bad reader provoked Susan to say, after a long pause, 'special reading classes'. She had little to say about what was good about being a good reader, and nothing about what was bad. This is not surprising as she has never filled that role. More ominously, however, it suggests that she has not even contemplated it.

Throughout the interview, Susan was pleasant, if dull, but most of all rather complacent. The contents of her responses show no burning anxiety about herself or about being a poor reader, nor does she give anything away about her family. It was indeed a depressing interview.

The second interview threatened to be a continuation of the first. She communicated boredom and lack of interest, yet the task was one in which she might conceivably learn something about herself and others. Eventually, I changed the interview radically by throwing her the following questions:

Q. Does your mother complain because you can't read and write very well?
A. Yes.
Q. What would she complain about if you could read and write well?
A. Nothing.
Q. Are you sure?
A. Yes, if my reading and writing was all right she would have nothing to complain about.
Q. Can you prove it? I know of no mother who has nothing to complain about.

Susan signalled her awareness of the challenge in this question by a smile and I ended the interview by inviting her to go home and think about proving it.

The third interview developed in yet a different way. As with Sadie in the previous case, I asked her to make a picture out of a line and put into this picture herself and four people who were important to her. In the execution of this task, there are two obvious components, the situation and the people. There are two less obvious components: the quality and the extent to which she communicates more or less than I had asked. In Susan's picture the situation was completely bare, the people were predictable and the quality was incredibly poor. In many ways her production echoed the reality of a subnormal girl that her mother had conveyed in the family interview. What would happen, however, if we take the poor quality as a communication over and above what was required? The following short exchange ensued.

Q. If an experienced teacher looked at this picture, how old would she say the child was who drew it?
A. Three.
Q. If I told the teacher that the drawing was done by a 15-year-old girl, would she think it was possible?
A. No.

Susan's responses to these questions was immediate, confident and interested, as though for a brief moment there was the possibility of a conversation that might make some difference to her. It did not last. I followed this with some other tasks and then took up the possibility of using the material she had given in the dialogue.

The procedure was for me to draw a picture which was both vague enough, and explicit enough, to reflect some sense of herself and her family. I then asked her for a story about the picture and promised, in exchange, a story from myself. The purpose of my story was to fill out some of the invisible messages that I deduced from the totality of the evidence. There is no pretence of infallibility in the reconstruction – only a stumbling attempt to create a plausible reality out of limited knowledge.

The picture I drew was of a family group in which a 3-year-old girl was the prominent figure. This girl was seen from behind and was shown holding something in her right hand. I ask Susan to tell a story as from a 3-year-old girl, and this is what she offered:

> Once upon a time, I was playing in the garden with a water pistol and my brother had one of his mates and another brother was listening to cassettes. Then Nan and Grandad came down with presents, it was Christmas.

(The last sentence was, in fact, extracted by my asking her to go beyond description and give an ending.) There is indeed little with which to work, but let us make an assumption that it represents a real situation. Let us also give mother a part to play, imagining in the light of what we know, what she would say. Let us also allow for the expression of feeling and let us also point out consequences. This is the story that emerged:

> Once upon a time there was a 3-year-old girl playing in the garden. She picked up her brother's water pistol and was just going to aim it at her brother when her mother, who was watching her out of a window shouted out to her to put ' that pistol down at once. You are a little girl, not a little boy' said her mother, 'and what's more you are not old enough yet to do that sort of thing'. The little girl was so angry with her mother for speaking like that to her and saying those things that she vowed that she would always be a 'perfect little girl' and that if she couldn't be grown up now she never would be. And the little girl's vow came true. Everyone thought what a nice little girl she was but they also thought what a pity it was that she didn't grow to be her age instead of always being tied to her mother. And that is how she is to this day. She can't read, she can't tell the time she chooses to meet her mother's wishes by not going out with friends. This girl is not Susan, but perhaps Susan is a little bit like her.

I asked her then to draw a picture of Susan who might be stuck at that age, and terminated the interview. To my surprise, after a few minutes, there was a knock on the door. It was Susan who had came back to thank me, a thing she had never done at either of the other two interviews.

At the resumed joint interview with the family, Susan was also present. For the first 10 minutes, mother angrily charged me with not believing in dyslexia, with offering nothing to Susan and with wasting everybody's time. She had completely forgotten the nature of the contract that I had offered, and indeed had probably not, psychologically heard it. How could she if she was committed to a reality in which my offer had no meaning? She then took pains to point out that the hospital dyslexic unit treated Susan as 'special – very special'. She was unable to see that in pressing this point publicly, she was both taking something away from Susan, and at the same time belittling her. She also demanded to know what had happened in my interview with Susan as though she and Susan were still in the relationship of mother and

2-year-old infant. I had to stand my ground and assert Susan's rights as a 15-year-old to her own thoughts and individuality. It was also apparent that although demanding change in Susan, she might not be able to recognize it. The demand for perfection is the guarantee for continued failure. I terminated the interview by hesitatingly making an offer of further family interviews, which father indicated he might be willing to accept, but mother is likely to reject. She cannot envisage the possibility of, let alone see, the invisible chains in the situation and would not be grateful if she could.

Mothers like this make the professional feel guilty and inadequate. The headmaster was certainly made to feel it and, in my turn, I felt impotent. In some ways Susan's behaviour and performance may also reflect her sense of impotence within the family system. Nonetheless, the girl had already changed. The dyslexic centre reported that her reading was now at the 8- to 9-year level. The remedial teacher at school said that within the last fortnight she was beginning to 'put things together', and the headmaster related how Susan was beginning to show some personal initiatives in her approach to himself and other teachers.

It is difficult to read the future. If Susan changes she will be committed to increasing autonomy and independence and involvement with systems outside the family. She will be made to feel guilty about this, and anger will arise between mother and Susan. This is likely also to produce tensions between other members, especially if they take sides. Thus the family stability will be seriously threatened. We cannot tell what the next accommodation will be.

Conclusion

The stories of Sadie and Susan bring my argument to a close but with a quotation.

> 'The action of picking up a label is the same action that lets go of fact and picks up opinion. We deny ourselves the chance of ever being alive to a living situation' (Swann, 1962).

I suspect that below the appearance of what I have presented, there is another reality – a reality within which whether a child learns or does not learn is seen to be intimately a part of his life and his living. My presentation of Sadie and Susan indeed are essays in constructing a view of their lives. In the process, I would like to think that I have shown something of my own attempt to be alive to their living situations. And is it not the hallmark of all true teaching that the teacher also is alive to the living situation of his pupils?

Chapter 7
To tell a story, to invent a character, to make a difference (1979)

This paper was prepared for a study day with educational psychologists who were interested in knowing about a PCT approach to their work. It offers an analysis of 'troubling' children, 'troubled' teachers and 'troubling' situations together with examples of psychological intervention.

This paper is about children in school whose behaviour gives rise to complaints: it is about those who complain: it is about the attempt to do something whereby the complaint ceases to have validity. The *dramatis personae* are children, teachers and psychologists. Parents are not included in this script although inevitably their presence offstage is recognized. The essence of the paper is placed in the middle: a critical analysis of the issues surrounding complaints and a theoretical framework within which action is both understandable and communicable. I should say at the outset that the paper may prove to be a trap for those who allow their thoughts and feelings to become engaged either by the contents or by the presentation. I should also say that although the obvious topic is precisely as I have presented it, there may be implicit topics that perhaps will only become apparent at the very end.

I shall start with the story of a primary school boy called Adam. Against this background I shall offer an analysis of the issues that lead a school to ask a psychologist for help. Next comes a discussion of some of the essential, but often unrecognized, aspects of what we call behaviour and this will be developed to include consideration of some of the 'whys' and 'hows' of change. I shall then illustrate the argument with ongoing work the success of which is still in doubt, but in which the failures illuminate the argument. This is the story of Martin, a 15-year-old secondary school boy, who, at the time I saw him, was under threat of suspension. In the final section I shall try to round off the matter by bringing into the open some of the underlying but unspoken themes which act as a substrate to the paper.

The story of Adam: a success

Adam, a 10-year-old boy, was referred by the head teacher. He was near to being excluded from school for rude and aggressive behaviour to some of the teachers, especially his class teacher, whom he claims to hate. He is rude with a rudeness that is worse than dumb insolence. He declines to give answers, and on occasion will respond with violence. Even where the teacher could give constructive help, Adam would decline the offer, or would not ask for help. In discussing the complaint with the head teacher before seeing the boy, the metaphor of 'prisoner in a prisoner of war camp' seemed a fitting description. The head teacher added that this also fitted the father on the few times when he visited the school.

My purpose in interviewing a child is to attempt an exploration of his ways of making sense of himself and his circumstances and the aim is achieved through the use of a variety of interviewing techniques. It is an essential part of this to establish with the child the basis for seeing him. Without this agreement, there is little chance of meaningful communications.

In general, Adam co-operated 'correctly' but all the time he was able to remain detached and uninvolved and was at pains to maintain his independence of me. At times, however, he allowed himself a smile, recognizing the incongruity of different points of view operating at the same time. The smile is the hint of a sense of humour.

Adam conceded that the head teacher would be worried because he fights teachers, but he did not admit that he himself would be worried. (By contrast his parents would be worried about his work.) In order to clarify the options involved in fighting or not fighting teachers, Adam was asked to say three things about boys and who did or did not fight them. All he could say of the former was 'when the teacher does something to them' and of the latter he could say nothing, almost as though this was an option with no meaning for him at all. As we also need to probe the possibilities of change he was asked how that could come about. For boys who fought it was a matter of 'don't want to fight', for boys who did not fight 'just a change of mind'. In other words, change for Adam was conceivable and would arise from a boy's internal decisions rather than from a demand that the world should change.

As I said earlier, the parents are offstage; nonetheless the family is ever present in the thoughts and feelings of the child. We need therefore to explore this aspect of Adam's sense of himself and his circumstances. We do this using three different techniques: a family drawing, a drawing in which the family may or may not be included and an interaction matrix within which is recorded Adam's answers to an enquiry about who each person in the family finds it easy or difficult to get on with.

There were two important features about the family drawing. The members were scattered widely across the paper, and Adam did not include himself. In talking about the picture it become apparent that all the children had Biblical names, and that Adam was fully aware of this. He himself added that his cousins also had Biblical names but neither family was particularly religious.

In the second technique, I draw a straight line, bent downwards at one end and ask Adam to make this into a picture in which he should include himself and four people who are important to him. (Some children do not include their families in the picture.) Adam made the line into a bus that lacked wheels and a driver. Brother Mark was excluded this time, and the family members, almost predictably, were placed one at each window. Thus the separated family is now presented in a public context but in fact powerless, directionless and, as Adam said, with nowhere special to go.

The interactions in the matrix confirm the potential splits and tensions in the family. In particular Adam identifies with his father but this is not reciprocated and the relationship between himself and his mother is based on potential misunderstanding. He confirmed that both he and his brother Mark were the two who were most uncomfortable within the family.

An awareness and understanding of feeling states are important aspects of how a child makes sense of himself, so we now turn to explore these with Adam. We invite him to say which of two faces is happy and which sad, and then to say three things about boys who would feel that way. We follow this with a request to illustrate faces that exemplify other feeling states, 'angry', 'worried', 'lonely' including one for a boy who 'fights teachers' and we end the sequence with an invitation to draw a face of his own choice.

Three themes emerge distinctly from his responses. The first is a powerful sense of isolation from his peer group, yet he is unable to describe a lonely boy. The second is that a concern for material things is important in the family and that Adam hints at a feeling of deprivation of things that rightfully are his. The third theme is his sense of equality with the adults. This appears especially in the context of the boy who 'fights teachers'. He says of such a boy 'the teachers fight with him'. 'The teacher tells him to do something and he doesn't want to do it' and 'the boy shouts at the teacher'.

There is another theme, separate from the other three, and perhaps more fundamental. It appears in the choice he made for the last face. Having filled in the details, he said that this boy was 'normal' and gave the following description: 'He doesn't fight the teachers.' 'He isn't angry.' 'He isn't sad.' In other words normality would seem to be a denial of an entitlement to negative feelings and also of the right to stand up for himself against an adult world, if he feels that this world is a threat to him.

We can now use the vocabulary that we have just developed as a means of finding out how Adam sees himself and how he thinks others see him. In his eyes, his mother would say he is 'sad' and 'worried'. His father would say he was 'worried' and 'sad'. His class teacher would say he 'fights teachers', and is 'angry' and 'worried'. He would describe himself with the words 'fights teachers', 'happy' and 'angry'. In other words he implicitly sees himself as 'not normal'. He agreed that I might offer my description of him and I gave 'worried', 'normal' and 'angry'. This clearly is an attempt to realign 'normal' along more ordinary lines and at the same time to dislodge him from his perception of himself as abnormal.

We brought the interview to an end with a technique that encouraged creativity and imagination both from Adam and from myself. I drew a picture that is loose and rather unformed but yet might be taken to be a representation of his family. I asked him to tell me a story about this picture with the expectation that it would present certain as yet ill-formulated issues that may be a cause of concern for him. I promised to give a story in exchange, and my story would attempt a reconstruction of some of the material that he has already given. It will suggest an alternative view of things and will validate certain aspects of Adam, which may not previously have been recognized and which may offer different ways of coping with the dilemmas that underlie his behaviour. Although this is the broad aim, there is no guarantee that a story will come which meets these criteria. Nor is there a guarantee that it will make any difference.

Adam's story was very short: 'Once upon a time there was a boy. He was going along with his two brothers and his mum and dad. And his dad was looking away and the boy followed his dad and the other two went with their mum.'

My story is rather longer and tries to capture some of the themes that have appeared in the interview. I ask Adam to close his eyes and listen. What follows is my recollection of the story I gave.

Once upon a time there was a boy, and everyone thought that he was very little, and he thought that he was very little. But really he wasn't because in his heart he was very big. Then brothers started coming into the family. And the boy thought 'I'm the oldest, like the Bible people. I'm the equal to them all, to nearly all the grown ups'. But he wasn't like that at school. At school everyone was bigger than him. [This part of the story provides a developmental account of the rise of his sense of equality with the adults.] He had an interesting family. They never said quite what they meant and even though they got on there were lots of rows. This boy did not know where he had to go to, to his father or to his mother. He couldn't sort it out so he got angry, and upset and worried. And he couldn't talk about it. If he told his family they would say he should be normal. [Here we present his feeling states as arising out of the idiosyncrasies of his family communication style and values.] In school it was a different world altogether. Nobody understood him and he didn't understand them. So he fought. He just hadn't learned that he could be normal and angry, normal and worried, normal and sad, normal and frightened, normal and lonely. [Here a model of normality is offered, which might have important implications for him outside the family.] But one good thing about this boy is that he can laugh a bit. He can see the funny side and that means that he can stand away from it all. [We draw attention to one positive aspect about the boy that perhaps had never been recognized, and we indicate that it may have utility value for coping in school.] The boy's name is not Adam, but perhaps Adam would recognize the boy if he met him.

At the end of the story Adam is relieved of the burden of having to be the boy in the story, but is given the opportunity of seeing an alternative to the boy he does know, which is himself. Adam was very intent whilst listening to the story and said that he liked it. This brought the interview to an end and Adam returned thoughtfully to his class.

The other half of the work, however, still has to be carried out. This involves bringing together the complainants, the head teacher, the deputy head and the class teacher, to share with them the raw material of the interview and any inferences that might be drawn. Whereas normally I go to great lengths to find out the teacher's ways of making sense of a child and his behaviour, on this occasion, for two reasons, I acted differently. The first reason was the simple fact that I had to be at another appointment and that left time only for a presentation of the interview. The second reason lay in the nature of the class teacher himself who, from previous experience, I knew to be inflexible in responding to children, and rigid in his understanding. I presented the interview, therefore, in almost a ritualistic way, punctuating my account with apologies for not being able to listen to the teacher's own view of things, and regrets that I had to leave early. At the end of my narration, I apologized again and left the school. This procedure was not planned, but in retrospect some observations seem apposite. I made no demands on him to change, but at the same time I gave him no opportunity to refute my own account. I did not criticize him, nor tell him what to do, but if he accepted my version of things it would be because of the inherent appeal of the material rather than because of my persuasion. Finally I respected his right to his own view of things by apologizing for not letting him give it.

In the event things did change. Late in the afternoon the teacher visited the head and said that Adam was a different boy. It is worth asking, 'did Adam change, or the teacher, or both, or neither?' Was it perceptions that changed? Or behaviour? No matter, the problem for which I was called in was apparently solved, and despite regular enquiries about Adam ever since I have not heard any further complaint.

This brings the story of Adam to a close, but in the telling, I have made comments and let slip remarks that already point to a way of looking at the problem of disturbing children. It is to this that I now turn.

Disturbing children in school: an analysis of the problem

Some children, by their behaviour, are undoubtedly disturbing to teachers, to parents, to other children and to society. It has become a commonplace to say that such children 'have problems' and 'need help'. Although, in some senses, there is an element of truth in these observations, the truth is not self-evident from the complaints as initially presented, and the problems that the children are supposed to have are certainly not the behaviour that they show. In fact to say that such children 'have problems' and 'need help' is to draw inferences that serve the purpose of deflecting attention away from the complainant to that which is complained about. If we are to arrive at an understanding of the issues surrounding these children we should start by asking questions about the context and circumstances out of which a request for the help of the educational psychologist takes place.

In the beginning a disturbing child's behaviour is such as to generate a wide range of thoughts and feelings, usually negative, in the teachers who have to deal with him. A request for help comes because of the failure of the teachers to make any marked difference to the child's behaviour, and because the behaviour is a threat to the smooth running of the school. It needs to be stressed that the basis for referral is not the behaviour itself, but the inability to make any difference to that behaviour through the normal processes of the school. The action of referral itself is, of course, selected from a tariff that would probably include exclusion and suspension as alternatives. Thus the presence of a disturbing child in school means that it is the institution which 'has a problem' and which 'needs help'.

A referral is an apparently simple message: there is a complaint about a child and a request for the psychologist to see the child and, hopefully, to do something about it. It is, of course, more complex than that as there are always many implicit meanings in messages and these need to be recognized. At the very least there are always three messages, one about the child, one about the teacher and one about the kind of help that is sought. On the basis of this, four separate categories can be identified, but any referral may be a member of more than one category. An awareness of these categories is important if the response is to match the request. I list them below, but a referral never comes as clearly defined as these descriptions.

- Whatever I do with this child it makes no difference, so I feel useless and impotent. This is an affront to my sense of professional competence. I think that there must be something seriously wrong with the child to make him impervious to what I asked of him. Please tell me what to do.

- No matter how much I puzzle about this child, I cannot understand him nor can I predict what he will do from moment to moment. This makes me feel pretty stupid as a teacher. Please help me to understand him.
- I know this kind of child very well. He is 'maladjusted' and should not be in this school. It is not my entitlement as a teacher of normal children to have to spend all my time with him. Please ascertain him as 'maladjusted' and get him into a different school.
- This child is a bit of a trouble and he is a bit odd, but I can deal with him now that he is still rather young. I am worried though that he will be very difficult when he gets bigger and I am afraid that future teachers will blame me for not doing something about it now. Please tell me I am doing the right thing and give me a report to confirm this to future teachers.

I should make it clear that I, too, affirm that there are some children who fit into each of these categories: there are some who are impervious to what a school has to offer, there are some who are difficult to understand and to predict, there really are some children who should be in different schools, either as an asylum for themselves, or as a protection for the rest of the school, there are some who will grow into really difficult young people. The point I am making, however, with this set of categories, is that a referral is always more complex than it seems, and that unless the psychologist is aware of the complexities he may well fall into the risk of colluding with the child against the teacher or with the teacher against the child.

In this analysis I have deliberately omitted two important facts. I have not mentioned the school as a system within which problems of disturbing behaviour arise. Nor have I talked about family factors. A full discussion of these would take me too far away from the central theme of this paper. Briefly, however, the argument still obtains whatever the school system, and although the child is obviously an extension of the family into the world of school, it is my view that possible change can be brought about within the processes and structure of the school. It is not always necessary to bring the family directly into the work. I take it as axiomatic that a school will already have had some contact with the child's family, just because of the school's concern about his behaviour.

The sense we make: theory and implications

It is implicit in this analysis that I view disturbing behaviour in school as also a disturbance in the relationships between teachers and pupils. The mutual influence no longer acts in a benign, or even neutral way, so teachers feel impotent and ignorant and the disturbing child fails to modify his attitudes and behaviour in line with reasonable expectations of co-existence within school. This, therefore, is an interactionist way of looking at the issues. It is also one sided. We need now to develop a complementary view that will illuminate the psychological as opposed to the interactionist account of things.

I would like therefore to suggest a fundamental proposition in which there are four interrelated statements. The first two are important for this paper. The second two are given for tidiness. I shall then redevelop some of the implications of this proposition.

- Whatever a person does depends on how he perceives things.
- Perceiving includes both being 'aware' and also 'making sense'.
- Making sense' also includes as an opposite 'failing to make sense'.
- Each of these, 'making sense' and 'failing to make sense' will be something of which a person is also 'aware'.

Underlying this proposition is the central notion that it is an essential aspect of humanity that individuals think, feel, act, react, touch, taste, dream and experience the whole gamut of human processes and that they are also aware of their experiencing of these processes.

The expression 'making sense' may seem to carry a basically cognitive mode of awareness, implying the use of thought and intellect. Such is not the case. 'Making sense' always involves in varying degrees, thoughts, feelings (and I include 'gut' reactions amongst these) values and action, real or potential and each of these seems sensitive to different kinds of information. Whichever carries the major burden, the sense we make depends very much on the individual himself and on the situation in which he finds himself. An ability to modulate his contribution to understanding is probably an important feature of growth and maturity.

Just as 'making sense' is a complex, so is that of which an individual make sense. It includes the whole of his internal thoughts and feelings, the external world of objects and people, and the interactions between all of them. Most importantly, he must 'make sense' of himself and of the difference his being in the world makes.

Thus, if we are to become involved in the process of working with disturbance in school, it becomes imperative both to find out and to give value to the sense which individuals are already making of themselves and their circumstances. The story of Adam included and exemplified this precept.

I have already said that, when disturbing behaviour takes place in school, it will invariably be associated with a wide variety of negative feelings both in the children themselves and in the teachers. At the simplest level there will be a sense of uncomfortableness because disturbing children are seldom happy, nor do they make their teachers happy. Such psychological discomfort should provide a basis for change but obviously it does not as the behaviour persists. For behaviour to change, the way a person makes sense will also need to change. There are three main reasons why this should be difficult, and one more.

- The sense a person makes now represents the end point of that person's whole history of making sense. It is an organized system of thoughts, feelings and actions that has developed over time as the basis whereby he has coped with himself and the world. It would be difficult, therefore, for it to change in any major way out of the ordinary experiences of living and it will tend to persist, even though it may lead to psychological discomfort.
- The second reason rests on the fact that feelings are an important component of our ways of making sense, and feelings are frequently intimately connected with our sense of ourselves. In many ways the child who feels that his identity is threatened is also the one who is disturbing in school. To open himself to change is to risk a threatening unknown. He therefore seeks to maintain his identity whatever the cost.
- Thirdly, we ourselves are at the centre of the sense we make of things and, therefore, whatever happens, it is very difficult to see new events and experiences in anything but the dimensions of our existing viewpoints. This argument is at the heart of Piaget's concept of egocentrism. Unfortunately he saw it as being transcended by the age of 6 to 8, whereas it is with us for life.
- In the general order of things, there is a fourth reason for change not to take place. When we are satisfied with things as they are, there is no need to change. Dissatisfaction is, therefore, a necessary ground for change to take place, but dissatisfaction is itself an aspect of experience of which we need to make sense. There is sometimes a satisfaction in dissatisfaction, as Berne describes in the game 'Ain't Life Awful?' and this therefore militates against change.

The task, therefore, if we are to resolve some of the discomforts arising from disturbing children in schools, is to find ways of freeing individuals from the inertia of their existing ways of making sense, to make possible a modification in their sense of themselves or, finally, to dislodge them from their egocentric vision long enough for them to open up alternative perspectives from which new thoughts, feelings and actions may spring.

To tell a story: to invent a character

At this point, theory and technique come together in practice. I have already given an illustration of the story-telling technique with the story of Adam. It can now be seen to take its place within a theoretical framework. The story is a traditional means whereby we can, for a short time, stand outside ourselves. If the listener can identify with the central character and recognize that the character's dilemmas are similar to his own, he may be able to take a different view of life. It will be recalled, in my account of Adam, that at the end of the interview I attempted to shape a story out of some aspects of Adam's sense of himself and his circumstances. I gave a developmental history and a family context that Adam could match against his own. Thus he could identify with the hero and his circumstances. Most importantly, however, I attributed to him a sense of humour, and pointed to it as an aid in coping with his life. Thus, out of this story, an option was created whereby he might be able to change. To assert that the boy in the story was not Adam but was recognizable was to enable him to become disentangled from his own egocentricity. In these ways the story I told is a move in the direction of freeing Adam from his existing point of view, and thereby making available a less uncomfortable existence in school.

When I now give my account of Adam to his class teacher, I am carrying out the same exercise. I give a slightly different but recognizable account of Adam himself. I attribute a sense of charity and competence in the teacher by appealing to him to forgive me, and by my assuming that he can take the material and use it. By discouraging rational discussion I put a premium on the teacher's feeling mode of receptivity. He is invited, therefore, to accept the possibility of being a different kind of teacher.

Thus the twofold telling of a story, one to the child and one to the teacher, represents an attempt to dislodge each from their existing viewpoints and opening up a chance for more satisfactory interactions. In this way, I identify with child and teacher in turn and by transcending the situation hopefully am able to relieve it.

When we tell a story as a means of offering alternative perceptions and alternative understandings, we look for change to arise as a consequence. It is possible, however, to operate in the reverse way, and use change of action as a means of bringing about change of understanding and perception. This cannot be attempted unless the client is dissatisfied with things as they are and is willing to do something different. The process has to be engineered, however, because spontaneous change does not arise easily.

One means of achieving this is called 'fixed role therapy' and was devised by Kelly (1955, 1991) out of his observations that when students acted parts in plays that mirrored aspects or aspirations of themselves it frequently led to lasting changes in their everyday behaviour. The procedure involves writing for the client a character sketch that he is asked to play for a period of three weeks on an experimental basis. It is pointed out that the part is not a prescription for him as an individual for life. The sketch has to be carefully worked so that the client can identify with the part, the psychological rationale needs to show some relationship to the client's ongoing sense of things, and the action that playing the part entails should lead both to giving and receiving new kinds of information about himself and others. In Kelly's version, the therapist is the 'producer'. In the version presented here, one of the teachers acts as 'producer' for the child, and if the psychologist is a 'producer' at all it is for the teacher, who implicitly is also being asked to play a part for this three-week period. As will be seen in the story that follows, carrying out the experiment is not so straightforward as this description would suggest.

In contrast to the story-telling technique, we aim here, experimentally, for a dislodgement, overt for the child and implicit for the teacher, from their existing roles. (Role here means the operational aspect of their current ways of making sense.) The hope is that, out of the new information that is given from playing those parts, there will arise a spontaneous change in perception and awareness, leading to a spontaneous change of behaviour. The story of Martin, which is still work in progress, is a case in point. As with Adam, I shall give extracts from the interview and these will show the links between Martin's account of himself and the final character sketch.

The story of Martin: work in progress

Martin is now 15 years old and attends a comprehensive school. I knew him some three years previously because of trouble in school and, by working through a series of family interviews with the head of Martin's year, Martin had been able to get by without causing too much concern. Now, however, the school was again seriously worried about him and had considered suspending him. He was said to be unpredictable; he was prone to doing dangerous things in the chemistry laboratories. He could not be trusted with property and money. He acted as though he had the right to override school rules and he would give no sign that he had registered what teachers had said. At home he was said to be staying out at night, and that his mother had said she wished he could be put down.

Disturbing as this description is, we should remember that the other complaint is Martin's imperviousness to the influence of the teachers and the threat he represents to the smooth running of the school.

He conceded that the teachers would be worried about him and that his behaviour was deteriorating. He specified that he was missing school without his mother knowing, that he messed about in school and that he was cheeky towards the teachers. He said that he got no pleasure out of this and he also indicated that he would like things to change. These opening responses gave some reason to hope that change might be possible: he gets no satisfaction from things as they are and he would like change. They do not however suggest in what ways change might be promoted. It was only at the end of the interview that a 'fixed role therapy' experiment seemed to be possible.

Martin clearly identified himself as a boy who did not get on with teachers, but we needed to know what option he was thereby excluding. After all, going through the motions of getting on with teachers could hardly be less comfortable than his situation as it was. We asked him, therefore, to say three things about boys who do and boys who do not get on with teachers. As we also wanted to know about Martin's ideas for change, we asked what would have to happen for each to turn into the opposite.

Of boys who *get on well with teachers* he says, 'they are always crawling round teachers', 'they never stick up for themselves' and 'they always think teachers are always right'. For these boys to change into their opposite 'teachers might have a go at them for something they didn't do' and 'they would just change altogether'.

By contrast, he said of boys who did not get on well with teachers 'they say what they think is right and stick up for themselves against the teachers'. 'If they had been bad in the past they could never be trusted again' and 'they have never been given a second chance'. For these boys to change, 'teachers would need to give them a second chance' and 'they would need to change altogether, to be as good as they can'.

For Martin, therefore, relationships with teachers seem to offer stark alternatives – submit whether you think them right or wrong or stand up and fight. Likewise change involves little compromise, either teachers change or boys do, and the change is total.

Against this background we next turn our attention to finding out how Martin sees himself. In response to a direct request to say how various people would describe him, all he could say was 'I don't know'. We approached the matter, therefore, indirectly by asking him to choose photographs of boys he thinks he might understand, and to describe them. This procedure, of course, also gave some idea of the verbal equipment he had available for communicating the sense he made of other boys. He gave a total of five different descriptions. For each of these we sought to establish an opposite, as these represent alternative ways of acting. The pairs are:

- 'Keeps himself to himself' elaborated to 'if trouble doesn't come my way I won't make it'. He agreed that the opposite for this would be 'goes out to make trouble'.
- 'Sticks up for himself.' Martin added, 'if someone picks on me I won't go and tell'. Martin agreed the contrast 'goes and tells on others when they are picked on'.
- 'Quiet'. This includes 'not sticking up for yourself'. The opposite is 'messes about a lot'.

- 'Tries his hardest'. The opposite is 'can't be bothered to work'.
- 'Good worker' has as its opposite 'lazy'.

Martin very much personalized this task so that we ended up with a small part of the structure whereby he understands himself and his peer group. We asked him now to say how different people would see him along the axes that these opposites offer. His parents had a rather different view of him from that of the teachers, and his view of himself was somewhat similar to the view his parents had of him. More specifically, he saw himself as a boy who kept himself to himself and who would stick up for himself. To some extent he messed around. He was not lazy but he was not much of a good worker. He was not a boy who can't be bothered, but neither did he try very hard. It is worth pointing to the high importance that Martin gave to independence and self-defence, and the low value he placed on school and schoolwork.

Martin was, however, most revealing in the next part of the interview. We systematically explored the complaints he might entertain about various other people using a sequence of open-ended questions that referred to the complaint, the psychological explanation, the remedy and the implications this would entail. Thus we were interested in his psychological theories and in his potentiality for change.

The trouble with most *boys* was that 'most of them aren't free to do what they want'. They are like that because 'people want to protect them' and because 'they just can't do the things they want to do'. It would be better if 'they were allowed to do something more than they can'. Then 'boys wouldn't behave so badly' and Martin himself 'would behave better'.

Martin ran into some difficulty with responding to the enquiry about girls. He said he didn't know, and when I challenged him said, with some asperity, 'I haven't got a clue . . . I don't know what a girl thinks, what she wants to do.' I pointed out that he is giving an answer to a question that I had not asked. I wanted to know how they affected him. This enabled him to reply.

The trouble with most *girls* is that 'they don't understand you properly'. They are like that because 'they don't really know you' and because 'they don't really think of you'. It would be better if 'they would understand you'. Then 'there would be better relationships'.

The trouble with *teachers* is that 'they don't understand you properly'. They are like that because 'they don't really think about it' and 'they just don't understand you altogether'. (In this reply Martin conveyed the sense that he had given up any hope that teachers could or would be bothered to understand him.) It would be better if 'they could understand you a little bit'. Then there would be better relationships in school and 'you would get on better with the teachers'. Martin also 'would get on better'.

The trouble with *brothers* is that 'they are too protective'. They are like that because 'they want the best for you' and because 'they want you to do well'. It would be better if 'they were not so protective'. Then 'there would be better relations'.

Martin gave exactly the same response for both *mothers* and *fathers* as he gave for brothers and for *sisters* his response was the same as for *girls*.

Martin has persisted with the use of 'relations' and 'relationships' in his answers and it might easily be thought that he was responding with a verbalism. We put this to the test in the following dialogue:

P. Tell me Martin, what is relationship?
M. It is feeling between people.
P. Are relationships based on good feelings, or bad feelings, or both?
M. Both.
P. Tell me, Martin, if there is no feeling, is there no relationship?
M. No, there must be a relationship.
P. Some people say there are three sorts of relationships. In the first you say 'yes' to each other, in the second you say 'no', in the third you don't give a damn. Which people do you have each of these relationships with?
M. The first relationship is with girls, the second is with teachers . . .
P. And the third?
M. I don't know . . . with people I don't like.

Thus Martin is very aware of the meaning of relationships and can enter into a constructive dialogue on the subject. His use of the expression, therefore, should be seen as meaningful statements about what is important to him.

We now return to the systematic exploration of complaints. This time Martin himself became the object.

The trouble with *Martin* is: '[I] don't get on well with teachers'. He is like that because 'I don't understand them, they don't understand me'. Another reason is 'school gets on top of me'. It would be better if Martin 'could understand teachers better' then 'I wouldn't be like I am in school'.

Thus, at the end of the interview the theme of getting on with teachers returns. It would be wrong, however, to leave the matter there. If things were as simple as Martin has described it would have been more comfortable for him at least to have gone through the motions of change. Presumably there are hidden gains and losses in both his 'diagnosis' and his 'cure'. We ask therefore for three bad things about 'not getting on with teachers' and three good things about 'understanding the teachers'. The sting, however, comes in the next question: 'what advantage do you get from the former and what disadvantage from the latter?' Let us look at his replies (Table 7.1).

Table 7.1: Martin's replies

Not getting on well with teachers	*Understanding teachers*
The three *bad* things about this are:	The three *good* things about this are:
1. They are always on top of you.	1. I would get on with most teachers.
2. You can never get on with school.	2. My work would be better.
3. You just lose interest in school.	3. I would have more interest in school.
The positive advantage is 'It helps me to stick up for myself'.	The disadvantage of this is 'I would lose my fight'.

We can see from this that, for Martin, teachers serve an important purpose. They provide a means whereby Martin can assert his independence and autonomy. If he gets on with them he loses his fight and become submerged beneath their authority. By not understanding them he can maintain the very fight that guarantees that he has an independent existence. The price he pays is trouble with teachers, and the risk of suspension. In summary we might perhaps say that Martin is a boy plagued by two issues, the need for relationships on the one hand, and for independence and autonomy on the other. This can now be recognized as a classic dilemma since the two needs are frequently antagonistic if their full implications are to be met. Is it any wonder that Martin claims not to be understood?

A fixed role therapy experiment: failure and continuation

It was at the very end of the interview that I made the decision to attempt fixed role therapy. Martin had shown dissatisfaction with the present position, and had said that he would like things to change. It was a reasonable hope therefore that he would accept an invitation to do something about his predicament. I explained the nature of the enterprise and he accepted the invitation. The experiment would start in the new term.

The interview with Martin was discussed fully with the head of year and he also accepted the idea of an experiment in fixed role therapy. He was prepared to be Martin's 'producer' for the three weeks, leaving me with the task of inventing a suitable character for Martin to assume.

It will be remembered that the character sketch needs to include three features. The first in relation to Martin is a prescription for action that will inevitably produce behaviour that is relatively 'safe'. The second is to write in a psychological formulation that bears some relationship to the issues that Martin raised in the interview. The third is to indicate the pay-off that Martin might receive as a result of carrying out the sketch.

The character has also to be given a name, in this case the name Antrim suffices as it is an anagram of Martin.

Character sketch for Antrim

When people see Antrim they get the impression of a boy of great modesty in that whether it is a case of praise or blame he maintains the same quiet unassuming attitude.

This, of course, is an appearance; the reality is more interesting and more complicated.

His great purpose in life at his present age is to understand other people and to be himself understood.

The feelings that go with this purpose are, however, difficult to deal with. He is gradually realizing that if he is able to understand other people, he is, in some ways, superior to them, whereas if he is understood by people, they will be in some ways superior to him. He never likes feeling inferior, younger or dependent. Because of this he has not solved the problem of getting on with people.

By acting as a person of great modesty, however, he may be able to suffer the hurts which come from not being understood and from feeling inferior whilst at the same time showing himself superior to situations.

A joint meeting with Martin and his head of year took place in the new term. I made it clear that I was leaving the whole task to the two of them and that I would only see them again during the next three weeks in case of emergency. In many ways this is a step that led to an unsatisfactory result, as I failed to brief the head of year on dealing with Martin in case of bad behaviour. By the time I had written him instructions, Martin had been a severe problem for a whole week and would have been suspended but for his involvement in this experiment. The second two weeks were peaceful, but Martin was away from school for nearly half of that time, and when he was there he did not once visit the head of year to discuss the playing of his part. Thus his commitment to the part seemed minimal. There were problems also in relation to the head of year. I had not been aware of the strength of his involvement in discipline and failed therefore to see that it would be very difficult to become a non-authoritarian 'producer'. Thus, he was unable to deal with Martin in anything but a disciplinary way. A player cannot easily play a part that is antagonistic to his basic sense of role.

Nonetheless, at the debriefing meeting at the end of three weeks, it was felt that there was enough at stake, both for Martin and for the school to consider a continuation of the experiment. The main practical difficulty was letting the head of year out of his dual role and freeing him to do his own job. The suggestion of using the drama teacher to act as 'producer', however, met with approval, and when we met again to restart the programme there was an immediate sense of urgency both from Martin and from this teacher. The difficulty was not completely resolved, however, for the head of year still has a part to play. He is now confronted with a boy who, by agreement, is playing a part but who also may be referred to him for breaches of discipline. We therefore need to negotiate a modification for the head of year so that he knows precisely what to do.

In this briefing it was pointed out that if Martin plays the part of Antrim, it is most unlikely that he will cause any breaches of discipline and will not therefore be sent to the head of year. If he is sent, then Martin almost certainly has failed to act in character. Under these circumstances, the head of year should point out the double meaning of Martin's behaviour. Should he deal with it as a failure in role, or as bad behaviour? Could Martin suggest what he, the head of year, should do? If Martin is unable to give any suggestions, the head of year should present some options from which Martin might choose.

This completed the briefing.

In summary, by means of fixed role therapy both boy and teacher undertake to play a part different from their habitual roles for a period of three weeks, the boy in his own right, the teacher in relation to the boy. Each therefore has accepted a dislodgement from their normal sense of self and their normal ways of making sense. The character parts are intended to be meaningful to both child and teacher. Unfortunately we made a serious miscasting error in the case of the teacher, possibly sufficiently serious to jeopardize the experiment. In the continuation, however, we take steps to bring in a 'producer' for whom the part fits easily into his existing professional role, and we modify the head of year's disciplinary role so that it can do justice to the new situation. If all three persons play their roles, or even take them seriously, without succeeding completely, they will be committed to changing their behaviour, and hopefully, their ways of making sense.

The end of the story

I now bring matters to a conclusion. As my title suggested, and the body of this paper elaborates, I see the task of the psychologist as 'making a difference', and if I were to write a character sketch for the psychologist, this would be the keynote. It is important to say, however, what this view of the psychologist's task implicitly denies. It is not to establish truth, nor to lay down correct ways of action. These may be left to philosophy, or religion. Nonetheless, as I have argued, to make a difference may need the adoption of alternative viewpoints and experimenting with alternative ways of behaving. Let me add, however, that the sole justification for this enterprise is that problems have arisen, within a school context, for which help is asked. It is, in my view, gratuitous to embark on such an enterprise in the absence of problems for which solutions are sought.

Although I ruled out the search for truth as part of the psychologist's task, yet paradoxically, the very attempt to establish alternative viewpoints will lead to improved understanding. If we did not have two eyes, each with a separate view, there would be no depth to visual perception. If I review briefly some of the contents of this paper, a sequence of alternative viewpoints will appear. I discussed the interactionist and the intra-psychic understanding of troubles in school. I represented the teacher's view of the trouble side by side with the child's view. I illuminated this with the child's story side by side with the psychologist's story, and the psychologist's story side-by-side with the teacher's. I then present two alternative ways of promoting change, through the imaginative use of words and the imaginative use of prescribed action. Neither side of any of these pairs contains truth, but jointly each pair can point to a deeper understanding. Out of this deeper understanding, there can flow action that is more congruent with the world in which we live. It would seem to me that I have in fact been describing a basic process out of which growth and maturity spring. This is true for the child; it is also true for the teacher, who through this process can achieve a greater professional understanding and wider range of appropriate actions. No less is it the way of growth of the psychologist.

Tailpiece

The child tells me a story, and I tell the child a story to make a difference.

The teacher tells me a story. I tell the teacher the story of the child, and my story to the child. This is to tell the teacher a story to make a difference.

This paper tells a story, and if it makes a difference, then the trap of which I gave warning at the beginning will indeed have been sprung.

Chapter 8
'Never, never, never give advice': an essay in professional practice (1980)

When a trainee psychologist is disappointed because she saw that you didn't give advice and yet thought that you should, what do you do? I said to her, 'Never, never, never let me hear you give advice.' This paper, written lightheartedly, but with serious intent, had to be written to justify my words.

From time to time incidents arise that provide an opportunity to reflect back on one's own professional practice and, from that exercise, perhaps, to see through some of the habits established over time by the too-ready acceptance of the expectations of others or a rather naive view of both ourselves and our clients. If there is one component of professional practice to which popular demand, professional teaching and task expectation would give assent it would be that a major part of the psychologist's task is to give advice. Typically an examiner will present a question in the form of a problem and then . . . A prospective employer will outline an issue and then . . . A teacher or parent will present a complaint about a child and then . . . In each case the likely completion of the sentence is 'what would you advise?' Thus, giving advice might be seen as the guiding principle behind the psychologist's investigations and the endpoint of his task.

This essay stems from the discrepancy between my own professional practice and the expectations of Margaret, an experienced but untrained educational psychologist who had joined my service as part of her formal training. It is important to stress that Margaret was experienced, as she had acquired from her trained colleagues something of the expectations of the job of educational psychologist, and expectations had by now taken on some of the status of axioms.

118

Part one

An incident and its sequel

Students in their first week accompany me and observe my practice. I use this experience as a basis for asking them what they thought I was trying to do, what they saw, and what their feelings were about what they had seen. The very first case that Margaret observed, proved, from my point of view, to be extremely interesting both theoretically and practically. The headteacher and class teacher were equally surprised at the quality of their own understanding as this was progressively revealed by the exploration of their own constructions of the child. Moreover, they received implicit validation for what they had already been able to achieve with a difficult case and could see the implications for their future actions. When, however, I discussed the case with Margaret, her response was very subdued giving the impression that the work she had witnessed left something to be desired and that in some way I had fallen seriously short of what she herself would have done in comparable circumstances. The gap between my positive feelings and her flat response was bridged by my intuitive awareness that what she had expected and what I had not given, was advice to the teachers. When I put this to her she immediately, and with relief, agreed. Her understanding was that the job was not completed until advice had been given. What she wanted to learn from me was how to invent, and give, better advice than she could. Hence her dissatisfaction and reluctance to comment. To her even greater consternation I gave a loud laugh and said in a mock admonitory tone of voice 'never, never, never let me hear you give advice'.

The very fact of my recounting this episode demonstrates that it had by now become second nature for me not to give advice. Yet in this situation I could not leave my student with a purely negative instruction, no matter how lightly given. Rather I had to help her recapture something of the logic of the healing process whereby I had arrived at my current practice. After all, as I was now in the position of teacher to pupil I carried the responsibility of furthering her professional development.

In pondering the twin issues, on the one hand of communicating my own buried professional development, and on the other furthering that of my student, I arrived at five aphorisms that to some extent defined the topic of giving advice. The aphorism provides a powerful means of instruction by virtue of its brevity, its memorability and its use as a shock tactic to stimulate thought. Inevitably, however, any one aphorism is likely to reflect only one fact of an issue so that the use of more than one is preferable in order to give a more complete view. These five aphorisms provided a teaching gift to Margaret.

Five aphorisms

- Giving advice takes place between two people; unfortunately it is usually good for only one of them.
- The giving of advice is good only when it can be rejected, otherwise it is a covert way of telling the other person what to do.
- If you want your advice to make an impact, ask your client what stops him carrying it out.
- If you want to ensure having your advice ignored, offer it when you have not been asked for it.
- Giving advice is like throwing a boomerang. If you are not careful it will come back and hit you where it hurts.

Two prosaic (and theoretical) arguments against giving advice

The reasoned case against giving advice can be presented in two arguments.

The first arises from the simple fact that advice of necessity carries a meaning content and is couched in verbal terms. At a fundamental level each person constructs his own personal world of meanings, implications and understandings. Even the representation of his phenomenal world carries each individual's personal stamp. This may present no difficulty in itself, but the communication of these meanings must be carried by verbal language. When, therefore, there is a verbal exchange of information between two people, what is given and what is received both reflect, and are related to, the representation of each individual's personal but hidden world. Even when there is apparent agreement between people by virtue of some commonality of language, their disparity is easily discovered by asking of any positive assertion either what it also denies or what else does it further imply. The giving of advice is merely one form of verbal interchange and suffers, therefore, from the failures in accurate communication stemming from the personalization process described above.

If the first argument is based on the informational content of advice, the second arises from the other simple fact that any verbal interchange carries a powerful relationship component. In the case of giving of advice there are two special relationship components. The first is the complementary relationship of 'giver' and 'receiver', the second the relationship of 'expert' and 'layman'. If the participants in the interchange accept these two sets of roles the interchange may be harmonious. People are usually, however, somewhat ambivalent accepting the 'one down' position implied by being either a receiver or a person of lesser expertise, parents and teachers no less than other humans. When the recipient of advice experiences these ambivalent feelings he is likely also to be ambivalent both about receiving the advice and the actions which the advice suggests. Under such circumstances even the best advice loses its power.

In sum, therefore, my two arguments point to the difficulties implicit in giving advice. On the one hand its informative content is likely to be less than fully understood. On the other hand, despite an apparent willingness on the part of the receiver, it might well be rejected or sabotaged. In either case it might have been better to give no advice at all.

Part two

If we should not give advice, what on earth are we supposed to do?

Margaret spent five weeks learning at first hand what we did instead of giving advice. She could not, however, receive a formal and systematic statement of the practice as that step was not taken until the writing of this essay.

At the heart of the matter lie two simple propositions. The first is that we are in the business of promoting change in situations, usually of academic learning, behaviour or social relations, where teachers and parents complain about children and where children fall short of the demands of parents and teachers. The second proposition is that the complaint itself arises from some failure in the ways teachers, parents and children make sense of themselves and their circumstances. By circumstances in this context I include the phenomenal world, the internal worlds of each individual and the demands implicit in the processes of living and learning. This failure is felt subjectively as a relative diminution of effectiveness and understanding, otherwise our help would not be sought. Changes therefore will need to be changes of awareness or changes of action, each in reality implying changes in the other, in order to promote greater effectiveness and clearer under-standing.

Bearing in mind the theoretical arguments against giving advice, together with the two propositions concerning change, I would suggest that there are four different approaches through which we might be able to increase the possibilities of bringing this about. It is extremely inter-esting, although perhaps not surprising, to find that three of these can be related to different psychological theories of change, each of which itself implies both a style and content of investigation and a wider range of potential actions.

The first approach is to illuminate the issue for which our services have been asked. In order to illuminate we need to see both beyond and behind our client's vision otherwise we can only tell him what he already knows. This approach requires of ourselves that we either see more than our client sees or that we recognize patterns where he has seen only isolated bits of information. We cannot do this, of course, without being prepared to ask many questions that our client would not dare to ask, or would not think of asking.

The corresponding theories of change here are those in which insight and understanding are seen as major means of promoting change, such as the pragmatic aspects of psychodynamic theories. As such the illumination approach would be useful both for the adults who complain and for the child who is complained about. In my view, whatever else the psychologist might envisage, to illuminate is the least he should do.

Before laying out my second approach I must warn of a trap to the unwary reader, the best precaution against which is to turn back and read again my second aphorism and my second argument. This approach calls for the writing of a 'prescription' for action that the client is expected to carry out. There is no optional aspect. The action could be a manner of communicating, for example paradoxical instructions, or a specific style of teaching, or the imposition of tasks designed to change the interactions between teacher and child, or perhaps it might even be to do nothing different at all.

Further, the client is told that he will be followed up to check the outcome of any prescribed course of action. When this approach is adopted the client is expected to accept the role of 'one down', i.e. he is both the receiver of instructions, and in relation to the given is the one who is a 'lay' person. The theoretical stances that correspond to this approach are the behaviour modifications systems in which the client is expected to carry out instructions to the letter, or a Haley-style systems approach involving paradoxical communications and tasks aimed to change the nature of interpersonal relationships.

The trap to which I pointed lies in the observation that the reader might well draw the conclusion that what I have described in this approach is precisely that giving of advice against which I have been arguing. His conclusion, however, would be false as my second aphorism points to the fact that good advice should be optional in order to avoid covertly telling other people what to do and the second argument points to the consequences of the ambivalence that accompanies the receiving of advice. People seeking advice quite properly have built in warning systems against advice that offends their intelligence, their feelings and their desires, and it is a matter of life experience that when advice is given that is unacceptable, the advice and the adviser will frequently be described in uncomplimentary terms, the client going on his way as though nothing had happened. In reality something of course has happened. The giver of advice has been devalued and in the process he has lost credibility. The end is worse than the beginning.

The third approach calls for psychologist and client jointly to explore their individual ways of understanding the problem and from the joint exploration to work out changes in the client's ways of acting on a 'what would happen if' basis. This approach allows a relationship of equality rather than 'one up–one down' and allows for each to find value in their total awareness rather than automatically giving preference to the awareness of the psychologist. It follows on naturally from the first approach described above.

The theoretical orientation corresponding to this approach is personal construct theory with its philosophical assertion that there are always many ways of understanding a problem, and with its pragmatic stance that being a scientist is not restricted to the scientist.

The fourth approach involves quite simply the telling of a story. The antecedents of the approach are the teaching stories of Taoism and Zen Buddhism in the Far East and of Sufism in the Middle East. In the West the stories and methods of indirect suggestion of Milton Erickson provide a related model.

It is part of the efficacy of the story that it simultaneously reaches the head, the heart and the will, yet the story itself leaves the client free to construct from his own resource a new vision and perhaps a new course of action. Moreover, it is less likely to generate ambivalence or resistance as the client is not asked to do anything, believe anything, or change in any way. Any change that does take place, therefore, is of the client's own devising. Thus the approach circumvents the two arguments that I put forward against giving advice. It is, however, the most difficult of all approaches because it demands of the psychologist that he have a powerful grasp of the problem for which he has been consulted, that he has access to a wide range of relevant stories, or that he is able, on the spur of the moment, to invent them. Not only must the story speak to the problem; it must also speak to the particular client and the particular situation. The approach goes far beyond orthodox psychological theories and points to a higher intuitive wisdom to which, perhaps, we can only hopefully aspire.

Coda: two tales

Just as the substance of this essay falls naturally into two parts, so does its ending.

The first tale

I met a teacher again after a lapse of about 15 years and she reminded me of a case in which we had then been jointly involved – the case of a girl having serious troubles with her family. 'You may be interested to know what happened to the girl' she said, and continued:

> At that time there was a young lady teacher anxious to help and she frequently counselled the girl about herself and her future. The girl however had laid out her own plans. She would find a young man who was likely to be a financial success, marry him, and produce three children. The young teacher was very worried about this materialistic approach and warned that it would lead to great unhappiness. She should marry for love and not for wealth.

The girl left school and, following the dictates of her head, married a likely young man. The teacher herself, following the guidelines of her heart, married the man she loved. Now, 15 years later, the girl is happily married with three children and material affluence. The teacher is obtaining a divorce from her husband.

The second tale

Mrs X and her son J were both clients of a colleague and myself. They attended for a final interview before the summer holiday but, alas, things had gone wrong: J had been picked up by the police for shoplifting and both were very worried as they did not know if a case would be brought or if J would merely receive a caution. They were also worried, each in their own way and for their own reasons, about the outcome. As it would be five weeks before we could see them again, and as they clearly needed some easement, I told them the following old Chinese story:

> There was once a farmer in a village in China who had only one son and only one horse. One day the horse disappeared and did not return. The villages crowded round him and commiserated with him in his loss. The farmer said 'maybe'.
>
> The next day, through the woods, came his horse, bringing with her six fine young stallions. The villages crowded round him and congratulated him on his good fortune. The farmer said 'maybe'.
>
> The next day the farmer's son was trying to break in one of the stallions. He fell off and broke his leg. The villagers crowded around the farmer and commiserated with him in his misfortune. The farmer said 'maybe'.
>
> The next day the Emperor's recruiting officer came to the village demanding that all fit young men should go to the wars. The villagers crowded round the farmer . . . congratulating him on the good fortune that his son could not go. The farmer said ' . . . '

We met Mrs X and J after the holiday and heard the outcome of the case. J had, in fact, been prosecuted, found guilty and fined £40, to be paid by him and not his parents. And now J was a transformed boy. From his earnings from a part-time job he was putting down £2 per week for his fine and also asking his mother to save £5 a week for him for the future. In mother's view he had suddenly become mature. My only comment was that the Magistrate had paid J the compliment of treating him as a person who was grown up and responsible for himself, and not likely to offend again.

Mother and son left the interview very grateful and quite confident that they would not need to visit us again.

If the reader still feels the need to give advice he should look again at the third aphorism.

Chapter 9
A drawing and its opposite: an application of the notion of the 'construct' in the elicitation of children's drawings (1980)

Over and above a description of this technique and its use, I discuss the relevance of children's drawings in relation to their 'assessment–therapeutic' value and the way in which the use of contrast brings out a child's possible meanings. This is demonstrated with two cases. The paper was written with an eye to publication but perhaps I did not try hard enough to find an appropriate journal.

The essence of the construct (Kelly 1955, 1991) is its bipolarity. A statement needs to be seen in the context of its opposite and takes on a more precise meaning when it is known what it both affirms and what it denies. When the contrast is personal rather than logical it conveys something of the individuality of the speaker.

It is usual practice to take a special interest in the contrast aspect of the construct, but less attention is paid to the commonality that necessarily unites the two poles. This commonality, however, may be very important when we wish to know how a person makes sense of things and I would suggest that the commonality points to an individual's underlying interests or concerns. Thus the construct 'Catholic–Protestant' would suggest that the user has a concern or interest in different forms of Christianity whereas 'catholic–narrow-minded' would point to a concern or interest in a person's breadth and flexibility of thought processes. When, therefore, we ask of a description 'what does it deny?' we are also opening up an individual's areas of interest or concern. In this context I would see 'interests' as relatively peripheral to a person's sense of self but 'concerns' as lying close to a person's core constructs. Potentially, therefore, 'concerns' may be important foci for anxieties, difficulties or conflicts.

The elicitation of both poles of a construct represents basic technique in personal construct interviewing where the currency of interchange is words, but it represents a novelty when applied to the use of children's drawings. The purpose of this paper is to describe and demonstrate the use of the notion of the construct in the elicitation of such drawings. Before developing the idea further, however, it is necessary to take a look at the way children's drawings have been used in the past.

Traditional use: three polarities

When we examine the traditional (and current) use of children's drawings we can distinguish three polarities. I shall put them in the form of three questions.

- Do we ask a child to accommodate to an adult's structures by asking him to draw something specific, or is he free to draw what he likes?
- Is the analysis of the drawing to be normative or in terms of personal meaning? Two points need to be made in connection with this polarity. The first is that it represents the 'nomothetic–ideographic' dichotomy. The second is that an analysis in terms of theory is just as normative as analysis in terms of psychometric scores because it involves measuring the child, through his drawing, against some general theory of development or personality. An analysis in terms of personal meaning, by contrast, involves attempting to arrive at some grasp of the child's own personality theory: his categories of under-standing, his options and his choices.
- Is the communication of the drawing and its analysis primarily for the enlightenment of the adults who are concerned about the child (such as teachers or social workers) or is the drawing and its analysis primarily to be used as part of a therapeutic dialogue with the child?

The thrust of these three polarities is in the direction of assessment as opposed to therapy. Task-orientated drawings, such as *Draw a Man* (Goodenough, 1926) or *Kinetic Family Drawing* (Burns and Kaufman, 1970, 1972) are used to provide norms of development and intelligence or indices of 'emotional disturbance' (cf. also Koppitz, 1968). Other workers, such as Di Leo (1973) and Schildkrout et al. (1972), use neuro-logical or psychoanalytical frames of reference as the basis for a diagnosis of children's problems or difficulties. At the opposite extreme, the documentation of the therapeutic use of children's drawings tends to be in the form of case studies and the analysis will be subjective and experiential. On occasion illumination may best be found in literary sources, for example Kahn's (1978) moving account of therapy with a young girl which carries the title: 'Recollected grief: "I, not remembering how I cried out then, Will cry it o'er again!"'

In posing these three polarities I am not arguing that one is necessarily good or bad. Each has a proper place. The choice of structure or freedom in the invitation to draw depends on the purpose of the interview. Therapeutic work at some point requires a reference to the outside world and therefore will carry a normative component. There needs to be some element of communication between the psychologist and others in order to safeguard against the limitations of the psychologist's own constructions. Stated in its simplest terms, any assessment process should have therapeutic potential and any therapeutic engagement should have an assessment aspect.

The 'one-off' interview

The reason why as psychologists we become involved in interviewing children is that adults (parents, teachers, social workers) are worried that these children fall short of the adult's expectations. This can be in terms of behaviour, learning or social and family inadequacies. The psychologist's formal task is usually to interview the child in order to assist the adult in understanding the child. This can be called the assessment/diagnostic function.

At the same time, however, these children almost certainly have their own problems for which their manner of functioning provides a current, if inadequate solution. The psychologist, therefore, has an opportunity of helping children explore the ground within which their dilemmas arise. Although this is not in itself therapy it provides a therapeutic slant to the interview and holds the potential for children to become aware of, and perhaps revise, their constructions of themselves and their circumstances. The setting for this process is the 'one-off' interview.

A personal construct approach to this task lays stress on the ways in which children make sense of themselves and their circumstances. Although much may be found out through a verbally structured interview, there are likely to be many areas of experiencing not so easily accessible. It is a worthwhile assumption that a child's drawings will point to aspects of knowing that exist at lower levels of awareness than that of verbal articulation. This then is the justification for asking a child to draw.

There is, of course, a complication. When a child is invited to draw a picture there is a hidden question underlying the simple request. The hidden question is: 'what are you able to tell me this way which verbal questions and answers are not able to reveal?' The invitation therefore contains an ambiguity and it is frequently useful, certainly with older children and young people, to remove the ambiguity by saying quite openly, 'and if you do this it may tell us something about yourself which you had not thought of before.' Such a comment makes clear the purpose of the task and allows the child to decide his or her level of response. It also prepares the way for the therapeutic use of the material at the end of the interview.

The 'elaboration of a line' and the elicitation of its opposite

The starting point for the invitation to draw is what I choose to call the 'elaboration of a line'. I draw a line about 3 inches long in the centre of a sheet of A4 paper. At the left end it curves downward at an angle of about 45° for a distance of about one inch. The child is then asked to turn this line into a picture that fills the page. If the child restricts his or her drawing to the representation of a single object he or she may be reminded of the task and then invited to draw in the background in order to complete a picture.

Single drawings are open to the ascription of as many meanings as there are observers. They will be the meanings of the observer and not necessarily those of the child. At the same time, if we accept that pictures may tap areas of awareness beyond the immediate range of words we would not expect children to provide more than a superficial under-standing of their own drawings. We are more likely to arrive at a child's meaning, however, if we can elicit from a child an opposite to the drawing he or she has already produced. At the same time, by the logic outlined earlier, we may gain some idea of the underlying interests and concerns that the polarity of the two pictures reflect. Hence the innova-tive step is to ask, quite simply, for the child to draw the opposite. This is done by clarifying the child's understanding of 'opposite' by using verbal examples and then saying something like 'look at your picture and draw for me what you think the opposite is.'

The significance of this request needs to be fully appreciated. The child now has to return to his or her drawing with new eyes and in the process become more fully aware of what he or she has created. Only when he or she has done this will it be possible for the child to discover some personal meaning out of the search of an opposite capable of pictorial representation. It is instructive to watch children do this. On occasion they will quickly reproduce the original picture but with some of the features altered to indicate the opposite. On occasion they will study the original very carefully and then suddenly, with great speed draw a second picture that is completely different from the first. On occasion a child will produce a second picture in which each object is changed into a logical opposite (day into night, sea into land, boat into car, and so forth).

A polarity arises from the execution of this double task that transcends the original drawing and points to areas of possible concern in relation to the child's experience of himself or herself and his or her circumstances. The penultimate stage of the technique involves getting the child to talk about the pictures. The associations that are then given provide for their use in a final stage in clarifying or illuminating the child's dilemmas.

In relation to the three polarities in the traditional use of children's drawings, on the 'structure–freedom' polarity this technique provides a minimum of structure with maximum freedom for expression. At the level of analysis it is possible to make normative statements according to the typicality of the first drawing. The line is frequently made into a house by girls, and a car by boys. It is common for the paper to be turned upside down and the line used for a boat. Less commonly, the paper is turned at right angles and the line made into a rocket. Alternatively a normative judgement may be made by reference to theory. Finally, although the drawings are used in the interview in a very personal way, they allow for assessment at the same time because the material of the interview may be communicated to the adult who is seeking help in relation to the child. Thus the use of the technique fits naturally into the 'one-off' interview and adds depth of understanding both for assessment and for the personal help of the child.

Two illustrative cases: John and Paul

These two boys were interviewed consecutively at a Social Services assessment centre. In each case there had been a breakdown between the boy and the 'carers' and the purpose of the assessment was to help the social worker decide on the next step. John's family had broken up many years earlier and, after a number of moves, John had been fostered with the same family for five years. This had broken down and so had subsequent placements. By contrast, Paul's parents had divorced when he was young and each had remarried. Paul had then had periods of living with each of the two new families. He was currently 'in care' for frequently running away from home. In his own words Paul did this in order to 'Make my parents see what I wanted. I didn't want to live the way I was living.' Normally my part in the assessment process is, informally as I described earlier, to help in the social worker's decision-making. I see my role as providing a young person with the opportunity to undertake a form of self-assessment that may in turn have therapeutic potential. It will be seen in the case studies that follow that the drawing technique appears late in the interview. The purpose of this is to generate a feel for, and an involvement in, self-exploration so that the invitation to draw fits naturally into the interview. At the same time the whole tenor of the interview is to involve the young person in becoming aware of some of the more hidden areas of his own experiencing.

John: 'The cat that walks on his own'

In presenting the case of John (aged 13) I give the whole interview in order that the drawings can be seen in context. It became apparent that the key worker's observations were very relevant in providing a further context for understanding them. Consequently I quote a part of his description:

> John is a very confused young man. He can be a Jekyll or a Hyde. When he went camping with a small group that had to be self-sufficient he could not have been better. He enjoyed the freedom of choice. This was Jekyll. As Hyde he can be very impatient. If he wants something he has to have it at once otherwise he becomes very aggressive. This could be verbal or physical. He deals with his difficulties by withdrawing from others and isolating himself. He will be part of a group but not a member. He will take companions as and when he needs them.

The interview, which was structured, fell into three broad phases. In Phase 1 the purpose of the interview was clarified leading in to an exploration of how John saw himself. The 'elaboration of a line' and its opposite, together with further exploration and clarification formed Phase 2. Phase 3 brought many of the ideas together by way of a third picture and its application to John's own dilemmas.

Phase 1

Who are you? (1)

I started the interview by explaining to John that I would like him to take it as an opportunity to take stock of himself and then commenced the exploration by asking him to choose three things which would say who he was (the 'who are you?' technique). His response to this request was 'I don't really know' (cf. the key worker's opening statement). I took this answer seriously and suggested that a way of finding out was through the roundabout way of seeing how he would describe boys whom he did in fact know.

Construct elicitation

In this task John was invited to give three descriptions each for two friends, an enemy and a boy whom he admired but did not know very well. For each description he was asked to give an opposite. His eight most important constructs (as selected by him) are given below:

- polite – they ignore you and walk away.
- always fighting other people – can walk away from a fight
- bad tempered – can keep calm.

- good general behaviour – always fighting.
- weird, don't understand what people are saying to them – they know what they are doing, what they are saying.
- speaks well (from a good family) – swears and moans.
- shares things with others – doesn't share things, selfish.
- always being naughty – always being good.

Who are you? (2)

These constructs were used as a basis for a self-description grid, the details of which are not given here. In the process, however, John was committed to defining himself on each construct. I then returned to my opening question 'who are you?' and this time he gave three answers, each of which was drawn from his list of constructs. It is important to follow up these descriptions by enquiring if they are important to John, and if so why. This was elicited by way of a dialogue, a summary of which gives John's answers in a sequential manner.

    1. I'm a bit polite.

This is important because 'then people will respect me.' In turn this is important because 'then you get friends.' In turn this is important because 'then you have people to talk to.' And this is important 'in case you get annoyed sometimes.'

    2. I've got good general behaviour.

This is important because 'Then you don't go round fighting.' And this is important because 'then you keep calm.' This is important because 'If you are in court and the judge says something, you don't like it, you get in trouble. You get yourself in trouble with the police if you are not calm.'

    3. I'm always being good.

This is important 'in case something goes wrong with your brother.' (This self-description refers specifically to disregarding his mother's instructions at home, thereby endangering his brother.)

Phase 2

The 'elaboration of a line' and its opposite

At this point I introduced the drawing task with the information that if he did it the drawing might tell us something about him of which he had not previously been aware.

Figure 9.1: John's elaboration of a line

Figure 9.2: John's contrast

He turned my line, on a sheet of A4 paper, into a car (Figure 9.1) but the drawing included neither people nor a sense of location. These he added when I commented that I had never seen a car just floating in space. His description of the picture was 'Just turning a corner, going to the airport, people going on holiday.' He was fully conversant with the idea of opposite, having already produced opposites in the previous phase of the interview. When I asked him to draw the opposite of his picture he studied it carefully and then produced the picture that appears in Figure 9.2, a male figure seated in an armchair. He described this as 'sitting at home, not going anywhere.'

In order to explore the associations of these drawings more fully I offered John a number of contrasting descriptions and asked which he felt most fitted the two pictures. They were:

- going away – staying at home
- enjoyment – sadness
- excitement – dullness, boredom
- being one of a family – being left outside.

John rejected the first three and readily chose the last. He added that the boy who had been left out 'would not know what to do, he would feel sad, unhappy.' When I added the query 'angry as well?' he said 'yes'. Of the boy going to the airport he said that he would be happy but then added 'he could feel sorry for the one who was left out.'

Underlying these two pictures there is a strong suggestion that inclusion or exclusion from a family is a major concern for John, and this is not surprising in view of his history. At a deeper level, however, there is a pervading sense of sadness, perhaps in turn as a cover for an even deeper sense of anger. John's earlier answers indicate that for him anger needed to be kept out of sight because of the trouble it could cause. In the light of these thoughts I offered John two constructive hypotheses which he could, if he wished, either agree or reject, or modify. The purpose of this offering is twofold. Whatever response John gives will provide an indication of how much I have understood things and, at the same time, the hypotheses offer a means of giving back to John a crystallization of thoughts that previously had been only loosely associated.

The first hypothesis was: 'John is the kind of boy who keeps his sad feelings to himself'. The second was: 'If he started showing them he could very easily get angry.' John confirmed each.

Phase 3

The exploration thus far has raised matters at a deep level of feeling. It seemed necessary to bring things back to a more ordinary level. To this end I invited John to draw a third picture but this time it should be one which was completely his own. His drawing was of a cat, curled up on the ground sleeping, with the patterning carefully shaded in a manner reminiscent of army camouflage.

This picture was completely unexpected and bore no obvious relation to his other two pictures. It represents a challenge as it is not obvious how one should respond to this drawing. My solution was to ask him 'if this picture represents three ways of solving your problems, what would those three ways be?' a question which brought John right back to his immediate and real world. These are his answers:

The first way is: 'you can go and venture. You don't have to stay in' (c.f. the key worker's description of the Jekyll aspect of John).

The second way is: 'You wouldn't have upsets.' Since the meaning of this is unclear I asked John to explain. He said that 'when you are a baby (cat) you get moved from the mother straightaway', i.e. before you make a relationship. In discussion the following ideas emerged: he had been moved many times after he had made a relationship and this had been painful and it was better not to be around long enough to make a relationship (cf. the key worker's description of John's self-imposed isolation and withdrawal).

The third way is: 'you can just run away from it all' (cf. the contrasts which he gave in his first two constructs).

In a way this third picture might well provide a metaphor, verbalized simply by Kipling as 'The cat that walked on its own', for John's current solution to his problems. John was familiar with the expression. Faced with this communication perhaps the most important response in a single interview is to accept its experiential validity and suggest that there are, perhaps, other ways, not yet explored, of dealing with his problems.

Comment

It is a proper question to ask what gain has accrued from using this drawing technique? I think it is clear that John's drawings provided material over and above that which was given through purely verbal interviewing. Moreover, it was material that was important at a deep level of experiencing.

From an assessment point of view a number of observations could be made, and these arise from the totality of the interview. Firstly, John's experience of frequent moves from one 'carer' to another needed to be seen as fundamental if one is to understand his current ways of making sense of himself and his circumstances. This was his normality, not an accretion to some more comfortable normality. Secondly, it was probably true that John was capable of experiencing great pools of sadness, if not depression, and that it was necessary for him to protect himself with a camouflage of politeness. Thirdly, his self-isolation was for him a further protection against the pain associated with disrupted personal relationships. All of these observations could provide subsequent workers with information that might maximize their chances of meaningful rather than superficial communications with him.

At the level of therapy, although words cannot express it, there was a depth of experiencing of which we were both aware. Important issues were brought into the open that, if not immediately resolvable, were available for future work. The possibility of change had been seen in the interview itself, and there was potential for change in the future.

Thus the interview as a whole served both as an assessment to help others in their work with John and at the same time offered John the possibility of gaining personal help through the process of self-assessment.

Paul: a question of life or death

The presentation of this case is short in comparison with that of John, because, as will be seen, the heart of the interview lies in the drawings. Nor shall I make any comments at the end, but rather let the material speak for itself.

Paul is very tall for his age, which is almost 15 years, and he interacts with adults as equals, yet without familiarity. The structure of the interview was the same as for John but, despite giving evidence of considerable intelligence and perspicacity, he gave no hint of deeper levels of awareness. Because of this I sensed either an inability or an unwillingness on his part to be open to this aspect of his experiences. I was, therefore, a little uneasy about asking him for a drawing. Consequently I prefaced my invitation to him to draw by saying, 'at this point I am going to take a gamble' and then proceeded with, 'I would like you to draw a picture for me and if you do you may well say something about yourself of which you had previously not been aware.' I drew a line and then asked him to turn it into a picture, explaining that the line was merely a way of getting a picture started.

Figure 9.3: Paul's elaboration of a line

He showed some hesitation but then turned the paper through 90° and produced the picture in Figure 9.3. The way in which he drew the tree suggested that his first thoughts were to draw one that was dead. However, he then added the foliage, the hole in the trunk, the surrounding bushes and the little animal. There was a freedom and ease in the way in which he carried out the task and he completed it very quickly. When he had finished, and without any discussion, I asked him to consider his picture and then draw the opposite. After a short pause he then produced the drawing that appears in Figure 9.4.

His descriptions of the two pictures were:

• Of the first: 'Two living things, the animal and the wood and leaves, a home. The bushes will provide food, so will the top of the tree.'

Figure 9.4: Paul's contrast

- Of the second: 'It's morbid, it's not very nice, there's no life or nothing. I could have put bushes.'

The interviewer should not be a passive observer but needs always to be trying to work out the logic of what he sees. My own thought processes were along these lines: 'these pictures, both by drawing and by verbal associations are about life and death. If the tree in some way represents Paul himself, then on the internal evidence of the second drawing Paul at some level of awareness has contemplated his own death.'

I then took my second gamble by asking Paul straight if he had every thought of taking his own life. Very seriously, Paul said that he had.

How should the interviewer respond to such a reply? One way would be to explore the details of what lay behind his answers, but in my view neither time nor the place was appropriate for such a course. Instead I gave a simple confirmation of the meaning of what he had said, together with a recognition that his feelings made sense in the light of his personal history.

Paul showed no wish to do any more work in the interview, as though he felt that enough had been done. All that was left for me, therefore, was to acknowledge the quality of what he had done and to wish him well for the future.

Surprisingly he shook hands and thanked me before leaving. This might have been a ritual between equals, but it felt more like a genuine expression of thanks.

Some final thoughts: the question of interpretation

I bring this paper to an end with just three final thoughts, and these are centred on the question of interpretation.

Firstly, a child's drawings should not be studied in isolation. They should be related to the situation in which they were produced, to the question for which the drawings provide an answer, the context of the child's own experiences and what the child actually says. Interpretations that ignore these factors are likely to be academic rather than related to the child's individuality.

Secondly, we need to bear in mind that there may be two kinds of interpretation, one that meets the needs of assessment and which might very well not be communicated to the child but to those who have made the referral. The other may be an interpretation of therapeutic value that is to be used with the child and that would not necessarily be communicated to others.

Finally, the 'truth' of an interpretation is not an issue. The inventive mind can produce many interpretations to a single drawing but the value of an interpretation rests on the extent to which it can clarify an individual's dilemmas or promote that individual's psychological growth.

The difficulty with children's drawings lies in their interpretation. The difficulty with interpretation lies in the fact that children's drawings provide a canvas on which interpreters may project their own fantasies. The application of the idea of the construct goes some way to limiting this occupational risk.

Chapter 10
The recycling of maladjustment (1984)

This was another reflective paper in which I attempted to give a reasoned analysis and account of the then current concept 'maladjustment', now re-labelled 'emotional and behavioural disturbance'. I did this within the broad framework already developing out of personal construct theory and allied theories. It was directed to my educational psychologist colleagues for whom the issue was a matter of considerable importance. To that end, it was published in their journal.

Introduction

The 1981 Education Act has now become law and with its introduction the old categories of handicap no longer exist in any statutory sense. The expression 'maladjustment' should, therefore, be quietly laid to rest. Such is the force of semantic inertia, however, that it will continue in common parlance amongst interested professionals for many years to come. It may never die.

This paper addresses the fact that the concept, whether in its usage as noun or adjective, has little commonly accepted meaning. There is always the temptation to redefine an unclear concept and to seek to win consensus for its adoption. That is not my purpose. Rather, I propose to approach the matter from a number of different angles in order to illuminate and not to convert.

The underlying problem for which the adoption of the concept was a solution was the need to label those children, of all ages, who defeat the best efforts of teachers to bring their behaviour into line with that which might reasonably be expected to obtain within the ordinary school. The existence of such children was recognized in the 1920s and the term 'maladjusted' was used to describe them. In 1945 the Handicapped Pupils and School Health Service Regulations described 'maladjusted pupils' as those 'who show evidence of emotional instability or psychological disturbance and require special educational treatment in order to effect their personal, social or educational adjustment'. In 1955 the Underwood Committee continued to use the expression but noted that it lacked clarification. It did not say anything about the means of identifying 'maladjusted' children. The committee's positive contribution was to point out the intimate relationship between an individual and his environment. The expression's continued use was justified because it carried legal connotations through it entitlement to special educational provision. In the light of the present Education Act that justification no longer holds. Thus the history of the concept reflects its purely pragmatic value. It has added nothing to the understanding of children so labelled, nor does it offer any rationale for their treatment.

The subject matter that is offered in this paper is developed through seven sections, each of which is relatively self-contained but each of which reflects the other sections. Sections, therefore, take on added meaning and depth as a result of this reflection. The argument moves from a consideration of the concept of maladjustment, through suggestions for a theoretical framework for investigating and understanding children and their behaviour, to possible strategies for action.

Section 1. The problem: a concept lacking in consensus

The problem that the concept 'maladjusted' presents is typified in the following examples.

At a conference in an education department a case was put forward of a secondary school boy who disregarded all requests from teachers, who declined to do any school work and in general treated the school and its staff as irrelevant. Thus he was unacceptable to the school. Outside school he was already established in a delinquent career. The probation officer in whose charge the boy had been placed was demanding of the case conference that the boy should be placed in a school for maladjusted children by virtue of the fact, in his eyes, that all of this boy's behaviour indicated that he was maladjusted and the Education Department had a responsibility to find such a place for the boy. The case conference turned down the request on the grounds that a community home with education on the premises was a placement probably more relevant to the totality of the boy's behaviour. The probation officer's notion of maladjustment was simply that the boy was deviant. It took no regard for the direction and nature of deviance.

Michael is a 10-year-old pupil who refused to accept the authority of teachers to tell him what he might or might not do. Nor could he tolerate the restrictions that the dependencies of friendship imposed. He was unhappy, isolated and closed to the influence of either adults or his peer group. An interview between mother and son, headteacher and psychologist revealed some of the dynamics of the situation and after this interview the head teacher asked the psychologist: 'Is Michael maladjusted?' The psychologist, wishing to turn the question to advantage asked in return, 'Are you asking if Michael is maladjusted, or if his behaviour is maladjusted?' The point was immediately taken but the head teacher, with a wry smile replied that life was simpler before she asked her questions than after the psychologist had given his answer. The essential dilemma that this question pointed to was whether or not a person and his behaviour are identical. The casual use of the concept maladjusted confuses the issue.

The third case is James, a second-year secondary school pupil who, during the last few months, had shown deteriorating behaviour. He was systematically distorting his presentation of himself to others by pulling faces, making odd noises, carrying out bizarre behaviour such as eating paper, head banging and putting lighted matches in his mouth. Without being 'naughty' he was consistently disruptive yet he refused to talk with his teachers who were anxious to sort out the reasons for his behaviour. The teachers were worried about him, both because of his behaviour and because of their inability to make any difference to him. When asked why they did not describe him as maladjusted they were horrified and replied that he was disturbed but in their eyes could be helped. By contrast, maladjustment referred to a condition that was 'more difficult to shift'. Their judgement of this boy was significantly affected by the fact that they had known him in his first year when he had presented himself as normal, active and happy, like other boys. For these teachers maladjustment was by implication a condition that was long lasting and not amenable to influence.

The fourth case, Peter, was a primary school boy. He was extremely aggressive to other children, he suffered irrational outbursts of anger and would stand up for the right not to be pushed round (his words for what was often a reasonable request) by teachers or anyone else. He had been excluded from school for a time and, when he was allowed to return, psychological help was offered in an attempt to help him bring some control into the expression of his feelings. If this help was ineffective it was suggested that Peter should perhaps go to a school for children whose behaviour was described as maladjusted. The mother was horrified by this word but was unable to put that horror into words. For her, maladjusted referred to some nameless indescribable condition representing the most awful thing that could happen to a child. The point that this case illustrates is the strength of feeling that its use might engender for someone for whom a special school place was meant to be a boon or an escape.

All four cases represent ways in which the use of the concept is idiosyncratic to the person using it, either in thoughts or in feelings. In reality there is little commonality of meaning even though there is some commonality in the situations in which the concept is used. Quite simply, the word 'maladjustment' is used in situations where:

1. There is a breakdown in the relationship between a child and others that is chronic rather than transitory.
2. The adults in the situation are worried by the behaviour, which points to a breakdown in relationships, and by their inability to do anything about it.
3. It is then a signal to others that the situation is intolerable, that the institution is entitled to some special help or relief and that perhaps the child should be placed in a more appropriate institution or be rendered 'normal' by treatment.

Although later sections of the paper will show that the logic connecting 1 and 2 and 3 is not necessarily valid, the use of the concept in this way is honourable because, at the simplest level, the description has some merit in reflecting what has happened.

There is, however, a further difficulty. The concept as currently used is made to serve a number of separate purposes. This appears in two ways. A child's behaviour may be described as maladjusted or alternatively he himself may be described as maladjusted because of his behaviour. Underlying these two options is some notion of cause and effect. Maladjustment therefore may be, according to the choice of the user, either cause or effect, description or prescription. A different pair of alternatives is revealed when the concept is used to refer to the manifest or observable aspects of a child on the one hand, or in reference to the hidden, deeper aspects on the other. Thus the concept is potentially so overloaded that there can be little guarantee of congruence of meaning between user and listener.

It is precisely this to which I referred earlier as the overt problem with which the paper is concerned. There is of course still the underlying problem of the breakdown of relationships between child and others. In the course of our explorations this also will become a major issue for recycling.

Section 2. Two polarities: adjustment–maladjustment

My first step in the direction of analysing the issue is to suggest that we are unlikely to create an understanding of maladjustment until we talk about its polar opposite, adjustment, because an assertion derives much of its meaning from that which is denied. The two polarities are, therefore, adjustment–maladjustment but I shall focus on the positive pole, in order to throw its opposite into relief.

At its simplest level, 'adjustment' would seem to refer to an easy, comfortable relationship between an individual and his environment based on an acceptance of roles and an agreement on goals and aims within that context. When this condition is satisfied within a school, a stable system already exists in which there is an appearance of harmony between its members. This might well be satisfactory if the school were closed to external influences. Unfortunately, it is not an isolated institution because it exists within the wider system of values and expectancies of the outside world and is made up itself of individuals each of whom carried something of those external values. Not all are congruent to those of the school. Maladjustment, under this argument, would represent the overt expression of a child's refusal to accept either the role relationships or the goals and aims of the school. The underlying reason for this is the existence of competing values and expectations stemming from internal idiosyncratic processes or from differing family and subcultural values. Maladjustment, in this sense, is specific to the institution because some of the children who behave in this way may be perfectly adjusted in their families and in their sub-cultures. There may, of course, be others with the same conflict of values but who have learned to conform by remaining silent and passive. I am not at all sure that this is the meaning we would really wish to give the concept adjustment. In fact the twin polarity, adjustment–maladjustment, would seem best fitted to the balance and regulation that occurs within static systems. By contrast, schools ideally should be involved with their neighbourhoods as well as containing the tensions and dynamics that stem from the developing independence and individuality of the children who form the school.

It is possible, however, to replace adjustment–maladjustment with the concept that Piaget called 'adaptation' (Mehrabian, 1968). It includes within it reference to ideas of stability, balance and change, the individual and his environment, internal and external processes. It is therefore more profound and more fertile.

All theories rest on metaphors, the metaphor underlying adaptation is biological. The organism is in a constant state of interaction with its environment. It takes in from the environment in order to live but in doing that has of necessity to transform its input to make it digestible within the organism's existing structures. At the same time, however, it cannot take in without making some accommodation to the outside world. The process is illustrated through the example of eating. Physical movements of muscle, mouth and jaw are necessary for food to be taken in but then the organism's chemical and physical processes transform the food to make it usable by the body.

In psychological terms the individual is in a state of constant interaction with his environment by way of receiving information and acting on it. The information is then interpreted within the individual's existing ways of making sense in order to give meaning to the environmental input and as a guide to appropriate action.

The twin processes are called respectively accommodation and assimilation. Accommodation always honours the 'not-self'. It may lead to imitation of and identification with others. In this sense it is extremely important and valuable in providing external models of thought, feeling and action for the growing child. By contrast, assimilation always implies a degree of distortion of incoming information (and this includes proprioceptive information) as it can be interpreted only in relation to the individual's existing schemas. These schemas are not purely cognitive. They include feelings, hopes, fears, anticipations and potential actions. Of necessity, therefore, assimilation is basically egocentric.

The joint operation of assimilation and accommodation leads to adaptation, a state that on the one hand balances the needs and wishes of the egocentric self against the claims of the outside world, and on the other allows changes and growth in the individual's ways of knowing and relating. Although each part of the process co-exists with the other, inevitably from time to time assimilation will predominate over accommodation and accommodation over assimilation. Maladaptation will arise from the long-standing predominance of one over the other. The two conditions are illustrated by the two cases that follow.

Stuart (aged 10) presented serious problems within school because he refused to be influenced by the reasonable and proper requests of the teacher. At these times he became very angry and insolent. During an interview with a psychologist it was found that, characteristically, he would interpret simple requests as orders and then complain that he was being forced, very much against his wishes, to submit to other people's will. This was a clear case of distorting adult requests in line with some internal scheme that the world was a place in which he was always under pressure from adults. This was a primacy of assimilation. His accommodation, when it came, followed the psychologist carefully pointing out the distinction between a request and an order. Stuart then complied but only in a surly manner.

By contrast Nick (aged 14) would settle into new situations with the appearance of a friendly, co-operative adjustment. Eventually, however, he would become violently angry over small incidents. At his own request he was sent to a school that trained potential merchant seamen but after a time he was expelled for outbursts of uncontrollable anger. When he was interviewed subsequently by a psychologist he presented himself as the model of a merchant seaman officer, both in dress and in manner of communicating. He gave his reason for leaving the school that one of the officers had not dealt with sufficient authority against the offence of another boy. This had made him furiously angry and he had walked out. In this case accommodation predominated over assimilation, but the hidden assimilation could be seen in his idiosyncratic distortion of the relationship between authority and the individual.

If we adopt this descriptive model of adaptation, certain corollaries follow in relation to children who are labelled maladjusted.

In the first instance we would expect these children to be those showing an excess of assimilation over accommodation because children with an excess of accommodation will tend to go along with the outside world even if they do not agree with it. The second corollary is that these children would tend to be egocentric in the sense that they make little or no accommodation to the realities of the outside world. A third corollary would be that in a world where situations are continually changing these children would tend to show a rigidity of response. Fourthly there will be discordance between the sense these children make of things and the views held by others. This follows from the observation that assimilation is in the service of the individual's own schemas. Finally, such children will be relatively impermeable to the influence of others. The maladaptation that occurs under these circumstances will progressively place these children at a serious remove from their peers and from adults.

An important caution needs to be made at this point. The model says nothing about the direction which adaptation would take. Adaptation in a delinquent culture leads to delinquency playing an important part within the person's schemas. Adaptation to a benevolent environment is conducive to a more morally acceptable development. From this caution arises the simple conclusion that those who create the environments within which children grow up carry a heavy responsibility for the adaptation that they implicitly promote. At the limit, adaptation leads to a way of life, and a different way of life reflects different cultural values rather than personal maladjustment.

This section brings to a close my recycling of the maladjustment concept. The sections that follow deal with recycling maladjustment when the concept of maladjustment is used to describe children and their behaviour.

Section 3. Three principles of perception, of creation, of action

We can move forward from contemplation about a concept to action about children, because, in the last resort, action is our major concern. In order to provide a bridge from the one to the other I offer three principles that, it seems to me, provide caveats to our own actions, perceptions and thoughts.

Principle 1: what is perceived is a function of the angle and distance of the observer from the object

The head teacher sees a child's behaviour as mildly provocative. The class teacher finds it extremely disruptive. The psychologist sees the same behaviour as fully comprehensible. The father says quite simply that boys always were like that when he was at school. The social worker finds the behaviour seductive. For whom is this child maladjusted? For only one of these five observers is the behaviour a problem; this is the teacher, because none of the others sees a cause for complaint or is likely to ask for help.

The principle is important in requiring of professional workers the willingness to see the validity of other's judgements rather than, in an egocentric fashion, insist on the correctness of their own view.

Principle 2: each person creates for himself his own personal world out of the raw material that life offers him, just as he himself is a creation out of the raw material which he presents to others

This principle stems from Mahrer (1978) and points in two directions. Of any individual it provides the questions 'how was he shaped by others?' and 'how is he in turn creating his world?' The practical implications, likewise, are twofold. We need to ask parents the function and purpose of the creation that is their child. Of the child we need to ask how he makes sense of himself and his circumstances. The principle provides, therefore, a logic for investigation if we wish to understand the child and his behaviour.

Principle 3: all actions serve some useful purpose for the actor

This principle is not immediately self-evident. How, for example, can an act of self-punishment be useful? How can an act of random violence have a utility value? In the first instance self-punishment may make a person feel better if he feels he has done something that deserves punishment but has gone unnoticed. In the second instance the doer may no longer feel at a disadvantage with a world that he sees as constantly on the edge of destroying him. To identify the positive value of actions is not to condone the actions but to suggest that we seek to find out what the positive value is. At some point it might be then possible to explore ways in which the positive ends may be achieved through different actions. The principle not only has therapeutic value but also encourages the professional to adopt a reflective and dispassionate view at times when the heart calls for an emotional response.

These three principles offer the beginnings of a constructive approach to children whose behaviour invokes the description 'maladjusted'.

Section 4. Four dimensions in the study and investigation of children

We now follow the three principles with four lines of enquiry that need to be followed if we are to study children and their behaviour.

The first dimension is the dimension of the observable. This might seem obvious but, in fact, complications arise from two separate sources: on the one hand, as I described in the previous section, what is seen is a function of angle and distance; on the other hand the reporting of what is seen involves categories of description, each of which is usually pitched at a high level of abstraction. A teacher might say, when asked to describe a child's behaviour, that he was disruptive, defiant and aggressive. Each of these descriptions is a generalization and if we ask the teacher what the boy actually does a different pattern might be seen to emerge.

'Disruptive' is elaborated as interference with others by excessive talking. 'Defiance' is a verbal refusal to do what a teacher asks. 'Aggressive' refers to verbal taunts and insults, not to physical activity. Thus the pattern that emerges is very much concerned with verbal rather than physical activity and this knowledge would be important in any subsequent interview with the child.

The difficulty of working in the dimension of the observable is that description given in this way pre-empts the development of alternative, and potentially more therapeutic, abstractions.

The second dimension refers to the context within which the child's behaviour takes place and describes behaviour in interactive terms. This dimension, when pressed to the limits, includes family, neighbourhood and culture as well as school, and poses the question 'within which, if any, of these contexts is the behaviour adapted?' If we can take the next step and change the focus away from the individual it becomes possible to study the system within which the behaviour takes place. The development of family as opposed to individual therapy is one current expression of the strategy of defocusing from the child to the context.

The third dimension is temporal. What is the sequence of behaviour over a short time and what is the pattern over a longer time? When this dimension is stretched it extends to the whole life history of an individual and perhaps to his family as well. The underlying implication of this dimension is that behaviour is not random and that by studying sequences and patterns it may be possible to fathom its roots in early times and its own internal logic. From this perspective stems the hope of predicting behaviour over time in contrast to the hope in the preceding perspective of predicting interactions. The two dimensions are complementary, and used together may give a full meaning to behaviour. There are, however, important elaborations of this dimension that I am deferring to the next section.

The fourth dimension is usually completely ignored because its very existence has not been widely recognized. Its acceptance is as powerful in the study of individuals as was the Copernican revolution in astronomy (Kelly, 1955, 1991). This dimension poses the question 'What does the child himself make of himself and his circumstances?' In other words, 'what are his schemas and his systems?' It is easy to assume that we have always asked this question but when we put it to the test we frequently find that in reality we have used a mind-reading process by projecting our own thoughts and feelings into the child rather than asking the child himself. When we actually do ask him we may well be surprised by his answers. To put the question to the child, and to accept that this view is not ours, represents a growth in our own wisdom and also a proper recognition of the child's own individuality and genius.

These four dimensions provide a framework within which it is possible to arrive at a more comprehensive understanding of the child based on a broad view from without, balanced by the knowledge that only the child can provide.

Section 5. The three histories of an individual

The third dimension of the previous section pointed in the direction of a person and his history. In many forms of psychological and psychiatric investigation, history-taking occupies a prominent place and is a highly valued skill. It is seldom recognized, however, that we should, perhaps, think in terms of three histories for each individual although the major consideration is usually placed on only one of them.

A traditional history is normally a compilation of the sequence of events that took place in the child's life. He was conceived, carried *in utero,* born. He passed through the developmental stages of locomotion, communication and self-help. He acquired social and educational skills. These happenings represent events in the child's life that, on the one hand, are the raw material out of which he creates his own world, and on the other hand provide the raw material out of which others create him. These events, however, mean nothing in themselves. They take on salience within the context of the other two histories.

The second of these I would call the child's experiential history. It is the history of the experiences that these events generated. Experiences, here, include thoughts, feelings and actions, and an awareness of them. They are included because a child is part of a system of interpersonal relations and interactions that constitute the system. Out of the dynamic of all these experiences, especially those stemming from the social interactions with others, he develops some notion of his own effectiveness within the world. Haley (1981) describes the process with reference to the styles of social interaction that various learning theories typify. If the style is similar to the procedures of operation conditioning the child will learn tacitly that he can, by his own efforts, bring about changes that will be to his advantage. By contrast, a child brought up where the prevailing style is comparable to Pavlovian conditioning will learn that his only way of surviving is to wait passively for his necessities to be brought, and to acquire a knowledge of the contingencies associated with them. A third style arises when parents play with their children. Through this form of interaction the child experiences the power of the symbol, the possibility of shared outcomes and the value of mutual co-operation. A fourth style is based on the principle of a random reinforcement. By definition, this is a conditioning procedure in which the response of the 'not-self' is essentially unpredictable. It renders the child, therefore, powerless in the control of what happens to him and under these circumstances he learns to adopt one of two strategies. He will either persist to distraction in order to have a need met, or he will abandon hope altogether, learning that he might just as well do nothing since no action he makes can guarantee a result.

The third history is constructed out of the first two through an awareness of the similarities and contrasts of events and out of his experiencing of what happens. To some extent this history becomes available through language but most of it is held at low levels of awareness. His deepest views of his own identity, of others, and of the world, are rooted in this underlying awareness which has become reified as schemas by Piaget and as personal construct systems by Kelly (1955, 1991). It can now be recognized that this third history is an amplification of the fourth dimension, which I described in the previous section. There can be no understanding of an individual without an exploration, with the child, of this history.

Section 6. Communication, behaviour and a sense of self

This section is the complement to Section 2. In that section I offered a theoretical model for maladjustment based on the adaptive development of the individual. In this section I offer a theoretical model for behaviour based on the recognition that behaviour is part of an interactive process. The model from which the thoughts in this section derive is that put forward by Watzlawick et al. (1967) in their study *The Pragmatics of Human Communication*.

Two assertions, each of which refers to aspects of the title of this section, set the scene:

- Behaviour can always be seen as communication.
- Behaviour, as a communication, always implies a message both about an individual's sense of self but also a sense of that which is the not-self.

Let me add also that because all behaviour takes place within a context there will also be a message related to the definition of that context. If we put these statements in a more elaborate way we must say that there are always three components to every communication. There is the actual content, words or gestures or actions. There is the component that defines the self and the other. This will be a non-verbal message and is, therefore, likely to be misunderstood. There is the component that defines the situation within which the interchange is taking place. The two parties in a communication are, therefore, mutually involved in defining their relationship and defining the context of that relationship.

The second part of the scene is contained in the idea that there are three and only three ways of responding to each or all components of the communication. One may affirm, one may deny, one may ignore – and this applies to the content – the relationship and the situation.

It follows from this analysis that in any communication there can be either congruence or incongruence between the definitions of self or situations that each holds. The issue is clear-cut when there is affirmation or denial. It is not so clear when a part is ignored. It may be that ignoring reflects a tacit agreement of basic issues that do not need to be made conscious. The effect may well, however, be to generate uncertainty in the person whose communication has been part ignored. I will for the moment defer consideration of the consequences of this.

Selective affirmation and denial are normal in all communications and congruity and incongruity are, therefore, logical outcomes. It is indeed through all of these processes that the individual acquires knowledge of the phenomenal world and a definition of himself and others. He learns to agree and disagree in ways that are socially acceptable. He acquires sensitivity to situations and the proper demands of the moment. He progressively develops sophistication in his dealing with the world and his fellows.

An awareness of incongruity in the individual's communications with others is not, therefore, a cause of a breakdown in relationships. The cause rests rather in an intolerance of incongruity. This is less likely to arise over matters of content and more likely to arise out of a mismatch in each other's sense of self. At its simplest level this may appear as a struggle over who has the right to determine the relationship, for example parent–child, teacher–pupil, the right to exercise authority over others. Frequently, however, this obscures a serious mismatch over context. In essence it reflects an unwillingness to give way to another's point of view and an insistence on one's own perspectives. The similarity of this analysis to the classical ideas of egocentrism, assimilation and accommodation, which I described in Section 2, is obvious.

I have so far stressed the importance of intolerance of incongruity. I return now to that uncertainty which stems from a part of a communication being ignored. I would suggest this uncertainty is also a normal part of communication. Its negative effect is associated not with uncertainty but with intolerance of uncertainty. Perhaps the commonest manner in which this disturbing behaviour arises is when a child persists in attempting to extort some recognition from others through what is loosely called 'attention-seeking behaviour'. The alternative to this for the child is to give up any attempt at maintaining a relationship. Either solution is self-defeating and therefore is maladaptive because neither solution achieves the outcome that the child is seeking.

These issues are illustrated by the cases of two 5-year-old girls. Tessa insists on drawing the teacher's attention to how clever she is and persists in this to the exclusion of all the other children. The teacher describes herself as one who believes in dealing fairly with all her children by giving them comparable amounts of attention. She sees this child as defining herself as the equal to the teacher and therefore having a prior claim on her time. She feels that the child is a challenge to her own sense of herself as a teacher who is fair to all her children. When the child's demands are ignored the child persists even more in demanding the teacher's validation.

Lena is very different. She is quiet and apparently gets on with her work. She does, however, frequently spoil it deliberately and in that way engages the teacher's attention. The teacher feels that the child is creating a situation in which she, the child, is the victim and the teacher is an oppressor. This seriously violates the teacher's sense of herself and underplays the school as a learning context in favour of a situation for the enactment of her own personal drama.

This theoretical analysis is concerned with the here and now of communication between individuals, in particular the teacher or parent and child. It lays stress on an intolerance of the incongruity and uncertainty that inevitably arise when individuals interact. It does not say how children became like this. The answer to that question can be found only by exploring the child's own construction of his own experiential history as I described in the previous section. Such an exploration may provide the keys to understanding the child's definition of himself, and the ways in which he defines situations. The two sections, therefore, point to a strategy of psychological enquiry in relation to children and their behaviour.

Section 7. The problem revisited: from thought to action

This final section brings about a return to the starting point, but with a difference. Whereas we started with a discussion of the concept of maladjustment itself, we now turn to dealing with the behaviour for which the concept was coined. We shall suggest ways in which hopefully there might be the possibility of bringing about change. The argument in the preceding section provides one analytic tool and three strategies. The tool is derived from the analysis of communication. Within any sequence of behaviour where problems of behaviour are manifest we look for the incongruity in the communication. This will arise from the mismatch of content, or in the definition of self, or in the definition of situation. In other words, we look for the ways in which the three components are selectively affirmed, denied or ignored. Analysing behaviour in this way reduces feelings of impotence and hurt and opens up the possibilities of constructive action based on understanding rather than emotion. Its use might be likened to first aid, sufficient in many cases but not enough for all.

The three strategies are related to this analysis and provide either a choice of tactic for moment-to-moment use or alternative plans for long-term intervention.

With the first strategy we aim to help a child construct his view of himself and his circumstances and in the process to envisage different ways of acting. As a long-term intervention this strategy constitutes some form of individual psychotherapy. When used as a tactic it involves inviting a child to see for himself the ways in which his constructions are leading him into behaviour that is potentially damaging to himself and others. We ask him to look backwards to the immediate roots of his actions and forwards to the possibility of change.

The second strategy requires a change in the interactions within the system in which the behaviour is occurring. Surprisingly, the use of behaviour modification techniques, ostensibly directed at the child, provides a way of changing the system. In essence, to change the interactions is to change the communications between its members.

The moment-to-moment tactic calls for an imaginative use of communications whenever and wherever it might bring about or consolidate change. The simplest device is the skilled reframing of parts of a communication in order to give it a different meaning, and when this is achieved the possibility arises of altered relationships. The following dialogue illustrates the point. The psychologist was asked to see John again as the boy had made considerable progress in bringing his bad feelings under control. The head teacher felt that this required validation from the psychologist in order to consolidate the change.

P. Would you consider that someone who climbed Mount Everest was a hero?
J. No.
P. Why not?
J. Because he might die.
P. And if he did not die would you call him a hero?
J. Yes.
P. And if a lady who was crippled won a gold medal at the Olympic games would you call her a heroine?
J. Yes.
P. (After a pause.) And would you consider a boy who had learned to control his bad feelings a hero?
J. (After an even longer pause, and a little smile.) Yes.
P. Then I think I have to say you are a hero.

The reframing here puts the control of feelings into the framework of great achievements – first, against physical odds, then against physical handicaps. Finally the control by oneself over psychological handicap is presented as the great achievement and on this count John qualifies as a hero.

We can use these first two strategies in tandem as when we explore with a child his perspectives and communicate these to his teacher, thereby influencing *his* perspectives. With his changed perspectives he can then change his communications with the child, especially at the level of honouring the child's own sense of himself. Thus the use of the first strategy by the psychologist with the child makes possible the use of the second strategy by the teacher in relation to the child.

With the third strategy we aim to change the situation. As a long-term decision this means placing a child, after discussion with parents, in either a day or residential school. As a moment-to-moment tactic this might mean simply putting the child into a different physical situation. More usefully, however, it means redefining the situation in such a way as to normalize the behaviour, thereby making possible a change in the relationship. In this way, what at first was disturbing behaviour becomes changed into communications that are under control.

Although I have offered what seem to be three separate strategies, they are separate only in that they reflect different aspects of the same issue. A change through the use of one strategy is likely to generate change in each aspect of the communication process. What is essential to all three strategies is a sensitivity to the meaning of a communication and a skill in responding because, in the last analysis, the only way in which we can expect to influence the child and his behaviour is by a change in the communications or a change in one's own behaviour.

Last thoughts

The focus in the second half of this paper has been children and their behaviour. I have treated the matter as a psychologist and have, therefore, used psychological theories to create an argument. It is a matter of personal belief that the most useful psychological theories are those which have relevance to the whole of mankind, even though developed on a small part. Thus everything I offer in this paper I consider to be relevant to adults as well as children. My last-but-one thought is, therefore, that we should apply the argument to ourselves as well as to children. My last thought is the hope that the words in which the paper is couched will generate experiences in real life that, in turn, will promote greater effectiveness in dealing with children who, whether we like it or not, will continue to be called maladjusted.

Chapter 11
Personal construct psychology and practitioners who work with children (1985)

A small group of personal construct theory (PCT) practitioners, all involved at some level with children, met regularly at the Personal Construct Psychology Centre in London to discuss matters of common concern. At their instigation, I prepared this paper for the Centre. It turned out to be a rather formal statement of PCT, albeit somewhat rearranged in a structure that reflected my own overview of the theory, specifically directed to people working with children.

The value of theory to the practitioner is to offer the possibility of transforming casual lookings into systematic investigation, 'Common Sense' understanding to precise formulation and unreflecting reaction to planned intervention. It is the value of experience to make these three processes look like their originals.

Structure

1 Background

1.1 Introduction

1.2 Four Facets of Personality Theory

2 Personal construct Theory

2.1 Epistemological Roots of the Theory

2.2 The Four Facets of Personal Construct Theory
    2.2.1 Attitude to Persons and Problems
    2.2.2 Attitudes to Intervention and Change

2.2.3 Contents of the Theory: Fundamental Postulate and Corollaries
    2.2.3.1 The Individual
    2.2.3.2 The Individual's own Theoretical System
    2.2.3.3 The Individual in Relation to Others

1 Background

1.1 Introduction

> This book [*The Psychology of Personal Constructs*] started out 20 years ago as a handbook of clinical procedures. It was designed for the writer's students and used as a guide in the clinic of which he was the director. At first the emphasis was upon specific ways of revealing and understanding the client's record of personal experiences and of seeing clearly the milieu in which he was seeking to find a place. (Kelly, 1991, p. xi)

> [Personal construct theory] actually started with the combination of two simple notions: first, that man might be better understood if he were viewed in the perspective of the centuries rather than in the flicker of passing moments; and second, that each man contemplates in his own personal way the stream of events upon which he finds himself so swiftly borne. Perhaps within this interplay of the durable and the ephemeral we may discover more hopeful ways in which the individual man can restructure his life. (Kelly, 1991, p.3)

The Psychology of Personal Constructs made its appearance in 1955 but the original publication has been out of print for many years [it was republished in 1991]. Thus psychologists and others who now wish to know about personal construct theory are dependent on the writings of Kelly's pupils, often at second or third hand. As the two quotations show, Kelly developed personal construct theory not only out of an academic interest in psychology but primarily from a profound awareness of himself as a practitioner. He operated a travelling schools' psychological service in the dust bowl of Kansas and was a therapist to troubled students on a university campus. These experiences led him to a rethink of the nature of man and his circumstances and out of the interaction of thought and experience he formulated the theory of personal constructs. It seems to be the case, however, that when the theory becomes a part of an academic curriculum, its practical roots tend to become ignored in favour of theoretical aspects. This becomes apparent when psychologists and workers in other helping professions, seeking to broaden their competency in dealing with clients, wish to explore the possibility of applying personal construct theory to their work. They will have been attracted by some personal resonance with the theory either from lectures or through reading, but cannot see its implications for use, almost as though, from what they had learned, these roots had never existed. Yet for Kelly the invention of personal construct theory was the outcome of dealing with problems similar to those that confront these workers. Typically, they equate constructs with words and words with theory, and ask whether children who are young, or of limited intelligence, or inarticulate can have constructs. They are not aware of the essential nature of the construct as elaborated and refined by Kelly and which lies at the heart of the theory. They show little awareness of the relationship between *behaviour, construing* and *constructs*. They wish to know about grids without knowing the connection with the theory out of which grids sprang, and frequently act as though the grid and the theory are coterminous. They are concerned over the detail of grid methodology without knowing how grids can properly and usefully be employed. In general they have an intuitive awareness that personal construct theory can help but have been given a false coinage of words whereby the theory's practical use has been devalued. The question arises as to why this should be so.

Individuals come to any psychological theory with widely differing personal interests. For some the prime concern is to find ways of understanding their fellow man within a framework of 'scientifically' validated theory. This may arise purely out of intellectual curiosity or because their work involves teaching others. For a different group a theory provides a systematic framework either for further elaboration through research or as a means of illuminating topics outside the theory's immediate frame of reference. There is a third group that consists of individuals whose interest is as much philosophical as psychological. They seek to locate different theories within some unifying scheme, usually by studying their similarities and differences.

These different interests are not necessarily mutually exclusive. They are likely to be found, however, in individuals whose work lies in such academic activities as teaching, research and writing. What they teach will essentially reflect their personal involvement with the theory.

There is, however, a fourth category of persons who differ widely from these groups in their concerns. These are individuals whose work is to ameliorate human problems within a wide range of contexts: schools, social service departments, clinics, probation departments. For them theory is not so much something to be proved, researched and taught, but rather a tool actually to be used in the understanding of, and intervention in, problems of living. Unfortunately, most of the people in this category receive their introduction to theory from people in the first three groups. It follows that what is important to academics will not necessarily be helpful to potential practitioners, and what might be important to potential practitioners may even escape the attention of the teachers altogether.

1.2 Four facets of personality theory

Fully to master another's personality theory may well be a lifetime's work – even then it will not be mastery but rather its personal reconstruction. Any theory can be studied from at least four different angles. Different theories will stress different facets and the separate facets of any one theory will have importance according to the interests of the user.

The first facet is the attitude a theory offers, either explicitly or implicitly, towards people and problems. For example, a psychoanalytic theory will tend to see people as battlegrounds between the forces of hedonistic wishes and social constraint. Problems arise within this context. Behaviourists will be likely to see people as elaborations of the processes discovered in the animal laboratory and their problems as the continuation of maladaptive learned responses from the past.

The second facet will be concerned with change and the ways a practitioner may profitably intervene in the resolution of problems.

These two facets are of considerable importance to the practitioner as, negatively, he will find it difficult to use a theory that does not fit with his spontaneous ideas about people and problems and positively, a theory may offer an orientation where previously his ideas had been muddled and confused.

The third facet deals with the actual contents of the theory. These include its basic assumptions, the processes, the language and the propositions that hold the language together. They can be likened to a map of reality. The map is, however, not the territory and the theory is not the reality it seeks to describe. It is easy to lose sight of the overall drift of a theory in pursuing the minutiae of detailed description and definition that the language carries. There is also the difficulty that the language of a theory is usually also the language of everyday life but the theory's inventor gives it limited constraints and meanings. It is a lack of awareness of this ambiguity that is frequently at the heart of the puzzlement that potential practitioners experience. This is no less true for personal construct theory – a matter that will be elaborated later.

The fourth facet lies in the need to relate any one theory to other theories that ostensibly cover the same areas. To continue the analogy of the map, this facet is concerned, through the exploration of similarities and differences, to establish whether or not the territory is the same. At a deeper level it is also concerned to determine the appropriateness of the underlying bases whereby the map was constructed.

In summary, a theory of personality offers a perspective on people and their problems that has implications for action and change. It offers a systematic framework for understanding people and intervening in their problems. It exists as one amongst other theories. From some it may gain support and illumination, towards others it may be set in opposition.

If at this point we take an imaginative leap and argue, as personal construct theory suggests, that we see each and every person as a personality theory in action, then this summary also offers a paradigm for growth through experience. Each person will have an attitude to his fellows and will have some ideas as to the ways in which they change. He will have developed a systematic way of understanding them and will use language not only in its ordinary usage but in a usage that is personal to him. He will be in constant interaction with others, each of whom will also be a theory in action. From some he will gain support and understanding, for others he will be in a state of antagonism. An awareness of this paradigm will provide the practitioner with an overview for intervention as the exploration of each facet of an individual's personal theory may open the door to furthering his growth and development.

2 Personal construct theory

2.1 Epistemological roots of the theory

Two fundamental principles form the roots of the psychology of personal constructs. The first is described by Kelly as the principle of *constructive alternativism* which states very simply that whatever view of things might currently be held it is always possible to construct an alternative. Developments in the various branches of science manifest this principle on a grand scale; variations in individuals' knowings manifest this at a personal level. It is the awareness that alternative views can be constructed that leads to the hope and expectation for changes in behaviour as alternative views offer the prospect of alternative actions. This principle therefore underlies the aims of practice.

The second fundamental principle rests on the fact that all knowing stems from the awareness of differences, and by implication, their complement, sameness (Bateson, 1979). A difference is known by the impact that it makes. The awareness of difference is in the perceiver and is, therefore, personal to him. For Kelly, this principle leads to the formulation of the *construct* as the central concept of the theory. But the implications of the *constructs* as a concept are seldom fully appreciated. Some of them are presented in the following observations:

1. The construct is an abstraction that
2. arises from an awareness of a similarity and a contrast between events
3. and is therefore bipolar.
4. This awareness will have cognitive, affective and conative aspects.
5. The construct arises out of an individual's personal experience and is therefore his own.
6. It provides an axis for discriminating between events.
7. It has predictive properties.

8. As one construct among others it provides an underlying basis for a person to make sense of himself and his circumstances.
9. For convenience the abstraction may be given verbal markers (a) to identify the two ends, (b) for distinguishing one construct from others and (c) for communication.
10. If a person takes another person's verbal markers as a basis for a construct he will invest it with his own personal meanings.
11. Because awareness of differences occurs from the earliest moment of an infant's life there will be constructs for which no verbal markers will be available. These can be called preverbal constructs.
12. Because of the essential continuity of human development constructs with verbal markers may have origins in preverbal experiences.
13. A person's system of constructs (as defined) provides the underlying basis whereby he constructs his map of 'reality'. It is not, however, the map, nor is it 'reality'. The construct, therefore, operates at a low level of awareness, and is not directly observable.

Just as the principle of alternative constructivism has implications for action, so the principle from which the construct is derived has implications for investigation. Quite simply: 'we do not know the meaning of a statement unless we also know what it also implies, what it denies and the context within which it is useful.'

This formulation provides a theoretical basis for investigative interviewing. In pursuing the answers to these three separate questions we elicit from the client his underlying bases for making sense, and in doing so we commit him to reflect on his own psychological processes.

Two caveats follow from what has so far been presented. The first is against equating the client's psychological processes with the theory. The latter is an invention of the theorist, developed for the purpose of making a better sense of his own experiences and those of his client. He then offers it to the world at large. It is essentially an assumptive framework that may or may not be useful for others either as a model of man, or as a tool for the practitioner.

The second caveat is concerned with language. Personal construct theory employs three cognate terms: *construe*, *construction* and *construct*, and their similarity may be a cause for confusion.

Construe is used with its ordinary meaning. '*Construing* means placing an interpretation. A person places an interpretation on what he *construes*.' To *construe* is to give meaning.

Construction ordinarily points in two directions. The first is to something that is made, such as a building or a model. The second is simply the noun from *construe* – 'meaning'. A *construction* is a meaning. Kelly takes the second usage, not the first.

Kelly departs from ordinary usage of the word *construct* and invests it with the detailed content described earlier.

Certain implications follow. It is possible correctly to describe a person as *construing* events and having *constructions* as these expressions vary in their commonly accepted meanings. We cannot, however, talk about a person's *constructs* unless we have already agreed with him that the bases for his *construing* are fully concordant with the description of the *construct* as used by Kelly. It needs to be remembered that, for the practitioner, the concept of the *construct* is a help in *his* construing of the client. The *construct* itself is not necessarily a part of his client.

2.2 The four facets of personal construct theory

2.2.1 Attitudes to persons and problems

The theory's stance is that people are active participants in their own ventures and not passive recipients of external stimuli. Kelly catches this view in the metaphor of 'man the scientist'. They shape and reshape their understanding of events and in the process each person creates his own experiential world because events are only knowable through the constructions that he places on them. The world in this sense includes both phenomena in the outside world and the thoughts, emotions and sensations that comprise the phenomena of his inner world. His constructions arise from his recollections and anticipations, his hopes and his fears, his planned intentions and spontaneous actions. If we are to understand this person we must understand both his constructions of the world and the underlying bases for those constructions.

A person's behaviour is made up from the choices he makes from moment to moment. These will always be in the direction of making the world (both internal and external) more predictable, more interesting, more bearable or whatever he senses to further his own best interest. For Kelly the metaphor is that 'behaviour is an experiment'.

Problems arise when a person's constructions fail to give meaning to oncoming events or when anticipations are consistently invalidated, or when, as between individuals, there exists serious mismatches in their construction of the same events, in particular when there is radical mismatch between a person's own construction of himself and the construction that others have of him.

It follows from these observations that there are important implications for the practitioner. The first is that he must honour the fact that individuals interpret the world in ways which are entirely their own, and secondly, that when problems arise the individual's personal interpretations, although honoured, should not, therefore, go unchallenged.

2.2.2 Attitudes to intervention and change

Personal construct theory, by placing its emphasis on a person's construction of the world and by stressing the essentially active nature of man, points the need for change of construction as a basis of change in behaviour, and the way of action as a means for bringing this about. Intervention, therefore, requires that the practitioner takes a careful account of the client's existing construction of his world but also poses to his client the question: 'If your current behaviour represents the best solution for you at the moment, what are the alternatives you are rejecting and in what ways do those alternatives offer you a disservice?'

The task for the practitioner is to help the client find ways in which he may revise his constructions or his construction systems. This may be fostered by exploring with him reflectively, either at a surface or profound level, his constructions of his inner or outer worlds, his self-identity or the identity of others. More actively, he may be directed to play a role whereby he is in the position of receiving a different range of validatory information. This is the experiential way.

Thus the attitude of personal construct theory to intervention and change opens up a wide range of strategies for the practitioner. It might be asked, therefore, what extra value lies in knowledge of the theory's content. The theory offers, economically and efficiently, through its fundamental postulate and eleven corollaries, a systematic model of the individual personality. The language within which it is couched provides a means of identifying phenomena and communication with others. It enables links to be made between information that otherwise might be considered unrelated. Finally, it provides an intellectual discipline within which practice and theory may mutually interact and develop.

2.2.3 Contents of the theory: fundamental postulate and corollaries

Personal construct theory is a theory about individual persons as well as being a theory amongst theories. Just as the four facets about theories in general, and personal construct theory in particular, can be recognized, so can the postulates and corollaries in the theory be grouped under the same four headings, i.e. statements about the individual, statements about growth and change, statements about the contents of the individual's own personal theory and statements about the individual amongst others.

The wording with which each postulate and corollary is couched gives precise meanings to each statement. To offer a gloss, therefore, is to risk weakening Kelly's original definitions. Nonetheless, it is a matter of fact that communicability and meaning frequently suffer as the precision of a formulation increases, and as nuances for the theoretician may well be different from the nuances for the practitioner, a commentary is offered for each cluster of corollaries.

2.2.3.1 The individual
Fundamental postulate. A person's processes are psychologically channelized by the ways in which he anticipates events.

Construct corollary. A person anticipates events by construing their replications.

Individuality corollary. Persons differ from each other in their construction of events.

The way a person goes about his business depends very much on his reasonable expectations of what will happen. He builds up this body of psychological knowledge out of his experiences, especially his awareness of similarities and differences in the events of his everyday life. This body of knowledge will be personal to a given individual so that even if happenings are thought by others to be the same, the meanings given by different people will be different according to their personal histories.

2.2.3.2 The individual's own theoretical system
Organization corollary. Each person characteristically evolves, for his convenience in anticipating events, a construction system embracing ordinal relationships between constructs.

Dichotomy corollary. A person's construction system is composed of a finite number of dichotomous constructs.

Range corollary. A construct is convenient for the anticipation of a finite range of events only.
Fragmentation corollary. A person may successively employ a variety of construction subsystems that are inferentially incompatible with each other.

The commentary on this cluster of corollaries has been to some extent anticipated in the discussion of the epistemological roots of the theory – in particular, the description of the construct. The content of that discussion can now also be seen to fit into this section.

Underlying a person's interpretation of events is a developed system of abstractions, each of which is two-ended, and each of which is limited in its usefulness to a restricted range of situations. This system will be personal to the individual and will be based on his personal experience. The abstractions are not all of equal importance, and they will tend to group into subsystems. An individual is not expected to be fully self-consistent at all levels of behaving and thus from time to time will act in ways that, to the observer, may seem out of character. Such a judgement might be harsh because, at some higher level of the system, a logic may be revealed that overrides the apparent inconsistencies at lower levels.

2.2.3.3 The individual in relation to others
Commonality corollary. To the extent that one person employs a construction of experience similar to that employed by another, his psychological processes are similar to those of the other person.

Sociality corollary. To the extent that one person construes the construction processes of another, he may play a role in a social process involving the other person.

Individuals live in various states of interactions with others. If people interpret events in the same way they will also tend to be alike in their behaviour in relation to those things. They will tend to find each other congenial to the extent that they broadly share the same understandings. By contrast, individuals who see things in radically different ways will tend to have difficulty with each other. These observations shed light on the interpersonal conflicts that arise when individuals fundamentally disagree over their interpretations of each other.

The sociality corollary is especially relevant when a person is expected to be engaged in some formal role with another, like, for instance, teacher and pupil. The corollary says that it is important, not so much to agree or disagree with an individual's interpretation of things, as to understand how those interpretations came about. Such an understanding, and the communication of the attempt to understand, makes possible a successful role relationship.

2.2.4 Personal construct theory and supporting theories

Despite the comprehensive grasp and range of personal construct theory, there are two areas of limitations for which the practitioner needs to draw support from elsewhere. The first stems from the fact that the theory was worked out in the context of adults who, in general, have well-developed construction systems. By contrast the status of children is one where development and change are the important characteristics. This aspect of theory is missing and, although researchers and theoreticians may properly direct their energies to rectifying the omission, the practitioner needs to get on with his job without waiting for the results of their enquiries. Thus within the overall orientation of personal construct theory he needs to use other theories that are both congruent with its orientation and that illuminate the growth and development of children's psychological processes.

The second limitation is that of pragmatics: 'what does the practitioner need to do in order to promote change?' In essence the question is about therapeutic interaction and communication, and although in many ways Kelly was ahead of his time as a therapist, it is from later workers with a primary interest specifically in these topics that the practitioner will gain most help.

2.2.4.1 Development

Three writers meet the double criterion of congruence with a personal construct orientation and the illumination of children's psychological development: Piaget, Vygotsky and Mahrer. Each promotes the view that the child is an active constructor of his world, but there are important differences of emphasis in their respective approaches. As a cluster of theorists, however, they compensate for each other and all three can be seen to add to personal construct theory rather than detract from it.

Piaget formulates the ways in which children construct the phenomenal world around them. He traces the stages whereby action is progressively transformed into the logical operations of formal intelligence by being successively freed from the illusions arising from perceptual dominance and the limitations of concrete operations. In order to give a full account of the child's psychological development he postulates a number of concepts out of which Mehrabian (1968) has created a theory of personality that provides a supplement to Piaget's interest in epistemology.

From a specifically personal construct theory point of view, Piaget describes the development of infants' primitive schemata, which always have reference both to what the infant has already grasped and what is new to him. This is an analogue to Kelly's experience corollary. Piaget almost casually makes the following comments:

> 'When the subject (infants under 1 year old) sees objects as distinct from himself, models can no longer be assimilated wholesale: they are seen to be both different from and similar to himself' (Piaget, 1951: 50).

> But sounds and movements which are new to the child, and yet comparable to those he has already made, give rise to an immediate effort at reproduction. The interest thus appears to come from a kind of conflict between partial resemblance which makes the child want to assimilate, and the partial difference which attracts his attention the more because it is an obstacle to immediate reproduction. It is, therefore, this two fold character of resemblance and opposition which seems to be the incentive for imitation. (Piaget op. cit.)

Thus Piaget instances Kelly's epistemological principle for similarities and differences as a fundamental psychological process in the child's progressive attempts to create meaning out of events.

Vygotsky (1962, 1978) offers a balance to Piaget's emphasis on internal psychological processes by pointing out the significance of the child's social world. For him cognitive development arises out of the internalization of actions that are basically social in origin. This viewpoint, therefore, gives importance to the influence, potentially both negative and positive, of the adults in the child's life.

Mahrer (1978) has developed a theory of psychology and psychiatry based on experiencing with special emphasis on the importance of *bodily feeling* as a root component. The bases of a person's behaviour lie in his potential for experiencing and he creates a world for himself in order to bring this potential to fruition. The events with which he comes in contact, either actively seeking or passively waiting, either jointly creating with others or through imagination, provide the building blocks out of which he constructs his world. The function or meaning of that world is provided by the potentials for experiencing. In this sense children also are building bricks that parents use in relation to their own potentials for experiencing. In their turn, children construct their worlds in exactly the same ways, at first sharing the meanings created by parents, later in terms of their own potentials. Mahrer describes the developmental sequence from the original unity of the parent-child field into individuality limited by the parents' willingness to let go and by the psychological inheritance of potentials from the parents. Thus to understand the foundations of a child's constructions it is necessary to seek them in the parents, and the younger the child the nearer he is to the parents' construction of the world.

These three separate theories therefore illuminate origins, processes and sources of the psychological developments that will eventually be described in personal construct theory terms as a person's construct system.

2.2.4.2 Pragmatics

The important conceptual analysis in the study of communication and interaction appears in 'The Pragmatics of Human Communication' (Watzlawick et al., 1967) and the following quotation gives an indication of the kinship between pragmatics and personal construct theory:

> Life – or reality, fate, God, nature or whatever name one prefers to give it is a partner whom we accept or reject, and by whom we feel ourselves accepted or rejected, supported or betrayed. To this existential partner man proposes his definition of self and then finds it confirmed or disconfirmed, and from this partner man endeavours to receive clues about the 'real' nature of this relationship. (Watzlawick et al., 1967: 259)

Two essential features in this analysis are that behaviour is always a communication and that problems that arise between individuals reflect breakdowns in communication. There are analogues in personal construct theory. Behaviour is an experiment (Kelly), behaviour is a communication (Watzlawick), whence it follows that communication is also an experiment and an experiment is a communication. Secondly, breakdowns in interpersonal communication rest on the participants' misconstructions of each other (Watzlawick). Problems arise out of an individual's constructions of 'reality' (Kelly).

By implication, the task of the practitioner is to find the communicational strategies that will lead to the modification of client's constructions, either of the world or of people.

More recently, Bandler and Grinder (Bandler and Grinder, 1979, 1982; Grinder and Bandler, 1976) have developed a detailed analysis of the communicational strategies of a number of successful therapists, such as Milton Erickson, Virginia Satir and Jay Haley, under the concept 'neuro-linguistic programming'. The principles that they elucidated were concerned with ways of clarifying individuals' representations of their worlds and in developing alternative ways of attributing meaning to these worlds. All of this is congruent with personal construct theory. In fact Lankton (1980) goes so far as to take over Kelly's postulate and corollaries and with the simple substitution of 'representation' for 'construction', describes them as consistent with the model of therapy and experience in his book. Thus the circle comes back full tilt.

3 Personal construct practice

3.1 When practitioners work with children

When the practitioner's work is with children, the logic of personal construct theory invites him to de-focus from an immediate concern with the child, and in the first instance, take a look at the wider situation that has brought the child to his notice.

Children do not themselves ask for help from a psychologist. Whatever issues or difficulties they may or may not have attributed to them, it is an adult, who by making a referral, is asking for help. It follows, therefore, that a referral is related to the constructions that a referrer is putting on the events that constitute the child and his actions and, at the same time, is also related to the referrer's construction of himself.

In relation to the teacher, a referral is always made against some normative notion of behavioural and educational standards. Typically a referral also can be reduced to one of four possibilities:

1. 'However I try to puzzle this child out I can never tell what he will do. He defeats my expectations.' With this referral, the child's behaviour leads the teacher to question her understanding of children and at the same time suggests that her construction system is expected to deal with events that lie outside its range of convenience.
2. 'Whatever I do I am unable to influence what this child does either in how he behaves or in what he learns, even though my expectations are reasonable.' This child, therefore, represents a challenge to this teacher's sense of professional competence. It also suggests that, because the role relationship is not proceeding smoothly, there is a failure in the teacher's construction of the child's construing.
3. 'I was trained to teach normal children. This one is educationally subnormal or maladjusted.' This referral suggests that the teacher has a rigid construction of himself as a teacher and an impermeable construction system for children in general.
4. 'This child has problems but whilst he is with me things are all right. I am worried, however, as to what will happen in the future, either with a new teacher, or in a new school.' This teacher is implicitly saying that the child's behaviour lies within the range of convenience of her construction system, but that other teachers may well not see the child in the same way.

A comparable taxonomy for parents' referrals might follow similar lines, but with the complications that normality will already be a function of family expectations and that the child's construction of himself and his circumstances have already been created by his parents. The issue is, therefore, more complex for parents' referrals than for teachers' referrals.

The import of this analysis is that the practitioner must explore and seek to bring about modifications in the constructions both of the referrer and of the child.

3.2 Questions at the back of the personal construct practitioner's mind

The practitioner, whatever his orientation, will always have certain key questions at the back of his mind, either to answer through direct enquiry or by inference. When he is a personal construct practitioner the following broad groups of questions cover the key areas of his concern and they follow naturally from the theory.

1. What are the events that are the cause of the referral? Who is complained about? Who complains? These questions help to pinpoint issues and prevent the practitioner from accepting from the referrer interpretations for events and prescriptions for descriptions.
2. What are the constructions within which the complaint takes on meaning for the referrer, and what are the constructions of the child about his circumstances that cause others to complain about him? For each description what is also implied and what is denied? These questions provide aims and suggest strategies for the investigation of a referral. The practitioner is concerned with meaning.
3. Which are the ways in which the protagonists' constructions may be changed? Is there new information for old constructions or new constructions for old events? Is change to be encompassed through reflection or imagination, through experimental enquiry or directed role change? Is the main work to be done with the child, or the referrer, or both? These questions reflect ways of intervening therapeutically.

The two cases that follow illustrate some of the ways in which these groups of questions provide the bases for action within a personal construct framework despite the differences in age and problems that the referrals offer: 'behaviour difficulties' in the case of 12-year-old John, and 'putative learning difficulties' in the case of 10-year-old Mary.

3.3 Illustrative cases

3.3.1 John

John was a pupil nearly at the end of his first year at a Roman Catholic comprehensive school. He was referred to the school psychological service because of behaviour that was described as 'disobedient and disregarding of teachers' reprimands. When thwarted by them he would get angry.' The work was carried out in two short interviews in school with the head of year present (this teacher carries pastoral responsibility for all the children in her year group). What is reported is the essential part of each interview.

At the first interview, John was required to clearly describe what happened to get him into trouble with his teachers. Gradually it became apparent that, in his eyes, his actions were faultless and he was therefore never responsible for trouble. The teachers were unfair to him for blaming him. His construction both of himself and the teachers was such as to land him in trouble and there could be no solution without some change of his present constructions. The logic of the dialogue that follows rests on John's membership of the Catholic Church.

> Psych: Do you believe in God?
> John: Yes.
> Psych: Do you believe in Jesus?
> John: Yes.
> Psych: Do you believe in the Virgin Mary?
> John: Yes.
> Psych: Have you ever met them?
> John: No.
> Psych: So it is a matter of faith?
> John: Yes.
> Psych: I wonder if, just for one week, you could show a similar faith in the teachers' judgement of you by accepting that perhaps you do in fact carry some responsibility for the actions that lead to trouble.

In this exchange John is invited to carry old constructions from one area of his experience in order to reconstrue the interactions which cause trouble. At the same time he is directed to play a role in relation to teachers that he had not previously envisaged – the role of a boy accepting responsibility for his own behaviour. If he can do this he will be in a position to experience events differently and also to receive a different kind of validation from the teachers.

At the second interview the teacher reported that John had had a good week with only one 'incident' and that really had not been John's fault. The interview commenced with a detailed analysis of the incidents and interactions that lead to trouble, with special reference to what he would think, what he would feel and what he would do. It became apparent that his usual sequence started with feelings that then led to action. Thinking came a long time after. In order to vary the content of the interview and include more information, John was asked to draw a picture. He drew a cup and saucer (at the corresponding stage the week before he had drawn a mug that was on the table). On the assumption that this picture carries meaning for John, the problem for the practitioner is to establish some of John's psychological processes. The dialogue that follows carries the gist of the linking process:

> Psych: Why would you use a cup and saucer and not a mug?
> John: When you have visitors. [There was, in fact, a visitor present in the interview.]
> Psych: What can go wrong with a cup and saucer?
> John: You can break it.

At this point I described and drew a tray that was used in a special school so that the children did not spill cups of tea when carrying them. The essence of the design was that the cup and saucer remained balanced however the child moved. The key word here is 'balance'.

> Psych: Which do you think is a better balance, to feel, think and then act, or to feel, act and then think?
> John: The first one.
> Psych: Could you then, for just three weeks, experiment with delaying your actions until after you have thought and felt about situations?

John accepted this suggestion and I then told him that I had no intention of interviewing him again unless he asked for it, thereby emphasizing the importance of his being responsible for his own behaviour.

Both interviews took place in the presence of the teacher so she was in a position to receive new information about John and could therefore modify her constructions of him.

This in turn makes possible an altered role relationship between teacher and pupil. Future interactions are likely therefore to be more effective.

Nothing was heard about John until some three months later when, visiting the school about another matter, I saw John going home in the middle of the day. I learned that he had been a perfectly satisfactory pupil since the second interview but suddenly he had 'blown up' with a teacher and had been sent home for two days. The teacher suggested I should interview him again but I reminded her that I would do this only at his request. When I enquired a week later she told me that John had emphatically refused another interview and had continued to be an exemplary pupil.

3.3.2 Mary

What follows is an annotated version of the formal report on the case.

Problem
This girl's mother had requested assessment of this child's special educational needs. The school report, however, was that, although she was a little behind the average for her class, the school in no way saw her as a problem for whom help was necessary. It was decided to interview the parents at school with the headteacher to clarify the issues.

Meeting with headteacher and family
It became clear that the school was satisfied with Mary's progress. Mother, however, for real and personal reasons, was very worried about Mary's educational future, partly on the basis of an unfortunately worded school report at the end of the summer and partly out of her projection of herself into the situation. The father was present at the interview and in general was constructive and helpful.

My detailed observations appear in italics.

1. Head teacher and parents hold different constructions of Mary as a child and of her educational progress. Hence this also constituted a problem since it created communication problems between parents and school and put Mary into a state of divided loyalties (cf. Ravenette, 1968).

Mary joined the interview, and when the matter of the mother's anxiety was raised she shed a few tears, but these did not last. While the conversation was going on, she was asked to draw a picture and when that was finished, draw either what was happening either just before or just after. She looked blank at this request, and I commented on the fact that various things were missing from the picture, including people. She then completed the task, the essential part of which was to take up the idea of people and fill her second picture with the same situation but with people. The other difference was clouds which had been apart were put together, creating an area of shading overlap. In commenting on this to the parents, I pointed out that, in the picture without people, everything was full of sunshine, but when people were present then there was shadow. I pointed out that this was a very wise observation that Mary had made.

2. Assuming her picture carried personal meaning at a low level of awareness the request for a further picture to make a sequence allows her meanings to be inferred using Kelly's principle that ideas that follow either elaborate the first idea or provide a contrast.

3. This is a minuscule alternative construction of Mary offered with a view to modifying the constructions of her held by both the headteacher and the parents.

It was agreed that I would interview Mary not from the point of view of a formal examination but in order to find ways in which anxieties could be alleviated and Mary's progress helped.

4. The expression 'helped' reframes the parents' complaint about slowness and failure to learn into one of continuing progress, i.e. positive rather than negative.

The evidence of the drawing suggests that, in Piagetian terms, Mary tends to accommodate to people, situations and things at the expense of assimilation. If this were the case, she would tend to be lacking in initiative, conforming to rule and looking to teacher for approval before action. In discussion with the class teacher, this was confirmed, as was her general unforthcomingness to him and her general lack of responsiveness.

5. Piaget provides a descriptive language which teachers understand but for which there is as yet no equivalent in personal construct theory.

Interview with Mary
The interview with Mary was in three parts. In the first, she was invited to co-operate in responding to the verbal scale of the WISC-R (6); in the second she was asked to draw two pictures that were opposites (7); in the third, we used the mutual story-telling technique (8).

6. The events that constitute an intelligence test offer an opportunity for a child to demonstrate his personal theory in action. This may well be more important than the IQ.

7. The technique used here applies the 'similarities–difference' principle as a specific interviewing technique. The interviewer can draw infer-ences from what stays constant across the two pictures and what appears as contrasts.

8. The mutual story-telling technique generates other aspects of the child's constructions but, more importantly, allows the interviewer delicately to suggest alternative constructions, preferably with implica-tions for action.

Behaviour in the interview
Throughout the interview, Mary was anxious and very talkative, but friendly and extremely co-operative, like a good accommodator should be.

Part 1
Her scores suggest a dull average level of verbal ability. There were two noteworthy features. The first was that she tended to use kinaesthetic frames of reference. The second rests in one anomalous response. To the question about what to do if a girl smaller than herself hits her she gives the immediate response 'fight back'. When questioned further – teacher would say 'not fight', mother would say 'not fight'. Her explan-ation for her own point of view was 'if you do not hit them back, they will have their own way'.

9. This suggests a spark of anger, defiance or individuality at variance with her accommodative behaviour and can be used in the subsequent reconstruction of her self.

Part 2
Mary elaborated a line into a very complicated picture that included land, sea, bridges, roads, clouds, rain, cars, and, most important of all, a monster trapped in a cage. When Mary was asked for the opposite, she repeated some of the features, including the monster but used different colours and made what was much more a situation with a potential for

play. Again, roads and weather and cars were in evidence. In talking about the pictures, having drawn the monster first, she then said nothing about it in her description. In the second picture, she said that the monster was dead.

Throughout this second drawing she continually talked, played guessing games with me like a much younger child, and was anxious to know if things were right.

1. Mary repeatedly talked about having done things wrong in the picture. She contended that she would be worried and that she would feel this is in her head, her chest and her hands. When asked if she was worried what people would think, she said 'I don't think sometimes that other people think about me.'

2. Three important differences emerge from the two pictures, against a background of essential similarity of scene. In the first there are many symbols of restriction and being hedged in; in the second, these are removed. In the first the monster was trapped; in the second it had been killed. A person is drawn in the second picture and according to Mary, this represents more than one person.

Part 3

I made a drawing representing two parents and two children, and invited Mary to make up a story. In exchange I would give one as well. Mary's story was:

> Once upon a time there was a girl named Ann. She had a little baby sister called Jane. She had a bow and an apron and she had this trolley with food and plates on it; that is why she had the apron on. Mum went out shopping to buy clothes, a jumper and a dress. The arms are too big. The man looks after the children; some of his clothes are torn, he has got a big nose. That is rain from outside.

The story I gave in exchange took up the theme that appearances are important from her story and the theme of the monster from her pictures, and integrated these with observations on her behaviour in the interview.

> Ann is a girl for whom it was very important that she looked right, that always how she looked was the right thing. She had to look happy and cheerful even if she was unhappy inside, even if she was angry inside, even if she was silly inside. To help her always seem to be looking right she would ask other people if it was right. She would talk and talk because that way people did not see what was happening inside. For a long time she did not have any trouble, but as she got older, she found that somehow she was worried that she would get things wrong and then she would be angry inside because things made her get worried, but always she had to hide the anger, like a dangerous

monster that was tied up. But just as she had tied up the monster, in a funny way she had tied herself up, because the monster was the way she could be brave and learn things that she did not know. One night she had a dream and in the dream a man came and told her what was happening inside herself, and he said that the only way she could get her freedom back was to tame the monster to become a friend. She thought that the man was really a bit silly, but when she woke up she thought about it. She decided that she would be very brave and let the monster become a friend that was tame, and the monster was always there when she wanted to do something new and the monster helped her to learn things on her own that she could not do before.

That little girl is bigger than you think, she is not Mary, but perhaps Mary in her heart recognizes her.

This story was meant to be therapeutic. The girl was very happy at the end of the interview and returned to the classroom very cheerful.

The interview was discussed with the class teacher in great detail in order to influence his construction of the girl. The analysis made sense to him and gave him the opportunity to work out a pattern of validating this girl for any initiatives that she took. It was suggested that a few signs of 'naughtiness' might indicate positive development. It was agreed to have a further interview with the family.

Follow-up: outcome

After three weeks, the girl was reported to have been 'naughty', to be talking much more readily to the teacher (which she had never done before), to be carrying out far more written work than she had before, and generally to be happy and cheerful. After a further three weeks the parents were interviewed again. They reported that Mary was much happier, she was no longer rejecting reading at home and, in fact, was taking the initiative. She was looking out for words in the environment and recognizing them. She was developing a strong relationship with her father arising from his acquisition of a computer.

4 The personal construct practitioner

The personal construct practitioner needs always to hold in his mind two polarities and to develop two further abilities. On different occasions, and probably more than once, Kelly made the following observations: 'If you don't know, ask. It is just possible that your client will give you an answer.' 'A pat answer is the enemy to a fresh question.'

As the practitioner always starts a new case with ignorance, his basic, and perhaps only tool, is the question, but because he may be given in reply a pat answer he needs to develop an attitude of *sceptical credulity* to what his clients say. Children frequently give answers that they have learned from adults, parents, teachers, social workers and so forth to be 'safe', and professionals' answers often derive from their theories. Thus the practitioner will always accept the answer that is given but he will not assume that it is a *personal* answer until he the client has been questioned further. An attitude of *sceptical credulity* is the first polarity.

Although a client's constructions may be easily elicited, his construction systems are far less readily available. The practitioner, therefore, needs the investigative acumen of Sherlock Holmes or Hercule Poirot to piece together the patterns of personal meaning that underlie behaviour. In order to achieve this he requires a degree of intellectual *detachment*. At the same time this needs to be balanced against feelings of *compassion, empathy,* and *concern* for his clients because his professional involvement with them derives solely from their human and personal predicaments. *Detachment* -*compassion, empathy,* and *concern* form the second polarity.

If the practitioner is to increase his effectiveness as an agent of change, he will benefit from developing two further abilities. The first of these is the art of story telling. This fosters the imaginative power to invent new constructions to match the client's circumstances and the fluency to present them as stories whereby he can influence those parts of the psyche that other forms of communication fail to reach. This ability is especially valuable in work with young children.

Alternatively, if his intervention is by way of requiring the client to act, he will learn a great deal from the skill of the stage director who, through his imaginative grasp of dramatic plots, is able to commit actors to playing roles that lead to constructive drama, rather than those uncomprehending disorders of relationships on stage that parallel some of the problems of actual living with which he has to deal.

When presented with these polarities and abilities as being important the practitioner may well ask what this has to do with Kelly's metaphor of 'man-the scientist', an exemplar of which he claims to be both as a human being and as a professional. The answer to this question, and the conclusion to this paper, is that whereas such a role requirement may seem to be in conflict with the public view of the scientist, and perhaps the view that some scientists have of themselves, the qualities that are advocated will be seen, on reflection, to represent the hidden side of the practice of science, the very processes out of which science as it is publicly known, arises.

The moon presents only one face to the earth. The hidden side has been seen only by those astronauts who actually visited it. So science also has a public face and those who join the scientific enterprise may need to unlearn the public face in order to develop the hidden. It is perhaps through the practitioner's special awareness that he is able to make a distinctive contribution both to the practice of science, and to the well-being of his clients.

Chapter 12
Personal construct psychology in the practice of an educational psychologist (1988)

This was my response to an invitation by the late Gavin Dunnett for a contribution to a book on PCT entitled Working with People. *On rereading the paper, I recognized that, in contrast to the preceding chapter, it was a rather gentle, informal account of PCT, specifically related to teachers and children. The first of two illustrative cases is especially interesting, demonstrating how working solely with a parent in the presence of the teacher was sufficient in promoting change and growth in a very disturbing handicapped child.*

The practice of an educational psychologist takes place in a context in which the role is shaped by the twin expectations of those who employ him and those to whom he offers a service. Each of these is also a function of their perspectives. Training provides a formal institution whereby role and expectations are transmitted. It was my good fortune not to be tied by either of these constraints. My training took place in a hospital context and seemed primarily to be a preparation for answering the questions of other professionals rather than taking a direct responsibility for dealing with clients' problems. Furthermore, the area in which I received an appointment had, for many years, no psychologist working in the schools, and the Director of Education gave me effectively a free hand to work out my own salvation. Thus, at one and the same time, I was both at an advantage and at a disadvantage. On the one hand, I was not really prepared for the role of carrying sole responsibility; on the other hand the possibility was there to develop practice which seemed to me to be relevant to the tasks. I had, indeed, recollections of what educational psychologists previously had done and I was determined not to repeat a style of work that appeared limited in conception and doubtfully illuminating to clients. By great good fortune, I was able to become conversant with Kelly's two volumes whilst studying for my professional qualifications and recognized that the psychology of personal constructs offered a stance that was positive to people as human beings (children, teachers and parents) and a theoretical basis from which it might be possible to respond meaningfully to the dilemmas that my future clients might present. Needless to say it has taken most of a professional lifetime to work out its implications, and doubtless the work is not yet finished. To anticipate what follows in the succeeding pages, the adoption of a personal construct approach effectively meant the creation of both a role and task that proved to be considerably at variance with the existing pattern in the practice of educational psychology.

In this work, children who fail to learn, who fail to behave appropriately, who show anomalies of development or disturbing features of personality are presented as problems. People making referrals will usually be teachers, sometimes parents, sometimes other agencies, and the work will usually be carried out in schools. On occasion a referral may be passed on to some other agency if the facts of the case make this seem more appropriate. The child guidance clinic, in particular, may be used if the problem seems essentially to be related to acknowledged tensions within the family. As will be seen later, personal construct psychology invites the psychologist to take more than a casual look at any referral.

The appeal of personal construct theory

It is proper to ask what is so special about personal construct psychology that I should see in it a basis for work as an educational psychologist. A number of themes that Kelly put forward made an immediate impact and provided the inspiration to adopt a Kellyan approach:

- 'Behaviour is an experiment' provides a way of giving a positive aspect to that which others see as a problem.
- 'Constructive alternativism', the insistence that there is always a different way of construing events, provides a challenge to the imagination and loosens the bonds that the notion of 'cause and effect' so often creates.
- 'No man need be a slave to his own autobiography' points away from the determinism of history whilst still acknowledging its importance.
- The fundamental postulate and its corollaries provide a basis for making sense of an individual's behaviour within a framework of relative simplicity.
- The implication running through the theory – that importance lies in meanings rather than events – leads to the evaluation of a person's history in experiential terms, thereby undercutting the view that personal history is a set of facts, each of which puts its mark on the individual.

Kelly's simple suggestion that if you want to know, then ask, his observation that 'A pat answer is the enemy to a fresh question' together with the corollary 'A pat question is the enemy to a fresh answer' all provide ideas for an overall style of enquiry. His stress on sameness and difference as the basis for all discrimination then suggests specific tactics for eliciting an individual's constructs and constructions.

Overriding all of these, his insistence on the provisional nature of psychological findings gives a freedom from the expectation placed upon us as 'experts' that there is always a correct explanation to be found and the consequent feelings of guilt when we fail to match up to those expectations.

In what follows I present the thinking and resulting practice that stem from my own interpretation of a Kellyan approach to being an educational psychologist. Although it is put forward in a number of sections each section is reflected in each of the others. The whole represents one psychologist's attempt to develop a practice out of a theory.

A restructuring of practice

Problems

By way of a preamble to this section, something needs to be said about what, in the context of a referral to a school psychological service, constitutes a problem. This is a difficult topic to resolve because, in construct theory terms, problems can only arise from a person's constructions of events. Let us say, quite simply, that there are events, and that individuals, from their construction systems, impose meanings, or constructions, on those events. When a person cannot make sense out of an event, *and feels that he should*, then he has a problem. The problem comes from the feeling that he ought to make sense, not from the event itself. Without that feeling there may be irritation, but not a problem. For example, a child fails to make the progress in school that a teacher expects. The teacher cannot understand why, but feels that he should. That teacher then has a problem. Alternatively, and typically, a teacher may construe a child as, for example, wanting to learn whereas the child has no such view of himself. His behaviour then becomes incomprehensible to the teacher, who in consequence may label him as 'lazy' or 'unmotivated'. If the teacher is satisfied with such a formulation, perhaps she does not have a problem. If she wants a cure for laziness then she has.

The personal construct psychologist therefore seeks to disentangle events from the constructions that people put on them in order to tease out precisely what the problem is. If we choose to see a person's actions as purposeful we may in fact go one step further and pose the question 'for what problem is this behaviour a solution?' But this is already a move towards problem resolution.

Clients

It follows from this argument that when a teacher refers a child, for whatever reason, the person with the problem is the teacher, and it is the teacher who is asking for help. The logic needs to be pressed even further. If things are proceeding relatively smoothly between teacher and child, no matter how little the child meets teacher's expectations, there will be no referral. It is at the point where a child's behaviour defeats the teacher's expectations that a problem arises and a referral might be made. When this is put the other way round – that a teacher's construct system cannot comprehend the child or his behaviour – it is clear that the teacher is the client.

This notion runs contrary to the popular view that the child is the psychologist's client, a view that at one time led to moves whereby educational psychologists should be subsumed under the label 'child psychologist'. Such thoughts take no account of the fact that a psychologist needs to be equally skilled in dealing with the teacher's problems that a referral reflects. To argue that the teacher is, at least in the first instance, the psychologist's client is not to deny that the referred child has problems, but I shall elaborate that later.

Teachers' problems

Returning to teachers and their problems, we have been able to recognize and categorize four types of teacher referral, and these hold whatever complaint is put forward as the basis for the referral. Sometimes the category can be inferred from the ways in which the referral is couched; at other times it needs to be elicited through subsequent questioning.

The first category reflects a failure in understanding a child and this failure represents a threat to the teacher's sense of knowingness about children. The request with this referral is for understanding.

The second category reflects a teacher's inability to make any difference to what a child does; the child continues not to learn, or continues with behaviour that is disturbing to the teacher. This relative inability is a challenge to the teacher's sense of competence and his request to the psychologist is to know how to act effectively.

With the third category, a teacher will speak 'with authority' that a child has 'special educational needs'. It is not this teacher's job to try to meet those needs because he has not been trained to do this. The child challenges the teacher's sense of who he is by making demands that the teacher considers inappropriate. The request here is for the child to be placed in some special provision.

Children referred in the fourth category are recognized by the teacher to have problems but that the present teacher can handle these in the here-and-now. The teacher is concerned about what will happen with the next teacher or the next school. Typically these referrals are made towards the end of a child's stay in a school and the teacher is asking for some guarantee that the child will have special considerations in the next school. By making a referral the teacher himself will not be held guilty of not taking action to have the problem dealt with. The referral represents an insurance policy.

Although I have identified four categories it is often more useful to look at any referral as carrying characteristics of more than one category. What follows is an instructive example. A teacher referred a child towards the end of the summer term of her last year in the junior school. The reason he gave was that some years earlier, in a different local authority, a psychologist had said that the girl was 'borderline' and should be followed up at six-monthly intervals. This had not been done but should be done now. When questioned further he said that although the girl could now read reasonably well she was impaired in her conceptual development and pointed to her inability to 'conserve length' and that she was not very good at 'numbers'. He claimed that he was not qualified to help the girl with handicaps such as these and that there should be some recognition in a formal statement that she had 'special educational needs'. My response to the referral was that at this point in her career there would be no action but that, should there be problems in the secondary school, action could be initiated from there. This decision, correct in its appraisal of the situation as it affected the child, was unsatisfactory since it did not recognize the teacher's problems, which underlay the referral. In fact he became quite angry, arguing that we were ignoring the referral (and of course the girl's 'needs'). Only when I recognized for myself that the referral was a combination of categories three and four ('it is not my job' and 'insurance policy') was I able to respond to the teacher in a way to deal with his annoyance. In effect this was to give him an assurance that the girl would not be 'lost' in a comprehensive school.

So far this discussion has been pitched at an interactive level. There is, however, a more profound way in which referrals are related to teachers' constructions, especially constructions of themselves.

It is a simple fact that any one teacher is unlikely to make more than a few referrals during his professional lifetime; he is quite likely, however, to grumble about many more children in the staffroom. When teachers do make a referral it is not usually the child who is worst behaved, the least mature, or the most chronic non-learner in the class. We are entitled to ask, therefore, what is so special that leads a teacher to refer an individual child.

Central to my argument is that the view the teacher has of herself will be based on peripheral and core constructs and these constructs are always open to invalidation. The invalidation of peripheral self-constructs will certainly lead to grumbles but the invalidation of core constructs is a much more serious affair. It seems to me that a referral of a child does in fact mean that a teacher's core constructs are being repeatedly invalidated by just that one child.

Two examples will illustrate the argument. A teacher referred an 8-year-old boy because of his continued failure to make progress in learning to read. She also described him as a boy who withdrew from contact with her, did not initiate communication and was generally distant. When I asked what, in her deepest sense of self, made her a teacher, she had to struggle for words and then said quite simply that she saw herself as a caring person. Having said that, she immediately recognized that it was the boy's distancing behaviour that upset her rather than the failure to learn to read. This was invalidating a core construction of herself. Significantly, a month later she said that she saw him now just as a remedial problem and that was something she could deal with.

The second case involves a teacher of a 9-year-old boy. His complaint was of the boy's impassivity and unpredictability both in terms of work and behaviour. My own interview with the boy confirmed the description of impassivity. The teacher said that even when he put on exaggerated behaviour in order to provoke a response, the boy remained unmoved. I asked the teacher what it was about the boy that got under his skin and his reply was that he saw himself as essentially good at making relationships with his pupils. This boy's lack of responsiveness and implicit denial of relationship, therefore, invalidated an essential construction that this teacher had of himself.

It follows from this analysis that personal construct psychology leads to an insistence on taking the teacher aspect of a referral very seriously. The psychologist needs not only to look where the teacher's finger points, but to the teacher behind the finger and the constructions which lie behind the teacher. In effect we ask of the teacher 'what is the problem for which this referral is a solution?' recognizing that behind the obvious answer – the complaint – there is an unverbalized (because it is unrecognized) answer that is personal to the teacher.

Children's behaviour

When a child is in school he is in a situation from which there is no escape. It is not of his choosing and it is a place where he is expected to meet the requirement of teachers that he should acquire skills and knowledge, become a social individual and progressively have control over the expression of negative feelings. The situation is essentially interactive and for this to run smoothly the child needs to have a reasonably comfortable sense of who he is. To some extent he is prepared for this by his parents who give him instructions as to how to behave, such as 'do as teacher says, be a good boy, work hard'. Out of all that he has heard about school (and the sometimes pious exhortations of his parents) and his own perceptions, the child makes some sense of school as a context in which he will spend much of the day. He will also develop simultaneously a construction of himself that will be an elaboration of the construction that has predominantly been shaped by the validations and invalidations of his family.

Just as a teacher's problems arise out of his constructions of himself and his situations, so too does a child's problems arise out of his constructions. Initially his sense of self will probably take some hard knocks from his social experiments with others and from his failure or success with the demands made by the teacher. In particular, there will be massive difficulties if the parents have created different and sometimes opposing identities for the child, leaving him in grave doubts as to which identity is appropriate in school. This, therefore, will be a ground for behaviour that is confusing both to this teacher and to other children. Alternatively, a child may be striving to refute the construction that his parents wish him to be, and if parents and school are congruent in their views, the child will then strive to refute the view of him that teachers naturally hold. Yet again, where family values are in opposition to those of a school, the child will be forced to go along with the parents in seeing the school as a hostile environment, or, if he sees the school as good, develop attitudes that are disloyal to this family. In either case, divided loyalties will lead to behaviour that is not easily understandable.

The ground for a child's problems is his constructions of himself and his circumstances, and the expression of those problems will be various, ranging from non-learning to disturbing behaviour, from self-isolation to excessive dependence on the esteem of his peer group. It is the exploration of these issues that provide a personal construct intervention with the child parallel to the enquiry with the teacher.

The aim of intervention

Stemming from the central proposition of personal construct psychology that an individual's construct system and constructions are at the heart of behaviour, the aim of intervention is simply to promote changes in that individual's construing. A referral from a teacher, therefore, calls for an exploration of that teacher's construction of the child, and of herself, in order to promote change. Interviewing a child in order to find out something of his construction of himself and his circumstances, and the communication of this to the teacher, provides a means whereby the teacher may change his constructions. At the simplest level a teacher who initially views the child with some hostility may, by being given a different construction, become sympathetic. The exploration of the child's constructions will, in fact, reveal something of the problems that underlie his actions. The problem will not be the one that the teacher has put forward. This dual exploration, of teacher and child, is already full of potential for change because it brings into the open undisclosed problems both in the teacher and in the child. At least when they are in the open, it may be possible to do something about them. Moreover, the exploration carried out in a non-judgmental way is frequently felt by the client as an experience of being understood, often for the first time.

I have described the need to interview both teacher and child. There is a further component. As I said earlier, the child is an extension of his family and carries their values and attitudes into school. The older he gets, the more he also carries his own feelings about them. Thus, to make an optimum sense out of the child's constructions, it is often necessary to interview the parents as well. In this way, we may learn something of their expectations of the child and of the school and the family construction systems that the child is living out. When this is carried out in the presence of the headteacher, the possibility arises of further modification of the headteacher's constructions, and consequently an improved understanding, of both child and family. In many ways, the joint interview with family, headteacher and psychologist, provides the most beneficial form of intervention.

An important aspect of the construct psychologist's intervention is to remind the client (teacher, child or parent) that the responsibility for change is theirs, not the psychologist's. It is the teacher who must find a way of maximizing her influence in promoting a child's educational growth. It is the child who has to master his learning in school. It is the parents' task to ease the child's load in school by finding better ways of understanding him and his dilemmas. It is the psychologist's responsibility to help each to achieve that end.

Questions and answers

The major, and perhaps the only, interviewing tool is the question. It is important, therefore, to elaborate principles whereby we may acquire a skill in questioning. Personal construct theory suggests a number of principles to promote this end, and in the process invites the psychologist to take very seriously the use of language – his own and that of his client.

The first principle is quite simply to go along with what the client says. The second principle is to be prepared to challenge what he says in the pursuit of meaning. These two principles imply an attitude of sceptical credulity in the interviewer. The third principle poses four questions, the answers to which lead to a clarification of what the client has to say. We need to ask:

- What does the client's answer deny?
- What does it further imply?
- What does the answer presuppose?
- What is the context within which the answer is valid?

The fourth principle takes care of the possibility of the client giving a pat answer by asking for a second and third.

The following dialogue illustrates some of these principles. All questions follow the first two principles. Question 1 uses the fourth. Questions 5, 6 and 7 all reflect the third. The dialogue is part of an interview with a 13-year-old boy:

Q. 1 Tell me three things about a boy who you respect or admire.
A. 1 He trusts his family and mates.
Q. 2 And the second?
A. 2 He shares things.
Q. 3 And the third?
A. 3 I don't know another.
Q. 4 You say 'He trusts his family and his mates.' How would you describe someone not like that?
A. 4 He doesn't trust anybody.
Q. 5 Is it important to trust family and mates?
A. 5 Yes.
Q. 6 Why is that?
A. 6 Then they will trust you.
Q. 7 Why is that important?
A. 7 It just is.
Q. 8 Is it important not to trust anybody?
A. 8 No!

In this dialogue what the final answer presupposes and the context within which it is valid were not taken up. They might have been taken up by asking what experiences led him to that belief and were there any situations in which he would give a different answer to that particular question.

A fifth principle requires that a client should respond to a precise question with an appropriate answer. Commonly a client will answer a question that was not put, giving a construction for an event or a diagnosis for a description. Not to take this up with a client leads to sloppy interviewing in which the interviewer and client do not come to grips with issues and this, in turn, reduces the chance of promoting change. The following is an example.

A teacher complained that a boy continued not to learn and whatever special help she offered made no difference. I asked her what specifically the boy did when she offered him help. Her reply was that he found it difficult to settle down. Unwittingly the teacher here gives a construct of events, not the events themselves. I pointed this out to her and asked again what the boy did. Her reply this time was very different. She said that he sharpened his pencil unnecessarily, he moved paper around, he went to sharpen other boys' pencils and generally declined to sit down and get on with the task in hand. I suggested to the teacher that an alternative way of understanding the boy's behaviour was to see him as deliberately avoiding the task. This construction, in the light of the teacher's overall knowledge of the boy made rather more sense to her than the one she had previously tendered and moreover led her to feel less guilty about her own relative failure with him.

The structured interview

With children the structured interview provides an efficient way of exploring their constructions. As a child lives in a variety of different contexts, and because problems arise out of his constructions, it is necessary to explore with him the sense he makes of himself and those contexts: himself and his family, himself and school, himself and other children, himself and his experiences, both in the outer world and within. The interviewer will need to sample some or all of these content areas, introduced, however, by an essential enquiry, namely, does he know why teachers are worried about him? Does he agree with their observations? Is he also worried? He needs to be told who is interviewing him and why. Without this preliminary enquiry the child will be at a loss to know how best to respond to questions and the psychologist will not know how to interpret his answers.

The process of interviewing is questioning and every question refers to some issue or event about which the psychologist is seeking the child's constructions. These referrals can be real people, such as his family, or pictorial representations of situations, such as school, or they can be himself and his experiences. Just as the referents to questions can be various, so can the mode of response. A child can be asked to give verbal answers, to demonstrate an action or to produce a drawing. The choice of referent, content area and mode of answering is part of the skill of the interviewer in weighing up what he judges will be both productive and within the child's communicational skills. Out of a number of interviewing techniques based on these parameters, I have chosen three to describe in detail, each of which I will illustrate with interview material.

'Who are you?' (WAY)

This technique represents a very direct request to a child to say who he is. The invitation is made along the following lines: 'I would like to know who you are. If I were to ask you to say three things to describe you, what would you say? Who are you?'

When these answers have been given the child is asked to elaborate each by saying what is special or important about them. A further elaboration can then be achieved by asking for the opposite of each of these responses.

The technique was used at the beginning of an interview with Timothy, a 12-year-old boy who had twice been found unconscious after sniffing an aerosol. Only the first of his descriptions is given because of the dramatic revelation that it produced. This self-description was, quite simply, 'myself'. His threefold elaboration of this was:

* 'I'm human', the opposite to which was 'dead'.
* 'I can move my body about' the opposite to which was 'can't move'.
* 'I can move my arms and legs about' the opposite to which was 'still'.

I then asked Timothy to describe the sequence of events involved in aerosol sniffing. He said 'You sniff, your head goes buzzy, you get lifted off your feet, you fall down unconscious.' He was rather shaken when I pointed out to him that the end product of sniffing was, in his own words, tantamount to a denial of himself. (Later in the interview he said, in fact, that at that time he wished he was dead!).

The family interaction matrix

This technique focuses on family interactions using as a construct the two polarities 'easy and difficult to get on with'. It draws on the fact that the child has lived many years with his family and by now knows fairly well the ease and difficulty with which members get on with each other. He is reminded of this and then asked to say with whom each member finds it easy and difficult to get on well. The child's answers are entered into a matrix that is drawn up and explained to him as part of the interviewing process. When the family has five members the child is asked for two choices for 'easy to get on well with' and one choice for 'difficult to get on well with'. With larger families, two choices are invited for each polarity. The child's spontaneous answers are also recorded. The technique is not useful for smaller families. The matrix can be analysed immediately by studying the *reciprocal* connections between pairs of members and drawing them graphically. The technique is illustrated here by a matrix produced in an interview with a girl of whom the mother complained that she had made progress with reading up to two years ago but had made no progress since then. Assessment of her reading attainment supported this complaint. In a family drawing she had omitted to include herself but had created her 2-year-old brother as a miniature version of her father.

The interaction matrix (Table 12.1) and its graphical representation (Figure 12.1) suggests that she has a neutral relationship with her parents and is in a state of misunderstanding with her brother and older sister. Moreover, the girl's judgements place her brother in a position of some influence in his family as she sees him as difficult to get on well with for both his parents. If her judgement is less on objective grounds but more a reflection of her feelings about him, then it is not an unreasonable inference to see her cessation of learning as coincidental with his arrival and growth.

Table 12.1: Family interaction matrix for Jo

		M	F	S	B	Jo
Mother	M		+	+	−	
Father	F	+		+	−	
Sister	S	+			+	−
Brother	B	−	+			+
	Jo		+	+	−	

+ 'Finds it easy to get on well with'
− 'Finds it difficult to get on well with'

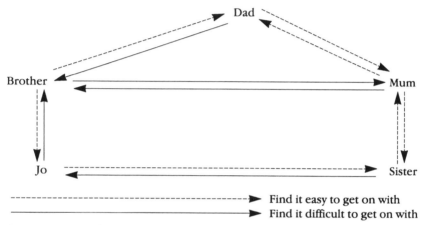

Figure 12.1: Graphical representation for Jo's matrix of reciprocal interaction

Personal troubles

The content area for this technique concerns times when a child feels troubled or upset. Drawings form the mode of response. A sheet of paper is folded into six compartments. The child is reminded that everyone has times when he feels troubled or upset and is asked to draw five pictures to show times when he felt that way. When he has completed that, or drawn as many situations as he can, he is asked to draw in the sixth space a situation when, by contrast, he felt good.

After the drawings have been completed he is asked what is happening in each situation and what his feeling would be. The next question is to ask him to say three things about a boy who would not be upset in those situations, followed by 'what would upset such a boy?' The final question brings the child back into the situation by my asking when in fact he has been this boy who would not be upset.

In this way the child produces both the view of himself with which he feels relatively comfortable but also the alternative view, which is its polar opposite.

As one example, I include Brian's response to the technique. Brian is 12 years old and is in temporary care because of persistent school refusal. At the beginning of the interview he strongly asserted that there was nothing wrong with him. He gave a free description of his family where everyone got on well with everyone else except father, who lived elsewhere. On the other hand he produced a free drawing which was of Frankenstein, which he agreed was a person with no feeling, and a contrasting picture of a girl who he said would have feeling.

With the personal troubles technique he chose to interpret the word 'would' in the instructions as pure imagination by denying any possibility that he might commit any of them.

His drawings were:

* Taking money from his mum's bag. He would feel bad after it.
* Nicking someone's bike.
* Ripping a chair in a house with an axe.
* Mugging an old lady.
* Picking on a little boy – spitting.

The contrast picture was:

* Playing for Arsenal and scoring a goal.

Even though these situations are imaginary they could actually be committed by an individual. He was asked, therefore, to say three things about a boy who would not be upset in those situations. The responses he gave were:

* He has no feelings (cf. his drawing of Frankenstein).
* His mum doesn't care about him (cf. cosy description of his family).
* He doesn't worry about anything he does (cf. his assertion at the beginning of the interview that there was nothing wrong with him).

The boy thus described would himself be upset if someone took something from him but he was unable to say when he had himself been this boy.

The technique, therefore, despite Brian's distancing himself from his own answers, seems to have produced responses that are of a piece with the rest of the interview and which suggest aspects of himself which he would like to ignore.

Two illustrative cases

I shall now illustrate some of these matters with edited material from two cases. In the first case, change is promoted through discussions with the teachers and an interview with the girl's mother. The method of interviewing is conversational but at the back of the interview is the question 'what constructs of the mother will the material exemplify?' In the second case, a boy is invited to take stock of himself by means of generating a formal structured interview, which includes the 'who are you?' technique and a 'self-description grid'.

Case 1

Sasha is a 12-year-old girl attending a school for children with physical handicaps. She has considerable problems of speech, hearing and mobility. She had attended the school from the age of 5 years but, for a variety of reasons, the family had moved away. Sasha returned to the school some months before the referral. The staff were very worried about her and had been given advice from a number of professional workers who served the school. Their reports only added to the confusion so that the teachers were at a loss as to how to help this pupil. I was asked to carry out with them a review.

Interview with the teachers

I met the headteacher, the deputy head and the class teacher and asked them what it was about Sasha that troubled them. Each time I put the question they described the girl's history, which involved not only moves to many schools but also to a different country. Alternatively they talked about the girl's mother. They described how, when the girl first attended the school, the mother always brought her dressed more like a doll than a child. She had extravagant claims about what the child would do, and represented herself as a *'grand dame'*! At this point, I asked the class teacher to say the three things that best described Sasha. After a long pause, all she could say was that the girl was isolated. I then turned to the deputy head who was equally at a loss but then said that she was a very different girl from the one who had previously attended the school. When I asked the three ways in which she was now different, I was given the answers 'then she was eager to initiate communication', 'then she enjoyed coming to school', and 'then she enjoyed school activities'. By implication, therefore, the girl's attitude represents a deterioration. A deterioration of performance based on known physical conditions was something they were accustomed to and, therefore, could understand. A deterioration of attitude without such an explanation was something with which they were not so familiar. The problem, which they were unable to articulate, arose out of failure to put a meaningful construction on the girl's change of attitude. The change was the enigma, not the behaviour.

It seemed to me that the 'non-description' given by the deputy head, together with the teacher's feeling that Sasha was isolated, was consistent with the girl behaving as though she no longer felt able to make any meaningful impact on her life situation. In order to communicate this construction the teachers were invited to imagine how Sasha might experience the constant moves to which she had been subjected. These were listed in sequence and set in the context of her handicaps. The teachers were then able to recognize the validity of such a construction and realized that their first task was to recognize and validate any initiatives that Sasha might make. Out of such validations she might become aware that she could be effective in promoting her own interests.

It became obvious that for me to interview Sasha could serve no useful purpose and might, to the contrary, merely add further conflicting information. It would be more to the point for me to attempt a further understanding of the situation in the context of what Sasha's mother might say. My next step was, therefore, to interview Mrs. P. (Sasha's mother).

Interview with Mrs P

Mrs P was interviewed in the presence of the deputy head teacher who had known her since Sasha was 5 years old. Although we were agreed that we were meeting because of a concern for Sasha's education, my own purpose was to listen carefully to Mrs P's construction of her life experiences in order to sense the polarities that gave them meaning. Right at the outset she said that *she would be frank*, a statement that did not take on full significance until after the interview had been concluded. In response to my questions she gave a full account of her background and her experiences. She was a Kenyan Asian married to a Punjabi Muslim, a matter of some importance since there were considerable religious and cultural differences that would not readily be recognized by the outsider. Her first employment had been as a cosmetic skin specialist. Her husband had trained as a lawyer but only did two or three days' work at a time. This was a cause of friction since it meant that she was effectively the financial mainstay of the family. Eventually, after a number of moves and financial ventures, they went to the Punjab with the husband and this only made matters worse. She then returned with her two children to England leaving her husband behind. Despite these marital problems she still argued that he was a good father and that she would willingly be the breadwinner even if it meant that he did the housework at home. The handicapped daughter's birth was medically traumatic and mother did not see her for 10 days whilst she was in intensive care. The father had then described the daughter as like a doll.

At the end of the interview the construction was put that the girl and the mother had much in common in relation to the various uprootings but whereas Mrs P had an adult range of resources, and could act in her own interests, Sasha had very few resources. Almost the mother might say to herself 'there but for the grace of God go I'. Mrs. P. was grateful for the interview, especially that she had been able to talk about her daughter. When I suggested that a tape recording of the interview might indicate that she had talked about herself she smiled and concurred.

The sequel

Reflection on the interview suggested that a construction that integrated much of the interview would recognize that it was crucially important for the mother to *put a good face on things*. This made sense of her early work as a cosmetician, the way she had presented her daughter in school, her own expectations of her daughter, her defence of her husband and perhaps her membership of a minority race in Kenya. If that represented one pole of an important construct she had already given its opposite when she had said that *she would be frank*, since to be frank means revealing the worst face. It was then significant that Mrs P turned up at the interview without make-up, something that had never happened before. A communication of this understanding to the school gave immediate relief for the anxiety generated by their inability to understand. Moreover, with considerable insight, they saw that a further way to promote positive change was by using the mother's knowledge of cosmetics for the benefit of the older children. Subsequent reports show that this has in fact happened. Sasha is now much more relaxed and is learning Makaton sign language quickly and creatively and the teachers feel more than competent in meeting her special educational needs.

Case 2

Whereas the interviews in Case 1 were basically conversational, the interview for Case 2 used two highly structured techniques, namely 'who are you?' and a 'self-description grid'. As will be seen, the interview ran into a hiatus early on but it was possible to turn this to good use.

Peter, a 14-year-old, presented problems to the school. These were a failure to present adequate work, but more importantly that he seemed to set up the world of his peer group against him. This led to behaviour in school that was disturbing to his teachers as well as the other boys. There had been a preliminary meeting between parents, Peter and the teacher who was the head of year. Whilst not giving the details of the interview, it can be said that Peter was an only child since the others had all died very young or as miscarriages. He was, therefore, somewhat special in his parents' eyes. The interview with Peter was intended to be the next, and hopefully the last, step in dealing with the case. The detail of the interview would be shared with the head of year in order to help her reconstrue Peter and the problems.

The interview with Peter

The aim of the interview was, quite specifically, to help Peter construct the different versions of himself as he thought he appeared in other people's eyes. In the process, he is of necessity involved in developing a construction himself.

Peter conceded that the teachers were worried about him because his 'work was suffering' and his behaviour was 'not good sometimes'. At home he felt that he was being 'pushed aside'. His elaboration of this was that other boys 'took the mickey' out of him when he could not discuss late night films on the TV with them because he had to go to bed at eight o'clock. They said he was a mother's boy. I then explained that the purpose of the interview was to help him work out who he was because this might help him disentangle his problems. I then moved into the WAY technique. 'If I were to ask you who you are what three things would you say?' Peter gave his name and then said 'I don't know what else I would say'. I recorded this as his second description adding that perhaps when we got to the end of the interview he would be in a better position to say who he was. This was the hiatus but it gave point to the decision to use a self-description grid. Its constructive use was to relocate the WAY enquiry to the end of the interview in order to see what difference the intervening part might make.

The self-description grid requires three stages: construct elicitation, completing the grid and joint analysis. In order to elicit constructs out of which he would describe himself, he was invited to give three descriptions each for two boys who were his friends, one boy he disliked and one boy he admired but did not know very well. In the event he would say nothing about a disliked boy. After he had completed this task he was taken in turn through each description in order to find its opposite. This is a procedure for eliciting constructs. His responses are those listed below. He produced nine constructs altogether but one was considered of less importance than the others and was omitted. The final eight were:

- good friends to his friends – can be quite nasty
- asks 'what's wrong, are you all right?' – doesn't pay any interest in who you are
- has lots of ideas – boring
- doesn't hang around all the time – bit of a nuisance, he's always there
- not too caring – doesn't care at all
- never ignores his friends – never says hello when they talk to him
- always talks to you even though he doesn't know you well – would say 'go away, I don't know you'
- would sponsor you even though he didn't know you very well – will deny the smallest request for help.

The aim of the self-description grid is to obtain from an individual the ways in which he thinks different people will judge him on a number of constructs. The judgement is given on a linear eleven-point scale.

When this technique was used with Peter, he was asked how the following people would see him: his mother and father, teachers he liked and disliked, boys he liked and disliked, girls, and last of all how would he see himself. These are represented in Table 12.2 respectively by M, F, T(L), T(D), B(L), B(D), G and S.

The analysis of the grid was carried out by simply drawing Peter's attention to his responses. He recognized that the values 5, 6 and 7 represented a neutral zone of non-entity between polarities. He was asked to draw the boundaries of this zone and observe for himself where most of his entries lay. A count shows that 52 lie in the neutral zone and 12 outside, 11 of which were given by people he did not like. Thus his assessment of himself was essentially that of a non-person.

In order to turn this material to advantage he was asked to locate in the grid the profile of himself when he was being a 'pain in the neck' and, by contrast, the profile of what he thought would be his parents' ideal. These two profiles are shown by the letters P and X respectively. Both now fall outside the neutral zone and are almost diametrically opposite to each other. Peter could see this for himself and conceded that he did indeed have a problem as to who he was. In fact, by becoming a 'pain in the neck' he ceases to be a non-person, but the alternative, to be the parents' ideal, could hardly be seen as acceptable as he was already judged by his peer group as 'mother's boy'.

It was now possible to return to the abandoned 'Who are you?' enquiry in order to see how his responses might change. This time he is able to give three descriptions and these appear below:

1. My name is Peter . . . with the elaboration:

• You've got a name.
• If people want you they call you by name, not 'here you'.
• If someone sends you a letter named Mr Blank, you wouldn't know who the letter was for.

2. Even though I don't know a person I can talk to him . . . with the elaboration:

• You can make new friends.
• You can find out more about a person.
• You can build up friendships all the time, not just give a greeting.

3. I would try to help people if they needed help . . . with this elaboration:

Table 12.2: Peter's self-description grid

1 Good friend to his friends	1	2	3	4	5	6	7	8	9	10	11	Can get quite nasty
			X		B(L)	S M D	T(L) G	B(D) T(D)		P		

2 Asks what's wrong, are you all right	1	2	3	4	5	6	7	8	9	10	11	Doesn't pay any interest in how you are
				P	D M	S B(L) T(L)	T(D) G	B(D)	X			

3 Has lots of ideas	1	2	3	4	5	6	7	8	9	10	11	Boring
				X	B(L)	S M	T(L) G T(D)	B(D)			P	

4 Doesn't hang around friends all the time	1	2	3	4	5	6	7	8	9	10	11	Bit of a nuisance, always there
			X		G	B(L) M T(L)	S D	B(D) T(D)	P			

5 Not too caring	1	2	3	4	5	6	7	8	9	10	11	Doesn't care at all
				X	B(L) M D	T(L) S	G	B(D)	T(D)	P		

6 Never ignores his friends	1	2	3	4	5	6	7	8	9	10	11	Never says 'Hello' even when they talk to him
				P X	B(L) M	S D	T(L) G	B(D) T(D)				

7 Always talks to you even though he doesn't know you well	1	2	3	4	5	6	7	8	9	10	11	Would say 'Go away, I don't know you'
				X	M D	B(L) T(L) S	G T(D)	B(D)		P		

8 Would sponsor you even though he didn't know you	1	2	3	4	5	6	7	8	9	10	11	Will turn down the smallest request for help
			X	T(L)	M B(L)	S D G	T(D) B(D)	P				

- Say a friend says 'will you help me with my homework or else I'll be in detention and my mum says I must get home early?' then I would help him.
- Someone cuts his knee. I would help by taking him home.
- Someone lost his keys. I'd help find them to get in.

These answers confirm that positive relationships with other boys are important. It is clear, however, that instead of giving a description of himself he has written a prescription for what he might be, and moreover, outlined concrete situations where this might be exemplified. To end the interview, I pointed this out to him and said that perhaps it would not be long before he would become this boy.

The sequel

I discussed the contents of the interview with the head of year who quickly grasped the essence of what Peter had said. She was a teacher of considerable acumen and when a boy was newly admitted to the school (described by his previous school as 'wet') she recognized that this presented a ready made experimental situation for Peter to work out in real life the implications of what happened in the interview with me. She asked him, therefore, to be responsible for helping the new boy become established in school. So far things seem to have gone well.

By way of a conclusion, six hard won lessons

- Any intervention to assess is at the same time an opportunity to promote change. The first interview, and it may be the only one, should therefore always be seen as an occasion for potential reconstruction.
- Language is the medium through which constructions are communicated. It is, therefore, a bridge. But language also comes between the experiencing of events and its communication. It may, therefore, be a barrier to the communication of that experience. It is the fact that a person has a problem that provides an authorization for a psychologist to challenge and explore his client's language and its referents.
- Just as problems in chemistry and physics may be resolved without necessarily isolating molecules and atoms, so may human problems be resolved without necessarily isolating a client's constructs, which are the units behind his constructions. Thus it is frequently more appropriate to look for the client's constructions and let his constructs look after themselves.
- In a free association test it is highly probable that the name Kelly would be linked as much with grids as with personal construct theory. Nonetheless, the grid is but one way in which a client's realities may be explored. For many problems, especially with children, there are other productive ways of exploring their constructions.

- Personal construct psychology does not bar the use of any technique from an interview – even psychometric tests – because it regards techniques as providing events to which a child is asked to respond. The immediacy of a child's behaviour then becomes an event for the psychologist to construe. He will seek an understanding out of the raw material that the child produces before his eyes.
- Finally, personal construct psychology is for the benefit of the psychologist as a means of helping him make sense of his task. It does not necessarily benefit the client. That a client fits neatly into the theory must be considered a bonus rather than a requirement.

Chapter 13
Personal construct psychology and the assessment of young people: the 'one-off' interview (1988)

I was invited to contribute to a conference on PCT, Deviance and Social Work. *This paper is a reconstruction of my talk, the contents of which arose out of my involvement with the local authority remand home. As of necessity, my involvement with a young person in that context was in a single 'one-off' interview and such interviews, therefore, provided the theme for my contribution.*

Context of the 'one-off' interview

The context for the thinking and work reported in this paper was a regional assessment centre for boys, which also included a secure unit. My part was that of the psychologist (educational by denotation but personal construct by persuasion and practice) in a multidisciplinary team that included a child psychiatrist, field social workers and the resident care and teaching staff.

The purpose of assessment in such settings is to help in the making of recommendations for action in respect of the young persons being assessed, not all of whom had committed acts of 'delinquency'. Therein lay something of an issue for those whose task was to assess. For children who had been placed in the centre as a result of 'voluntary reception into care' assessment might well be academic because there could be no guarantee that any recommendation would be implemented. For children who had been placed on a full 'care order' there were severe restraints on the extent to which the team's recommendations for the young person could be carried out because of the lack of matching resources for the young person's putative needs. Young persons in the secure unit were usually held there for the preparation of reports for the court. In this instance, I did not see myself as filling that role because I had no professional relationship with the legal system. I therefore made it clear that my assessment was to help the staff, both field staff and residential, in their understanding of the young person, but also, as will be seen later, potentially for the benefit of the young person himself.

Given these circumstances, the question arose as to how a personal construct psychologist might play a useful part in an assessment procedure where the involvement was extremely transitory and the practical outcomes doubtful.

The essential point about the 'one-off' interview is that it will happen only once. This is in contrast with the ongoing nature of therapeutic counselling or supportive interviews, where there is continuity from one interview to the next, there is a tacit or overt concession that the young person has a problem, and there is time to let the client take the lead with minimum intervention from the interviewer. Consequently the 'one-off' interview needs to have a structure, a beginning, a middle and an end, in order to promote the meaningfulness of the event for the young person but also to maximize the efficient use of time.

The young person is not an 'object' to be weighed and measured against some psychometric yardstick or theoretical model. He is a live human being, operating his own personality theory, having thoughts, feelings and strivings, and living in interaction with his environment, and this includes the residential setting in which he currently finds himself. The very act of placement for assessment in such a setting is, in fact, already an intervention that, for better or worse, he will reject as meaningless, or that he will strive to interpret. Inevitably this experience will in some ways be incorporated into his future expectations of life and himself, just as his present placement will, to an extent, have arisen within the context of his past experiences.

In the light of this, the solution to the question of what role a construct psychologist might play lay in shaping the assessment interview as an occasion that young persons might be able to use for their own growth. The material from such an interview might then be helpful to other professionals in the understanding of the young person. Such an approach, therefore, very much determines the content of the interview. It will be an exploration of some of the ways in which the young person makes sense of himself and his circumstances. As a consequence, because this involves the young person taking a close look at himself, it will also, paradoxically, be a form of personal self-assessment.

Personal construct psychology and assessment

I propose to outline just four issues that stem directly or indirectly from personal construct psychology in order to illuminate the practice of the 'one-off' interview.

Firstly, it is a central tenet of the theory that what people do is, amongst other things, very much a matter of how they make sense of themselves and their circumstances. In abstract terms, this is their *construction* of themselves and the world. The world in this context is the subjective world of personal action, interaction and experience, not the phenomenal, the objective world, the study of which falls into the realms of formal education. (This boundary is drawn for convenience only because there will always be subjective knowing and experiencing of this phenomenal world.)

Secondly, a sense of self is crucial in an individual's encounters with life because people usually have a fairly clear notion of those actions and attitudes of which they would say 'that just is not me'. This sense of self includes, at varying levels of awareness, consciousness of one's own thoughts, feelings (with their physical substrates), striving and actions, real and imagined. It includes core and peripheral notions of 'Who I am' the invalidation of which can cause the individual to suffer respectively serious psychological distress or minor irritation. This issue is extremely relevant in interpersonal relations because when individuals miscon-strue each other there are likely to be failures in communication leading to massive misunderstandings and, in turn, covert, if not overt, hostility. This is especially likely to be true in the specific context of 'deviant' young persons and the professional workers with whom they are involved.

Thirdly, and at a practical level, the theory is profoundly concerned with meaning. What is the personal sense that a person makes of 'events'? What are his or her constructions? There are, however, practical difficulties here. The theory, at a highly abstract level, deals with *constructs* and *construct systems*. It is an essential feature of the theory that constructs are *two*-ended and are based on similarities *and* contrasts. A descriptive assertion requires for its amplification some statement of what that assertion also denies, i.e. its contrast, and the search for these personal contrasts is an important part of interviewing. The following example points to the practical importance of this.

A group of psychologists agreed that 'aggressive' would be an attribute they would all be comfortable to use when describing people. When I asked them to write down their personal contrast with 'aggres-sive' and share this with each other they were surprised at how little agreement there was between them. It follows that for each, therefore, over and above some commonality of meaning, their personal use of the word 'aggressive' also probably had varying connotations.

There is, however, the further danger of failing to recognize that the *communication* of constructs is usually through words and then to assume that the elicitation of these words ends the task. But the words are merely verbal markers, they are not the constructs themselves and may well have powerful feeling and experiential overtones. By way of an analogy, a buoy at sea may indicate underwater hazards or sunken treasure but is itself neither the hazard, nor the treasure. The implication follows that the pursuit of an individual's *personal,* as opposed to his purely *verbal* constructs, should not rest with the superficial elicitation of words but should include some exploration of what those words imply.

The fourth issue drawn from theory is the principle of *constructive alternativism,* which means, quite simply, that there is always at least one other way of seeing things. The value of this principle is that it provides an aim for the assessment interview. Can a young person come to some alternative sense of himself and his circumstances, thereby creating the possibility of freeing himself, at some point in the future, of the burden of those past constructions out of which his actions have arisen? At the same time the corollary also obtains: might it be possible that the other professionals who are involved may also see the young person in a different light in their ongoing dealings with him?

These theoretical considerations now provide a logic and a purpose for the 'one-off' assessment interview.

Strategy of the interview

It may be a statement of the obvious, but it is worth restating that the basic tool in the interview is the question. To quote Kelly 'A *pat answer is the enemy to a fresh question*' but the inverse also applies: 'A *pat question is the enemy to a fresh answer.*' 'Patness' here includes superficiality, of-the-cuff answers and perhaps triviality. Pat responses have their place in casual social encounters but in a 'formal' interview may serve as a defence against revealing what is personal whilst at the same time, under a cloak of seeming conformity, they may implicitly deny a commitment to the situation.

The value of the question is that, at its most effective, it sets off those internal thought and feeling processes that are the beginnings of personal self-assessment. Hence the importance of choosing questions that are likely to be effective towards the end. If the value of the question lies in its search-promoting quality, the content of the question directs the attention to where the search needs to be made.

It is certainly true that questions about external events have their place and may be very revealing in an indirect way about how a person sees him/herself. Nonetheless, where the aim of the interview is self-assessment there is a strong case for asking directly how the young person sees himself or herself. 'Self-description', then, in a variety of ways of asking, forms an important part of the assessment interview.

As indicated above, responses can be given either at a seemingly superficial level or at a meaningful personal level and a personal construct approach is very much concerned to elicit the latter. In order to achieve this, questions need to be posed that are a challenge to the superficial response. A number of interviewing techniques are available to this end and, out of their use, the interview acquires a structure and a meaningful shape. The first of these is to ask not for one answer to a question but for three. The effect of this is quite interesting. It recognizes the possibility of more than one answer to the question, which may be a relief for the interviewee in not having to find the 'right' one. At the same time it is an effective challenge to the pat answer, usually the first that is given, but requiring a search for the second and third. Experience shows that not infrequently finding the third answer proves to be very difficult, thereby fulfilling the purpose of the question in promoting an inner search.

The second technique, and this was pointed to earlier, is to ask for a contrast to what has been said: *'How would you describe a person not like that?' 'What sort of situation would be the opposite of the one you have described?' 'You say that is important to you. How would you describe someone who says it is not important?'* It is a further benefit that the two answers, the overt description and the elicited contrast, afford the opportunity of asking what it is that holds the two ends together. As an example 'friendly–cool' may reflect a concern about warmth in personal relationships whereas 'friendly–unhelpful' may have, as an underlying dimension, co-operative helpfulness. This dimension itself then provides an opportunity for further exploration. The third technique is to ask for the importance or relevance of an observation in the life of the interviewee and then to pursue that to more and more fundamental levels. The basic question is *'is that important to you?'* followed by *'and that?'* . . . *'and that?'* The use of a subsequent non-motivational *'how come?'* then aims to find some of the experiential bases for these answers.

Each of these is intended to serve the purpose of leading to some clarification of the ways an individual makes sense of things. To put into words what has been hidden, or ill formulated, or half-sensed, is to allow a degree of self-understanding and, therefore, also a self-direction that was not previously possible. This can sometimes further be achieved by putting forward for acceptance or rejection constructive hypotheses that attempt to link meaningfully some of the material that the interview has brought forth. These are not necessarily alternative constructions, although they may be, but they provide a view of how things seem to be and this may be a starting point for a young person to offer a different presentation of self to the outside world.

From an assessment point of view, the sharing of the information in the interview with the other professionals makes possible their altered constructions of the young person. This, in turn, may lead to them communicating with him in ways that respect rather than ignore or invalidate his sense of self.

An illustrative case

A verbal account can never do justice to what happens in an interview.
What follows is material from the two major explorations of which the
interview comprised. Its presentation is primarily to demonstrate the
strategy and some of the techniques already described.

Background

John was 14. He had been 'in care' since the age of 6 years and was now
in the secure unit at the assessment centre. He had been a chronic
'runner': from children's homes, from schools, from open assessment
centres. When he was on the run he tended to gravitate to where he
thought his mother was living but her address was not known. On the
last occasion of running, he was thought to have been involved in a
incident of 'buggery' with another boy, but the evidence was unclear so
no criminal proceedings were instituted. It was considered, however,
that for his own protection, and in order to make plans for the future,
John needed to be in a place from which he could not run, hence the
secure unit.

His family background was somewhat complex. His mother had
been a pupil at a special school for children who could not easily make
educational progress and was remembered by her previous teacher
because she suffered from 'tunnel vision'. John also had the same
handicap, for which he had special glasses. There were doubts as to
who his father was and the social environment showed few clear-cut
family boundaries.

He had attended a special school for pupils whose behaviour was
disturbing to others. The headteacher there had said that he was like
none of her others pupils: it was not possible to communicate with him,
he was immature and when he was in a mood he had said 'the Devil
takes me over'. (This information only became available after the interview.)

The interview

The resident care worker introduced me to John and I interviewed him
in his room. I asked him if he knew why I was interviewing him and he
replied vaguely 'for assessment' but did not know what that meant. I
explained that the official purpose of assessment was for professional
workers to plan what should happen for a young person, and then went
on:

> I am not very good at knowing what ought to happen but I am sometimes
> able to help a young person to take a look at himself. My questions are like a
> mirror to see yourself in, or perhaps like your special glasses, which help you
> to have a wider view of things.

This introduction makes clear the purpose of the interview, and in the special case of John uses the reality of his visual handicap as an explanatory metaphor.

The interview involved the use of two techniques, one verbal, called 'who are you?' and one through drawings ('a picture and its opposite'). The content of each, however, was the same – John's sense of self. In presenting the material the nature of the interviewing techniques will progressively unfold. The dialogue represents a rather simplified reconstruction of what happened. 'I' stands for myself as interview, 'J' stands for John.

'Who are you?'

This is a direct questioning in which the young person is invited to define just who he is prepared to say he is.

    I. *I would like to know who you are. If I were to ask you 'who are you?' what three things would you say?*
    J. *Name, age, date of birth.*

John has given a formula but he has not answered the question. I point this out and then:

    I. *So what is your name, what is your age, what is your address?*
    J. *I am J . . . E . . . P . . . I'm 14. But my mother's moved, I don't know where she is.*
    I. *Is it important to say you are J . . . E . . . P . . .?*
    J. *I don't know.*
    I. *I am thinking of a different boy who says that his name is not important, how would you describe a boy like that?*

This is the use of a contrast 'John himself, who say he doesn't know,' and a 'different boy, who does know' but denies its importance.

    J. *It's silly, it's important to know your name.*

The challenge of using a contrast has been effective in leading John to concede and answer that he had either declined or had not clarified.

    I. *Why is it important?*
    J. *It deals with your whole future.*
    I. *Why is that important?*
    J. *You earn money to live, you have to get a job.*

As this is a concern with the future, can we now use as a further contrast someone who refers to the past?

I. *A different boy said it was important because you could know your past.
    What would you say about that?*
J. *The past and future is the same thing.*

(Sadly my recording of further exploration of this is lost because of indecipherable handwriting.)

We now turn to the second description.

I. *You say you are 14. Is that important?*
J. *Yes.*
I. *Why is that?*
J. *You learn more about life than when you are 10 or 9.*
I. *A different boy said it was important because 'you don't have to be young any more'. What do you make of that?*
J. *Yes. As you get older you have more responsibility.*
I. *How come?*
J. *You drop your mother's vase when you are 9 or 10 and you sit on your bed for a week. When you are 14 you say you are sorry.*

Next, his address:

I. *Is your address important?*
J. *Yes: people have to know where you live.*
I. *Why is that?*
J. *If you have a job, they put wages to you in the post.*

Underlying all of these responses is the polarity 'past–future', hence we need to explore some of its implications.

I. *What's special about the future?*
J. *It will affect your whole life.*
I. *Yes?*
J. *I will feel better like the past.*
I. *What's special about the past?*
J. *You get older, you get away from it.*
I. *Just like running away?*

In all of these interchanges, although John has used the dimension *past–future* he has given no unequivocal judgement about whether or not they have been 'good' or 'bad'. Moreover he has denied the difference between them by saying they are the same. A similar hiatus appears in relation to space: his address is important *(for the future)*, it is where his mother is, he does not know where his mother is. One is tempted to pose the nonsense question 'for John, where is now?'

A picture and its opposite

The use of drawings is sometimes a relief from intensive verbal exploration but it also provides a way of opening up areas of personal knowledge that are not available at high levels of awareness. In this particular technique I draw a line, bent at one end, in the middle of a sheet of paper and then give the following instruction:

> *I would like you to draw for me a picture, and if you do, it will probably say something about yourself that you had not been aware of. Will you turn this line into a picture?*

John turned the line into a house in which my line was used to make the roof. He then added a heavily shaded fence or palisade round the house but in front of the door drew a path, and on the path a mat with 'WELCOME' printed on it. He then carefully drew, and counted, six flowers. Although the palisade and the 'WELCOME' suggested conflicting messages I did not know what the picture meant. Consequently I said:

> *I do not know what your picture means. Will you look at it carefully and then draw me another picture that you feel is the opposite?*

This time he repeated the house from the previous drawing but encircled it with a 'balloon' emanating from the head of the figure of a man.

John said that the first picture represented *'Future – he went to a house he had dreamed of in the past'*. The second picture represented *'Past – the person was dreaming of a house he was living in the future'*.

The drawings were executed with a level of skill more appropriate to a much younger person, which is not, however, to say that this was necessarily the limit of his ability. It is a matter of rather more than speculation that the skill level shown by young persons in this content frequently reflects the age at which they went through some rather negative experiences. To test this I told John of a school where drawings were highly valued. The drawings of 5 to 7-year-old children were hung on one wall, those from 7 to 11-year-old children on a different wall and drawings of 11 to 16-year-olds on yet another wall. I then asked him to show where a skilled teacher would put his drawings. He immediately said with the 6 year-olds (c.f. the carefully drawn and counted six flowers). Then:

> I. *Tell me, John, what happened when you were 6?*
> J. *I went into care.*
> I. *Did you know why?*
> J. *No, and my mum didn't know.*

(In reality early reports suggested that he had been abused, probably sexually.)

In some ways these pictures seem to represent riddles about 'living' and 'dreaming', 'past' and 'future', and it would be easy to lose oneself in trying to disentangle unambiguous meanings out of the verbal markers that accompany them. They are reminiscent of the infinite regress when a mirror is reflected in another mirror, and where the addition of yet another mirror adds nothing new to what is reflected but a reflection of itself. In this context it is perhaps worth recalling the metaphor with which I opened the interview. Rather than risk further confusion it seemed a better option to offer some constructive hypotheses for John to accept, modify or reject, but that might clarify some of the underlying issues behind his responses. The important point here is not that the interviewer has to be 'right' but that he puts forward a way of seeing things that John might find useful.

Each of the following statements, then, is a constructive hypothesis about how I see John, based on the things that he himself has said.

I. *John is the kind of boy who finds the past too painful to talk about. Am I right or wrong. If I'm wrong what should I have said?*
J. *I don't know.*
I. *John is the kind of boy who looks to the past and thinks that something good was taken away from him. Am I right or wrong? If I'm wrong change it.*
J. *Right.*
I. *Before he was 6?*
J. *Yes.*
I. *His running away is like trying to find that good thing that was taken away from him.*
J. *Yes.*
I. *But he does not think now that he will find it.*
J. *Yes.*
I. *So growing up he will have to learn to make his own happiness.*
J. *Yes.*

If these hypotheses give a tentative view of John in the present, that view is about the one certainty that John's drawings implicitly ignore – the 'present' itself. Since he had already said that 'past' and 'future' were the same thing it might be useful to treat them as a unity and ask John for a contrast by now drawing a picture to represent the 'present'. Such a request would provide a fitting final task in the interview.

John drew a picture of a road, which he called a motorway. Cars were going in both directions and exhaust fumes coming from the rear marked each car. (The reports of putative incidents of buggery may well be relevant in this context.) There was a large road sign on which was marked a roundabout, but without names. There were steps leading to an underpass and a boy on a moped. He added two 'suns': one with a 'happy' face, one 'sad'.

Of this picture John said that the boy on the moped should not be there. He wanted to get to the other side where the road sign was to see if the road sign had the name on it. But it didn't. Of the two 'suns' he said that the sad one was 'good' and the happy one was 'bad' (which is contrary to what most young people would say). The 'bad' one was happy because the boy was going the wrong way, a man was telling him but the boy wouldn't listen: he was happy (to continue going the wrong way). The 'good' one was 'sad' because the man was telling the boy he was going the right way (and he would rather not).

From this it would seem that the 'present' for John includes an awareness of choices of 'goodness' and 'badness' but that these might not necessarily lead respectively to happiness and sadness. Nonetheless he is effectively in a 'no-man's land' because there is no positive indication as to where he is, nor how he can get to where he wants to go.

I brought the interview to an end by commenting that John had indicated some choices in his mind and that I hoped that they would work out for him. I thanked him for the hard work he had done in the interview and wished him well for the future.

Two conclusions

This paper tells two stories: one, the story of John, inside another, the story of the 'one-off' interview. It calls, therefore, respectively for two conclusions, one referring to the interview with John, the other to the paper as a whole. Each conclusion should refer back to theory.

Within the personal construct psychology framework Kelly suggests that it might be useful to take the client's words seriously and allow that they may have some validity as an expression of his or her thoughts and feelings. We might then reflect on the totality of what he or she says in order to trace out any consistent patterns. With this suggestion in mind we might look again at what John has produced in the interview.

His opening response to the personal question 'who are you?' was an impersonal formula. This is reminiscent of the situation of the serviceman who has been given the instruction that, in the event of capture, and for the sake of security, all he should give when interrogated should be his name, rank and number. When actually captured, however, he does not give the formula, but the elements that the formula specifies. By contrast, John gives the formula and it is only under challenge that he actually gives the content.

At the stage of exploration he first of all gives a defence 'don't know', but then tends to give abstractions rather than personal details and talks about a distant future rather than the present. Even in the drawing tasks he consistently moves away from the here and now to the past and future. The present, if anything, would seem to be a dream state. Moreover a number of his answers include opposing messages, leaving it to the listener to make of it what he may. At times, indeed, one is tempted to say 'what a philosopher!' (some of his answers might not seem out of place as quotations from TS Eliot's *Four Quartets*), or 'what on earth does he mean?'

Effectively a construction can be put on to the material that John is constrained to offer a minimally articulated view of himself as a 'little boy lost' or, more seriously, that he needs to camouflage himself with abstractions and ambiguous communications against a world seen as hostile and invasive. Those contrasting options are part of the theme.

Two questions then arise: assuming this construction to have some validity, 'under what circumstances might this make sense?' and relatedly 'how on earth did this come about?' To take the second question first, John's reported *actual* history is one of a problematic early life with possible abuse from adults leading to his being taken into care at the age of 6. We do not know the pattern of life after that but the evidence of disturbing behaviour leading to a special school placement suggests serious breakdowns in his relationships with adults. In the light of this I would suspect that his *experiential* history has been one of massive invalidation of his sense of self and of his expectations of the essential goodness of his 'caretakers'. What he now presents arises from the progressive development of his ways of safeguarding himself against the pain of further invalidation either by creating circumstances where, whatever the approach from 'the other', John cannot be wrongfooted (metaphorically becoming the mirror reflecting the mirror), or, quite simply, by running. And this provides an answer to the first question.

My second conclusion is very short. Kelly puts forward as part of the formal theory the Sociality Corollary which reads:

> *To the extent that one person construes the construction processes of another, he may play a role in a social process involving the other person.*

In more ordinary language, it is not so much a matter of understanding other people (which may indeed be patronizing) but of understanding how they arrived at where they are. This implies a respect for their individuality that transcends the question of agreement or disagreement, approval or disapproval.

As I see it, the 'one-off' assessment interview represents the putting into action of this corollary and is therefore an exemplar of the use of personal construct psychology in the assessment process.

Chapter 14
Who are you? A structure for exploring a 'sense of self' (1989)

I had become increasingly aware of the importance of 'sense of self' as a major theme in relation to problems within a school setting. This, then, is the paper I wrote systematizing my thoughts about the theme and describing the practice whereby I investigated a person's 'sense of self'. The structured interview has proved very illuminating for adults participating in PCT workshops.

Using the process of self-observation, we may be able to realise that our own view of the world isn't even singular and constant, that we have many different and conflicting views inside us all the time. The process of self-observation may convince some part of us (I don't know which) to give voice to alternate views and actions. (Robert Ornstein, 1986: 188)

Not only did it seem that the words man uses give and hold the structure of his thought, but, more particularly, the names by which he calls himself give and hold the structure of his personality. (George Kelly in Maher, 1969: 56)

We have seen persons change as a result of carrying out new commitments and we have seen them change as a consequence of their redefinitions of themselves . . . How often the client in psychotherapy says, in effect, 'I see what I want to do; I see how to do it and where; and I see how someone like me could step out into an entirely new way of life; but I cannot picture myself – me – ever becoming anything other than what I was.' (George Kelly in Maher, 1969: 56, 57)

These quotations might have brought this paper to an end instead of being placed at the beginning because the first was spotted and the second rediscovered long after its contents had been developed. Nonetheless, in essence, they convey the gist and purpose of the paper's intent. It may well be the case that the quotation from Kelly passed unnoticed when first read in the 1960s but acted like the biblical seed falling on fertile ground. Unfortunately it took the seed a rather long time to come to fruition. Be that as it may, the material that appears here represents the culmination of interviewing developments over time in three areas: in technique, in elucidating personal meaning and in theory. The original context of the work was with children and subsequently with young people; however, the interviewing structures have also proved valuable in consultative work with adults and in workshops. The paper is, therefore, a further essay in professional practice.

'Who are you?' technique

The starting point for these developments was a paper by Bugental (1964) in which he published the results of a postal enquiry made to a specially chosen sample of adults. His request had been for the recipients to respond to the question 'who are you?' with *three* statements. I have italicized 'three' because that seemed to me to be an essential part of the invitation. To ask for three answers implies that there may be many more than three possibilities and that the client has freedom to be selective in what he/she may choose to give – in how to present himself or herself. The invitation for three, therefore, became integral to the whole of the subsequent structure of the interview. Bugental analysed the responses in relation to various social and demographic categories but made the further point that some of the 'deviant' responses might be of clinical interest. He did not, however, develop this further.

Applying the technique with children and young people certainly produced answers, but in the absence of normative data (which seemed at the time to be important) and lacking the ways of using them meaningfully, the technique was dropped. It did, however, lead to a constructive variant: instead of asking the individual to give his or her own self-definitions the idea occurred to ask what three things his or her mother, father, siblings and so forth might say to describe him or her. This variant then formed a step in a different direction – the development of self-description grids (cf. Ravenette, 1977c, 1977d).

Relatively recently, however, following parallel developments in ways of elucidating personal meaning, it was found useful to resurrect the idea (Ravenette, 1988). It then became apparent that individual responses to the question 'who are you?' tended to fall into one of two groups, one of which was a categorical description, e.g. name, age, status, the other that of personal qualities, e.g. friendly, kind, clever. This observation, therefore, suggested two separate enquiries: 'who are you?' requiring a categorical definition and 'what sort of a person are you?' requiring a personality description. These two, together with the variant described above 'what would (significant others) say?' now provide three root questions as the basis for the exploration of a person's 'sense of self'. Useful and interesting as the answers to these questions may be in themselves, they represent the surface rather than the depth of a person. Their real value lies in opening up the possibility of going beyond the verbal description of an individual's 'sense of self' into, for want of a better expression, the person's 'sense of being'.

Elaboration of personal meaning

In essence the elucidation of the personal meaning of a statement (in this context the responses to the root questions) required exploration in four areas:

- *What is the statement's contrast, i.e. what does it deny?* This clearly is an extension of the contrast principle underlying Kelly's formulation of the construct. A word of caution needs to be made at this point. Kelly makes the construct the major building block in a person's constructions (or meanings) and there is a danger of pursuing constructs as ends in themselves. In the therapeutic enterprise, however, we need to go beyond the constructs to what lies behind them. Hence:
- *What does the statement further imply?* The use of 'laddering' (Hinkle, 1965) and 'pyramiding' (Landfield, 1971) are valuable techniques in this elaboration.
- *What is the context within which the statement makes sense?* The context here can be of different kinds: e.g. intrapsychic, interpersonal, professional, developmental, historical, and is very much concerned with the question of personal relevance.
- *How important is the statement in the client's view of things?* It is certainly the case that the client should be listened to carefully but it is not necessarily true that every statement that is made carries equal importance. In fact sometimes its importance may well be denied and we do not know unless we ask.

An example drawn from the responses of a psychologist taking part in a professional workshop will illustrate some of these issues. Her first definition of herself was her name.

Is it important to give your name?
No.
How come?
Because most people know me.
How would you describe a person who says that her name is important?
Fairly precise, she didn't want herself to be misunderstood.
How might that have come about?
Something they needed to do in their role – it might be confusing.

(And finally, for this mini-elaboration, a further, self-referent, question.)

Has this ever been true of yourself?
Yes. (But not further followed up.)

There are two more optional questions that become important when the purpose of the interview is consultation or therapy.

* *Under what circumstances would a 'positive' description be disadvantageous and a 'denied' description advantageous?* The purpose of this question will be taken up later.
* *Has there been an occasion when you found that you either were, or afraid that you might have been, the kind of person defined by the 'denied' descriptions?* This is the self-referent question in the above illustration and which points to a coming into awareness of a client's shadow or negative self (cf. Ravenette, 1977a).

These elaborative questions now provide scaffolding around the three root questions out of which an individual's sense of self may be explored. The full structured interview is given as an appendix but in summary the three parts, via the root question and its elaboration, are concerned with:

* *Who are you?* – how the individual chooses to locate himself or herself in self-chosen categories, with an elaboration through the use of questions about personal significance, contrast and the experiential bases of the individual's responses.
* *What sort of person are you?* – seeks a personality description, using contrast to establish constructs, and further elaboration as above. It is in this part of the interview that questions are asked about advantage and disadvantage and, on occasion, the negative self.
* *How would (significant others) describe you?* – the extent to which individuals can make sense of how others see them, which can then lead to the exploration of interactions, especially in the family. The elaborative questioning is, through contrast, in the elicitation of others' constructs, and the importance of these constructs as indicated by rankings. This rank may then be used to develop either or both of self-description and personal values grids.

Theory: 'sense of self' and core constructs

Persons' problems

The use of the word 'sense' in the expression 'sense of self' is intended to convey the meaning of the perhaps rather loose notion 'intuitive awareness'. The expression has the added value of being free of the accumulated luggage attached to the more familiar 'self concept'.

A sense of self lies behind all our actions and colours our interpretations of the multitude of situations in which we find ourselves – witness the positive or negative feelings attendant on confirmation or disconfirmation of our expectations. This personal sense of self also varies from situation to situation, because happenings that validate or invalidate it may vary in meaning and implication according to the spatial or temporal context. For example events that, say, a teacher might find especially pleasing or hurtful in front of a class may lose all relevance within recreational or family contexts. Alternatively those same events may carry different affective connotations if they occur first thing in the morning or late in the afternoon, at the beginning of a term or at the end. To put this more generally, a person's sense of self is at stake according to the nature of the event and the situation.

More particularly, within a personal construct framework it will be recognized that the development of this sense of self is intimately related to the pattern of validation and invalidation over time of those constructs, core and perhaps peripheral, whereby a person maintains some stability of response to the outside world. When problems arise for an individual this sense of self will always be in some way involved yet, instead of taking a close look at this sense to see what might be being invalidated, there is a constant temptation to look only at the outside circumstances both for a cause and for a solution. Each of these may just possibly lie in the individual's sense of self, as the following example illustrates.

A teacher referred a child ostensibly because he was not making progress in learning to read. She also described him as a boy who withdrew from her approaches, stayed very much to himself and was generally uncommunicative. These attributes were in evidence in an individual interview with him. In some despair as to how best to help I asked the teacher to tell me what, deep down, was her sense of herself as a teacher. After some little time she commented on how difficult the question was and then said she supposed that she was a person who cared. She then saw for herself the link that the boy's behaviour was effectively a denial of this aspect of herself. When I saw her a month later she said that things were now all right as the boy, in her words, was just 'remedial'.

Implicitly the invisible problem of personal invalidation was no longer an issue and she was, therefore, free to help the boy with his reading in an objective manner.

The alternative self

The second part of the structured interview 'what three things would you say to describe the sort of person you are?' is a means of eliciting verbal markers for an individual's self-constructs by going beyond immediate responses. It is a matter of experience to observe that clients, seemingly operating a hidden moral dimension, usually give a positive self-description as the first response and a negative description as the contrast. Nonetheless, they frequently also concede that the contrast description might indeed be also true of themselves. These constructs, both in their overt and contrast poles, have their roots in a client's experiential history so, as I indicated earlier, they may very well define 'alternative self', the recognition of which, and its implications, would be important in a therapeutic or counselling context. In the example given in Ravenette (1977a), a 13-year-old girl was interviewed because of her stealing. The description of her 'alternative self', elicited in this instance through the verbal elaboration of her drawings, was:

> She did not care about anything that happened, she must not have feelings, she would not care what happened to her.

When asked when she might be this girl she paused and then said, very softly, 'when I'm stealing.'

The potentiality for change

Ideally techniques of personal enquiry should contain not only information for the interviewer but the potential for change for the client. In a paradoxical way, information for the interviewer may well also be information for the client, certainly when elaborating his or her immediate responses. This is so because the elaborative questions throw light on areas of knowing held at varying levels of awareness. On occasion the new information will, in fact, be new links between old information, which are now forged for the first time. This is tellingly illustrated by Jane's account. As part of a consultation process in connection with her psychological research she took away the structured interview material and applied it to herself. The following is an extract from the letter she wrote to me with observations on what she learned from it.

> *Father* 'unsure of' . . . 'someone he could relate to'. I think this is pretty self-explanatory, particularly if I tell you I had real difficulty trying to think of a description my father would give me at all. In the end this one just about summed it up. *This really stung me when the realization hit me of what I had said (or not been able to say):* speaks volumes don't you think? The reason it was so telling was that I had thought that my relationship with my father was fairly normal. I really respect him as a kind, fair, clever, hard-working person, and that difficulties I had in relationships I might have traced back to some ideas inculcated from my relationship with my mum. In fact *(and this is something that literally only occurred to me for the first time when I did my technique):* it seems that there is rather a gaping hole where I thought my dad was. [my emphasis]

To quote Jane again: 'I think this is pretty self-explanatory'. New information and new links open up the possibility for new constructions. These observations mean that, for Jane, it might now be possible to change the interactions between herself and her father.

A second important way in which change might be promoted is through the exploration of contrast. In a specific sense clients, as I said above, tend to operate a moral dimension when giving their self-description constructs: one pole is implicitly 'good' and the other 'bad'. By asking for the relative advantages of the 'bad' and disadvantages of the 'good' clients are committed to revaluing both neglected and under-valued aspects of themselves and of those situations in which these aspects might be important.

In a professional experiential study session in which John agreed to be interviewed, his second self-description was 'thoughtful', to which he gave as a contrast 'impulsive'.

Is it important to be thoughtful?
Yes.
Why is that?
I can anticipate what I have to do next.
How did that come about?
Through need, dire desperation, in case I couldn't make a decision.
What is the disadvantage of being thoughtful?
That's fatal.
How come?
Feelings win over thoughtfulness. Spontaneous (!)
[Turning to the other pole]
How come a person might become 'impulsive'?
Through anxiety: you don't learn the strategy of coping with anxiety. You jump to the nearest thing.
When might being 'impulsive' be an advantage?
Avoiding danger: delay might lead to really dire consequences.
[His third description was 'selfish' with the contrast 'altruistic'.]
Is being selfish important?
Yes. It's a mechanism for self-protection.
What might be the disadvantage of being selfish?
When it gets in the way of responding spontaneously with people you know: it stops genuine feeling.
[Turning to the other pole.]
How might being 'altruistic' have come about?
You would have resolved problems aroused by core needs: to be able to respond properly.
When might being 'altruistic' be an advantage?
When you look at it, thoughtfulness pushes you to help other people.

This material offers many interesting ideas that might have been taken up in a consultation. For example, the different frames of reference suggested by these two constructs and the double-faced implications of 'spontaneity' implied by them. Such action would, however, not be appropriate in what was a study session.

At a more general level, the operation of the contrast principle itself opens up the possibility of promoting change. This is exemplified in the following extract taken from a letter from an art therapist who came to me for a consultation in connection with her work and in which the use of contrast played an important part.

> In the fortnight since I've seen you, I've pursued the notion of contrast more explicitly with my clients, with useful results, in that several people with whom I had similarly been stuck [a reference here to the personal 'stuckness' which led to the consultation] came up with just what was not being represented, and began to act on it: it stunned me when you picked up my explicit and implicit labelling of 'good' and 'bad' poles: the alternative context comes a shock to the system.

A third way in which change becomes possible arises from the simple fact that, in pursuing the structure of the interview, the client has to look systematically at a number of issues that had previously been ignored. A resident social worker, whilst eliciting the descriptions which significant other people would use to describe her, repeatedly insisted, and with great feeling, that she was not the sort of person that other people said that she was. In completing a self-description grid, however, using these descriptions, she finally said 'oh, but I see that I am like what they say, and I thought that I wasn't'. Having recognized this she also saw the possibility of choosing the kind of person she might be rather than through her negative reactions to others' perceptions of her.

Some observations on practice

It cannot be too strongly stressed that this enquiry into a 'sense of self' is invitational. In other words the client can decline to accept the invitation. Nonetheless, when the invitation is put into the context of problems to be solved, as in consultation or therapy, or experiential workshops, the invitation is usually accepted. There are limits, however, as to how far the exploration should go with any individual and his or her reticence should be respected. This is especially true in workshops where the exploration will probably be in front of others.

The style and form of this enquiry originated in working with children and the question arises as to the age at which children can respond in a meaningful manner to the interview. There is no firm answer to this question. Rather it is a matter of experiment and judgement as to whether, with any individual child, to proceed or not. Needless to say, the posing of these questions to a child represents an event for which s/he has to make some sense. Any response, therefore, is a communication of some aspect of his or her sense of self. The fullest response to the structured interview, however, is likely to occur with older adolescents and adults.

In the matter of timing, the 'who are you?' and 'what sort of person are you?' parts of the structure fall comfortably early in a first interview.

After agreeing the basis for the interview, it is quite natural to broach the issue by saying something like 'I would like to know just who you are: if I were to say to you "Who are you?" what three things would you say?' – i.e. the root question which starts the enquiry. The second part, 'what sort of person are you?' then can be seen to follow quite logically. The third part, 'what would other people say?' may best be left to a separate interview because it is much longer and in some ways more demanding.

A cautionary tale

A professional worker who allowed me to demonstrate one of the techniques on her in a study group commented 'I feel threatened'.

Such a comment is likely to generate anxiety in an interviewer, as it did with me. How, then, should one deal with it? The comment is itself a communication, and a very immediate communication, of some aspect of her sense of self, hence, in line with the structure of the interview, I continued with: 'how would you describe someone who did not feel threatened?'

> They would think the interview was a waste of time.
> So you do not think the interview is a waste of time?
> No.
> So although you felt threatened you did not feel the interview was a waste of time?
> That's right.
> So you feel all right now?
> OH YES

. . . to the relief of the interviewer, and perhaps also the interviewee, through the simple expedient of eliciting a contrast in order to provide a context and a range of convenience for her comment.

Appendix: structured interviewing for exploring a 'sense of self' – three techniques

1. The three root questions are:
   - Who are you?
   - What sort of person are you?
   - What sort of person do other people say that you are?
2. In order to know what lies behind a description we need to know also:
   - what, in a personal as opposed to a semantic sense, it denies – i.e. its contrast;
   - what it implies, which may include the kind of events that justify the description;
   - the circumstances under which it makes sense and its experimental basis;
   - its personal importance.

These four requirements provide the bases for exploring the client's responses to the three root questions given in 1. above.

3. The procedure involves asking the client for three answers to each root question and then carrying out the further exploration as indicated below. The wording for the exploration is neither mandatory nor restrictive, but suggestive and open to further elaboration.
4. Answers to the root question should be recorded on the left and contrast answers on the right, leaving space underneath each for elaborations. This allows the interview to remain on course and facilitates recognizing patterns in the client's responses.
5. Clients do not always answer the question that is put; sometimes they answer the ones that they construct for themselves. It is necessary to note what they say, gently to point out their error, and then return to the original question.

Technique 1: a question of personal identity

Root question: 'I would like to know who you are. If I were to say to you "who are you?" what three things would you say?'

Exploration 1

'Is it important for you to be ...?'
If YES – 'how come it's important?'
If NO 'what sort of person do you think would say that IT WAS important?'
'Why might that be?'

Exploration 2

'You describe yourself as . . . and say that it is important. What sort of person would deny that being . . .was important?'

'How might that have come about? What might lead them to that view?'
Repeat the enquiry in turn for each response to the root question.

Technique 2: a question of personality

Root question
'This time I would like to know not just who you are but what sort of a person are you. If I were to ask you "what sort of a person are you?" what three things would you say?'

Exploration 1

'How would you describe someone NOT like that?'

Exploration 2

[Initial response.]
'Is it important for you to be like that?'
'How come?'
[Contrast pole.]
'How might a person get to be that way? What kind of experience might lead them to be like that?'

Exploration 3

[Initial response.]
'Tell me occasions when this might be a disadvantage.'
'How might that be?'
[Contrast pole)
['Tell me when being this might be an advantage.']
'How might that be?'
Repeat for each response to the root question.

Technique 3: what do other people say?

Root question (for children and young people): 'I would like to explore with you how you think other people might see you. If I were to ask your mother (father, siblings, peer group, teacher, up to seven or eight) what sort of boy/girl you are, what three things would she (etc.) say?'
    For adults use a selection from the client's 'significant others', e.g. parents, spouses, friends, etc., up to seven or eight.
    When three responses have been given:

Exploration 1

'How do you think she might describe someone NOT like that?' Repeat for each of the remaining seven or eight significant others.

Exploration 2

There will probably be many repeats: ask the client to reduce the list of *positive* descriptions to seven or eight by eliminating those that the client feels are most trivial. Finally ask the client to put these into rank order as he/she thinks each of the 'significant others' would. This material is then available for analysis through a rank-ordered self-description or personal values grid thereby giving some indication of the client's interactions with the value systems of these 'significant others.'

Alternative exploration (intensive) (with older pupils or adults)

This should follow exploration 1 (above) and should be reserved for use with two or three of the most important of the client's 'significant others' such as parents, spouses, teachers, etc.

Exploration 3

'Does (your mother) think it important for someone to be like that?'
(Left hand side description)
'Why do you think that is?'
'What experiences do you think led her to that way of seeing things?'
'What for her is so bad about being (right-hand description)?'
'What reasons would she give?'

Exploration 4

'Which of these (mother's) views do you go along with?'
'Is it important to go along with her views?'
'How come?'
'What happens when you don't agree?'
Repeat for the other one or two 'significant others'.

Chapter 15
Asking questions within a personal construct framework (1992)

I was invited to give a talk to teachers attending an introductory special course on personal construct theory at the Institute of Education in London. My original brief was 'asking good questions of children' but as the text says, I broadened it to the much more general 'asking questions', developing some of the implications and illustrating with case material.

> To ask a question is to invite the unexpected.
> (Kelly, 1966 in Maher 1969: 8)

The word belongs to its own world. Beyond every word lies another and another and another and so ad infinitum. We bridge the gap between the world of words and the world of experience by a series of imaginative leaps.

The original invitation to me was to speak to the title *'Asking good questions of children'* with the implied reference to a teacher–pupil context of counselling or personal help rather than academic teaching. This title, as it stands, seemed to me to be rather restricted in scope and yet difficult to encompass in a short time without a great deal of background preparation about theory and practice. Nonetheless, by the simple process of pruning out 'good', which implies some set of unspecified values, and 'children', which implies that questioning adults is a separate domain, the title can be reduced quite simply to 'asking questions'. This now might provide a fruitful topic for developing a set of ideas about questioning within a framework of personal construct psychology and practice. Indeed Kelly (1966) himself saw questions and questioning as serving an essential function in promoting personal growth. The topic might also suggest some notion as to what might constitute 'good' questions.

The nub of the paper is the recognition that the posing of questions points in two different but complementary directions. A question to a person is a communication that inevitably involves interaction and it is necessary, therefore, to take a careful look at what this entails. At the same time a question always arises out of people's existing ways of making sense, their own personal theories of things. These theories, implicit or explicit, give purpose to a question, provide a range of expectations as to what answers might arise, give meaning to answers when they are given and suggest what might be a fruitful continuation. At an everyday level the whole process usually proceeds on an habitual or intuitive basis. For the worker involved in communicating in a professional capacity, however, as in an interview, there will be an espousal of some formal theory. In this paper the theory in question is, by definition, *The Psychology of Personal Constructs* (Kelly, 1955, 1991). For my observations on interactions I draw heavily on *Pragmatics of Human Communication* (Watzlawick et al., 1967). Although using different approaches, each of these protagonists is concerned with meaning and the ways in which meaning is derived from construing the sequence of events. Their similarity and (not necessarily valid) difference is perhaps best conveyed in the following quotation:

> A similar concept is at the basis of Kelly's monumental Psychology of Personal Constructs . . ., although this author does not consider the question of levels and presents his theory almost exclusively in terms of intrapsic, not interactional, psychology. (Watzlawick et al., 1967: 263)

Communication and interaction

In any communication between two people there are always three components and always three ways of responding. There will be an overt content (the expressed message), an implicit statement of 'how I see myself' and 'how I see the other' and an indication of the context within which the communication is taking place. There is a complication in that some of the messages are explicitly expressed, whereas others are expressed non-verbally, for example using tone of voice, physical stance, facial gestures. These may be very subtle and sometimes culturally determined and may very easily be misunderstood.

The threefold response is to confirm, to deny or to ignore each or any of the three components. Thus the act of communication is a complex affair, a large part of which takes place at a low level of awareness. An argument over some apparently purely factual matter may become a battle over who has the authority to determine what is right and wrong. As such, it is implicitly an issue of definition of 'self' and 'other'. By contrast, a refusal to answer a question may be tantamount to a denial that this is the right time and place to pose the question – a denial of the context.

A simple way of summarizing this description of the communication process is by means of a 3 x 3 matrix (Figure 15.1).

	content	sense of self/other	context
confirm			
deny			
ignore			

Figure 15.1: Communication matrix

In general, troubles arise when the communicants are not in agreement about one or more of the components and do not recognize the basis for this. Sadly, such disagreements often end up as a battle over each other's sense of self commonly signalled by angrily asking 'who do you think you are?' or 'who do you think I am?' In the long term, repeated misunderstandings, especially of the sense of self, may lead to a chronic breakdown in interpersonal relationships. It is highly likely that similar phenomena underlie the disaffection of some pupils who sense that what a school has to offer is tangential to their sense of self and their personal concerns. Likewise, current legislation about education is felt by some teachers to be a denial of their professional sense of self and their role in shaping the form and content of education.

Two simple personal experiences will illustrate the value of the model in helping to avoid a breakdown of communication. The first took place in an experiential workshop in which I was demonstrating a form of elaborative questioning with one of the participants. I noticed that the respondent was giving a number of more and more banal responses and this was making me less and less comfortable – my sense of self in this teaching situation seemed to be at risk. In order to do something constructive I initiated the following mini-dialogue.

> Me. I get the feeling that we aren't getting anywhere with this exploration. Why do you think I should be feeling that way?
> Pa. Because it's very superficial.
> Me. Yes I agree with you. So what question should I ask for it not to be superficial?
> Pa. Oh! I thought this was just an exercise.

This response indicated that we were clearly not in agreement about the context in which the communications were taking place, hence my discomfort. It is almost inevitable that a misunderstanding by the one leads to a further misunderstanding by the other and this can then easily escalate into hostility. Fortunately the situation was changed by my second question, which tacitly helped to redefine the context and to reconfirm my own sense of self without challenging that of the respondent.

The second example is even more simple yet could have led each person to label the other (or themselves) as 'stupid', 'forgetful', 'inconsiderate' or what you will. After a long period of being out of touch, a friend and I agreed to meet again and fixed a time and date outside Liberty's, a well-known shop in London's West End. By way of confirming that we knew the rendezvous we each stressed that it was necessary to turn left outside Oxford Circus underground station. Come the day, come the time, we each arrived at Liberty's and paced the pavement for half an hour. Alas neither saw the other. Finally we each went our separate ways.

In trying to puzzle out why this had happened I hazarded the thought that perhaps there were two completely separate entrances to the shop. When we compared our experiences on the telephone that night it was apparent that that was indeed the case. One entrance was in Regent Street and the other in Great Marlborough Street. She had been at the former and I had been at the latter. Each of us had agreed a location (the content of the message) but each of us had filled in the full meaning of the content out of our individual and separate personal experiences. And these were radically different, an issue which takes on salience a little later.

This discussion has concentrated on the nature of communication and interaction. The asking of questions is indeed a special instance of communicating and interacting and, therefore, the same potential problems arise i.e. misunderstandings of a person's sense of self, disagreements both overt and covert over content and context, and the selective validating and ignoring of each other's messages. In turning to the theoretical component of the paper, however, it will immediately be seen that the same issues: meaning, a sense of self and context are central to personal construct psychology.

Theory

As I said earlier, the importance of theory in relation to asking questions lies in the fact that it gives a direction to the questions one wishes to put, it indicates a range of responses that might arise, allows the questioner to come to some understanding of the answers and suggests what might be the next step. Finally, it provides an aim for the interviewing process. Any theory has a number of essential properties. In the first place it provides a language for describing what happens, and to learn the theory involves learning this language.

It then sets up a number of propositions, axioms, postulates, corollaries, whereby this language holds together. It thereby provides a basis for understanding whatever constitutes the focus of interest of that theory. The testing and extension of these propositions provides programmes for research, that is the posing of questions within a theoretical framework. Their application to human dilemmas leads to the posing of questions for the practitioner. Secondly, and in the context of this paper more importantly, a theory is based on a set of beliefs and attitudes both about the nature of 'things' and the nature of 'knowing'. Personal construct psychology offers such an overview and, within that, provides a coherent framework of understanding and action both for theoreticians and for practitioners. What follows is a summary of the special features to the theory, numbered sequentially in order not to lose their separate importance.

Persons create their own personal meanings of themselves and their worlds (1); out of their awareness of similarities and differences (2); arising from the succession of events with which they are confronted (3). These discriminations lead to the development of two-ended constructs (4); which themselves progressively become interrelated into systems (5); which then enable the persons to anticipate with varying degrees of success the likely outcomes of their encounters with the world (6). Central to these systems are the core constructs by which individuals define themselves and these are essential for the maintenance of a sense of self (7). They may operate at different levels, e.g. personal or professional and on occasion may lead to definitions of self that are in opposition and this may cause deep distress for the individual (8). People's behaviour at any moment (and this may involve long- or short-term views) stems from their constructions of themselves and their circumstances at that time (9); and they choose the alternative that seems to them most apt (10). The theory is underpinned by the principle of 'constructive alternativism' – the notion that there is never an inevitably 'right' view of things but rather that there will always be alternatives, some of which may not as yet exist (11).

There is a danger that this formulation might lead to seeing individuals as functioning in highly conscious, deliberate and verbal ways. Such a view would be illusory and stems from the necessity of stating the theory in verbal and precise terms. But constructs appear as words only when we try to explore or explicate them, they are not themselves the words. Behind the verbalized construct is a history of personal experiences involving thought, feelings and actions, and patterns of validation and invalidation. Moreover, constructs and construct systems exist at a low level of awareness and thus usually operate smoothly and of themselves. Indeed some constructs, such as those arising out of an infant's earliest experiences, may have no words available to represent them. It is when things go wrong, when events defeat the smooth running of the system, that persons may usefully be brought to an awareness of their constructs and construct systems, the better to puzzle out what is happening and how to review their sense of self and their circumstances. Although I have chosen to present a broad overview of the theory, two formal corollaries represent important guidelines when we are concerned with asking questions.

- *Commonality corollary:* to the extent that one person employs a construction of experience that is similar to that employed by another, his psychological processes are similar to the other person.
- *Sociality Corollary:* To the extent that one person construes the construction processes of another, he may play a role in a social process involving the other person (Kelly 1955, 1991).

Implications for asking questions

In the light of these observations and corollaries, the logic of the theory suggests that the overarching direction for asking questions will be towards exploring an individual's personal constructions of events – his meanings – with a view to opening up the possibility of personal reconstructions when things are going wrong. To that end, because asking questions takes place in an interactive context, the commonality corollary suggests that part of the questioning will be aimed at arriving at some common ground in relation to experience so that meanings can be agreed, whereas the sociality corollary suggests the need to explore the bases whereby a client arrives at where he or she may be. Without manifestly attempting to satisfy these needs, communication is likely to be at best trivial and at worst tangential. Questioning involves verbal interchanges, so it is necessary to enter a caveat about words. It is a matter of considerable importance that we should have special regard to the fact that there are always two aspects to word meanings (and these loosely relate to the two corollaries quoted above). For any individual there is the commonality aspect, which includes dictionary meaning, the meaning as required in a vocabulary test, and the meaning of common usage and knowledge. At the same time there is the individuality aspect, which, as I indicated earlier, is a personal, private meaning based on the history of an individual's experiencing of events (c.f. the Liberty anecdote quoted above). It is this latter meaning with which the theory is particularly concerned and that the theory invites us to explore through our elaborative questions. In the process it may then become possible both to arrive at some commonality of understanding – agreement on meanings – and also some awareness of how the individual's experiences led him or her to arrive at those meanings. When this happens there is occasion for a potentially therapeutic interchange to take place.

In summary form, and again I use sequential numbering to indicate the importance of each part, elaborative questioning would be based on the following set of propositions:

We do not fully know the meaning of a client's descriptive statements (1), until we also have knowledge of what the statement denies (2), what it further implies (3), the context within which it makes sense (4), and the experiential grounds on which it is based (5). We also need to know

(6) the importance and relevance (7) of the ideas in the statement to that client (8).

Elaborative questioning is built around, but does not necessarily pursue, all of these ideas, and the interview becomes a collaborative venture in the search for personal meaning. In the upshot, questioning of this nature goes beyond immediate and obvious responses and commits the client to search deeply within for answers that honour the question and which satisfy the client's sense of self.

Illustrative material

The following material is taken from interviews with Eric (not his real name) and is intended primarily to exemplify a number of propositions listed above rather than stress the content. Some background information about Eric, however, is necessary to establish a context for this content and in the light of that information many of his responses can be seen to be very informative.

Eric is 18 years old and comes from an army family that is stationed abroad. Currently he is a student at a residential extension college for young people with 'special educational needs'. He was presented to me as extremely limited in ability, not able to do simple addition and subtraction of numbers and not able to remember information over even short periods of time. Despite this, in the first interview, the detail and quality of his figure drawings was consistent with above average ability, which was indeed matched by his humour and manner of response. Nonetheless, it also became apparent that Eric found it very difficult psychologically 'to put two and two together'.

Example 1

> Me. I would like to know who you are. If I were to say to you 'who are you?' what three things would you say? [Eric was surprised by this question and at first gave only one response. Later he added more but I quote only the first.]
> Eric. Eric Arthur Jones.
> Me. Is your name important?
> Eric. Yes.
> Me. How come?
> Eric. You need it to get in and out of the country and if you get a criminal record it stays with you all your life.
> Me. How would you describe someone who says his name is not important?
> Eric. Doesn't care about himself.
> Me. How would he get that way?
> Eric. The way the family brings him up they show him to the world outside . . . He picks up things from the world outside, like swearing.

Example 2 – (same interview but a little later on)

> Me. This time I would like you to tell me what sort of boy you are. If I were to
> say 'what sort of boy are you?' what three things would you say?
> [Eric found this easier. He gave three answers and I quote his third.]
> Eric. Smart.
> Me. How would you describe someone not like that?
> Eric. Dirty.
> Me. What does he do that leads you to say he's dirty?
> Eric. By not washing . . . living outside on the street.
> Me. How would he get that way?
> Eric. His family didn't want him any more. They threw him out.
> Me. Is it important to be smart?
> Eric. Yes. If you go for a job you have to be smart, they won't take you on.
> Me. How would a person get that way?
> Eric. If your dad's smart you get to be like that. When I dress up in a tie mum
> says 'you look too posh'. Maybe that's not the right word!

At the risk of being inferential it would seem that underlying Eric's sense
of self are powerful thoughts and feelings about family and his place in
that family. Moreover his final remark hints at differences between his
parents about him. This became even more apparent in subsequent
interviews.

Example 3

In this interview I invited Eric to use his imagination in making up
stories to a sequence of pictures. The situation itself then becomes part
of the exploration. I present, face down, a pack of cards each bearing a
titled picture.

> Me. I would like you to choose three cards to make up a story. Will you
> choose? Or would you like me to choose?
> Eric. (After a long pause) You choose.
> Me. What kind of person would choose for themselves?
> Eric. A keen person.
> Me. And what sort of person would want me to choose?
> Eric. (With no confidence.) A kind person.

I challenged this as not really being satisfactory and Eric laughingly
agreed. Then:

> Eric. I made the problem myself
> Me. What do you want to do?
> Eric. Pick for myself?

I pointed out that his tone of voice showed that his answer was in fact a
question, again making me responsible for the outcome. As this seemed

to be almost an habitual technique for offloading responsibility for choice I queried that perhaps this was something he had been doing all his life by presenting himself as not being able to learn and not being able to remember things.

Eric then chose three cards and was offered the choice of making a story around all three or making a different story about each one. He chose the former.

> Eric. Dad comes home and meets his wife. The children have been a pain, so father sends them to bed. His sister-in-law comes along, and then says, 'I'll baby-sit, and you two can go out for a drink.'

The aim of my questioning around this rather thin story is to flesh it out with thoughts, actions, feelings and implications and perhaps to arrive at a construction of events which might be relevant for Eric himself.

> Me. What sort of day did the father have?
> Eric. Chaotic.
> Me. How come?
> Eric. Too many problems.
> Me. So what did he do about it?
> Eric. Comes home when they've all gone and talks about it.
> Me. This was not in your story. Was there no one at work to discuss with?
> Eric. Maybe they're not interested.
> Me. How would he feel?
> Eric. Upset.
> Me. What sort of day did the mother have?
> Eric.She'd been having a chaotic day with the children.
> Me. How come?
> Eric. Looking after them, they'd been a pest.
> Me. Doing what?
> Eric. Doing things . . . touching tablets . . . playing with fire . . . not going to bed.
> Me. Were they putting themselves at risk?
> Eric. Yes . . . But they didn't know it.
> Me. So when mum was telling them off would they understand it?
> Eric. No.
> Me. What sort of day did the children have?
> Eric. That would be chaotic too.
> Me. How would they feel?
> Eric. Upset . . . confused.
> Me. So would the children grow up confused?
> Eric. Yes.
> Me. Would they have difficulty learning to read and write?
> Eric. Definitely yes.
> Me. Would a boy who was confused like that be easily hurt?
> Eric. Yes.

I reflected that perhaps Eric was describing some of his own history and that one way of protecting himself from the hurt might be by looking dumb and proving himself incapable by not learning. The sequence reflects an attempt to help Eric 'put two and two together'. If in fact we are right in seeing this as a prime difficulty for Eric it is not surprising that he should place 'chaos' at the heart of his story.

Good questions? Good answers? A prescription? Or a hope?

The questions people put will arise out of their awareness of inter-actional issues and their orientation to people and events. Within the framework of personal construct psychology the questioner will ask of him/herself 'how might these events make sense?' 'How might they come about?' 'Is it possible to promote the creation of new construc-tions in order to widen the choices for action?'

Of the client the interviewer will ask questions that explore the client's individuality of meaning and this entails going beyond the obvious, to ask about what has not been said. He or she will need to listen and observe carefully in order to note apparent discrepancies and gaps in what is said and to use the principle of contrast to illuminate these non sequiturs. He or she will be cautious against settling for mere words rather than personal answers and will be prepared to take risks in the pursuit of achieving and agreeing meaning. All of this will take place within an ambience of validating, and working with, the client's sense of self.

Coda

Questions are keys to unlock, often to the surprise of both interviewer and client, the hidden treasures of the client's buried knowing and experiencings, in order to reconstruct old personal myths and metaphors or to create new choices, the better to breast the march of events that constitutes living.

Chapter 16
Triadic elicitation: academic exercise or key to experiencing? A mini-paper (1993)

As the text shows, this is another paper that arose out of a specific incident. It shows the very simple use of the 'triadic' procedure for construct elicitation, not for assessment purposes but as a means of promoting change. The incident was written up with publication in the EPCA Newsletter *in mind.*

A mini-preamble

The account that follows might have been given a variety of titles but the one I have chosen points to its own moral. Kelly (1955, 1991) was certainly theoretically correct in pointing out that three elements are necessary for the elicitation of a construct and used the formulation as a technique for developing a list of a client's constructs. He did this by applying it systematically to three people at a time, drawn from a sample of known people, each filling a specified role. The resulting constructs in turn provide the basis for a grid that might then reflect something of a client's construct system.

So far so good, but it must be conceded that the total procedure of triadic elicitation can too easily become a formal exercise, taking a great deal of time and occasionally generating feelings of boredom and artificiality. More seriously, the essential focus of the technique is a client's constructs and construct systems – the real people constituting the elements are merely there to meet role specifications. But why not shift the focus of interest away from the constructs as such in order to create personality profiles of the people with whom the client is in a problematical relationship? It is a matter of some good fortune that this is what happened in the consultation that follows.

A mini-consultation

The setting was a residential school for very disturbing children, and my services were available for children and staff. I had been asked if I would offer an interview to Jane, a residential care worker of the school, and she had agreed to this.

In answer to my question as to why we were meeting she said that in her eyes she didn't have a problem but her supervisor thought that she had and that it might be helpful for her, Jane, to have an interview with me.

> So what is this problem that she thinks you have?
> Well, she says it's my attitude, people have been complaining.
> What people?
> I don't get on with the men, not all of them.

I did not know how to play this as there was no acknowledged problem as such and it seemed that 'not getting on with some of the men, not all', was just a fact of life, not a problem. The thought then occurred to me that it might just be worth while to invite Jane to explore – to share her discriminations about men – and that triadic elicitation of constructs might he a useful way of doing this in a systematic and efficient manner. To that end I asked her to give me the initials of four of these men, which she did. As she had difficulty in holding on to their initials in her memory I wrote them in four slips of paper numbered 1 to 4.

> Tell me Jane, in what important way are two of 1, 2 and 3 alike and different from the third?
> Higher status . . . lower status.
> And of 2, 3 and 4 which two are alike but different from the third?
> Tender . . . tougher.
> And of 1, 2 and 4?
> More chauvinist . . . less chauvinist.
> Which of these four men do you have most difficulty with?
> Oh, 4.
> How does he fit on these descriptions?
> Higher status . . . and tougher.
> And more chauvinist?
> [with a laugh] Yes!
> [and now the key question] Where do you fit on these descriptions?
> Lower status . . . (pause) . . . tougher. . .

With astonishment and also amusement she said that perhaps she too was more chauvinist!

> So it is a problem of 'like' with 'like' not getting on with each other?

Jane then told me that when she had started at this school her first meeting was with a male residential worker who had said that there was a pile of ironing downstairs and clearly expected her to go and do it. This made her very angry as she felt that he was typecasting her and fixing her in a limited role. She had never forgotten that and was always expecting that the men workers would see her in that way.

And what did you do?

[very softly] I went and did it.

And you've kicked yourself ever since? . . . Is the attitude of the men like that here now?

No, not really.

So it's like you got a splinter in your finger and didn't get it out. It got infected, and infected your finger and then your hand and then the hand was very sensitive. Perhaps the task now is to get it out.

Jane said that she would try to make things different. I pointed out that 'trying often doesn't work and can then cause more bad feelings because of it.' Could she be more charitable with herself?

I suggested that she experiment with the following technique:

Since we can never control where thoughts come from [which Jane agreed], when the negative thoughts crop up, just recognize them for what they are, acknowledge their presence without judgement, figuratively doff your cap to them and send them on their way with a smile. And as a bonus the other person may think you are smiling at them!

Jane was quite taken with this proposal and recognized that it might be useful in other situations as well. We agreed that there was nothing further to be done and ended the meeting. (This consultation had taken about 15 minutes, hence 'mini'.)

Some further thoughts (not so mini)

A number of other observations now become relevant. Firstly, Jane had been delegated as the staff member to meet me at the station. On the way we had some desultory chat included in which was a half-complaint that men did not share in all the chores in the home – some were considered to be 'women's work'.

Secondly, after my consultation with Jane I joined the staff for a case discussion. Jane's supervisor was the senior care worker present. When the meeting finished there was more informal chat with her in which she mentioned that her husband complained of pains but just how typical of a man, he was in refusing to go to the doctor (or take his wife's advice?). Thirdly, whereas a year ago there had been only one man on the staff, now a change in policy had led to changing the balance from predominantly female to one of comparative equality between the sexes.

Mindell (1987) suggests that gossip (the informal chat of which the observations above are examples) includes unintended communications and that these often point to unresolved issues. So perhaps there was a pattern of incipient chauvinism in the air arising out of the changed balance of staff. Rather than this being acknowledged and dealt with as a staff issue, Jane was seen to have the problem and was asked to work on it through me. No wonder she said that she didn't have a problem and that her supervisor said that she had. And whose problem was it?

Jane was not on duty on the day of the consultation so she was not required at the staff meeting and was free to do as she pleased. Nevertheless she stayed around and after the staff meeting was over came into the room, shook me warmly by the hand and thanked me.

In the light of my title to this mini-paper I suspect that she felt that the 15 minutes' consultation had generated for her some valuable experiencing: for my part, it had been both illuminating and instructive.

Chapter 17
Transcending the obvious and illuminating the ordinary: personal construct psychology and consultation in the practice of educational psychology (1993)

This was another invited contribution to a personal construct theory book, this time from Larry Leitner. As its title suggests, the contribution was written with a special concern about the dual nature of language. Arising from that there are warnings against the seductive power of a client's words and a parallel risk of the blindness that may be occasioned by an uncritical acceptance of the 'obvious'. The paper has an especial, for me, significance as it was my last major intervention in a case before retirement.

A school asks for help in relation to a child whose behaviour is causing concern. After a long and detailed discussion about the child with head teacher and teacher an understanding is developed that puts the child's behaviour in a new light, possibly leading to a resolution of the difficulty. At this point they will be duly appreciative but then add, with some surprise, 'well that's obvious, isn't it?

An analysis of this situation may well go something like this. When a person's seemingly obvious understanding of a situation no longer works, that person has a problem. 'Obvious', however, is only so in the eyes of the viewer. In the event of help being sought to resolve the problem both helper and helped will need to transcend what was previously seen as obvious in order to establish a new, jointly held 'obvious'. In the process there may then be an illumination of what had previously been accepted as ordinary or commonplace, hence the surprise and, of course, the comment 'well, now it's obvious isn't it?'

What follows is the elaboration of these ideas within the practice of consultancy in a school psychological service using the theoretical framework of George Kelly's personal construct psychology.

Introduction

One of the features of personal construct psychology which made a profound impact on me when first it came my way was that it treated ordinary events seriously and saw deeper meanings behind the commonplace. This was equally true both for a person's behaviour, which Kelly saw as always serving some useful purpose, and for his or her language, which gave pointers to the person's ways of making sense out of life. Moreover, the theory suggested ways in which one might explore and come to some provisional understanding of how a person did, in fact, make such a sense. It offered, therefore, a viable basis for practice as an educational psychologist.

The material that forms the substance of this paper derives from applying personal construct theory in a service where psychotherapy and counselling were the exception but where consultation with teachers about individual children constituted a major part of the enterprise. In retrospect I suspect that where I have been maximally successful it has been through mutually 'transcending the obvious and illuminating the ordinary' with those who have asked me for help.

The nature of an educational psychologist's interventions

The work of an educational psychologist in a school psychological service characteristically involves responding to teachers' requests for advice in relation to individual children. It needs to be pointed out that neither teachers nor children ask for help themselves and this provides a marked contrast to those situations in which clients ask for help for their personal problems and for which some form of psychotherapy or counselling might be offered. There are two further complications in that teachers make their referrals through a head teacher (or, in a secondary school, through a head of year) and in that families of referred children need also to have been involved in the referral process. Thus, whilst at an obvious level there is one problem, namely with the child, there are likely to be differing problems at every level – teacher, head teacher and family – arising out of their own constructions of the child and what the child does or does not do. The following case illustrates some of these points and, incidentally, gives in advance an indication of a personal construct style of interviewing.

The headteacher of an infant school referred John, a 7-year-old boy, because the teacher, Mrs A, was finding difficulty in coping with his behaviour. In discussing this the head teacher said that she felt the problem might well be with the teacher, who had recently been divorced and was in considerable personal distress, for which she was receiving psychotherapy. I interviewed John in the presence of the head teacher and it became apparent that he was healthily, if a little exaggeratedly, concerned about his masculinity.

After Mrs A had given a spontaneous account of John's behaviour she was asked to give three separate adjectives which would best describe him, and then to say for each what was her opposite. She gave 'aggressive–peaceable', 'noisy–quiet' and 'active–still'. These three pairs of opposites can be used to frame a three dimensional box with two diagonally opposite corners formed by 'aggressive, noisy, active' and 'peaceable, quiet, still' respectively. I presented this to Mrs. A. in a drawing and hazarded the guess that she would place the children in her class towards these two corners. 'No,' she replied whereupon the head teacher immediately intervened with 'Oh! But what about those six boys you keep telling me about? Aren't they here?' pointing to the 'aggressive, noisy, active' corner. In effect this was a confirmation that, as the head teacher saw things, Mrs A was, in fact, construing children along this complex axis, boys in particular, with John being an exemplar of the 'aggressive, noisy, active' extreme.

In this example it is clear that at each level there is a different issue. The headteacher is concerned about the class teacher's coping in the classroom. Mrs A is explicitly concerned with John's behaviour but implicitly with personal matters following her failed marriage. John is concerned with sorting out his masculine identity. Unfortunately John's behaviour seems to have resonated with his teacher's underlying problems thereby involving the head teacher's necessarily over-riding concern with both teachers and pupils and with their satisfactory interactions within the school. Bringing these matters into the open seems to have been sufficient to resolve the difficulties because no further difficulties were reported, either in relation to the teacher or to John.

The form of intervention illustrated by this case can best be seen as a series of consultation interviews with one, two or more participants, according to the nature of the case. The aim of these consultations will be to move the participants through problems and difficulties which, ostensibly located within a child, inevitably involve the constructions and the concerns of the adults in the situation. The intervention having been made, its effectiveness will depend on the impact that it has made on them. The psychologist would certainly be very interested to see what happened as a result of the intervention and to become involved again if necessary but not to undertake therapy or counselling for the participants.

The 'Janus' nature of language

It is within the context outlined above that language, which is the major medium of communication within the interview, calls for special consideration. When I refer to the 'Janus' nature of language I am pointing to the fact that language has two aspects, a 'commonality' aspect which serves the purpose of communicating meaning to others and an 'individuality' aspect in which language provides verbal markers for personal experiences and private meanings. My use of the expressions 'commonality' and 'individuality' echo, but are not identical with Kelly's use of these terms in two of his corollaries:

- *Commonality corollary*: to the extent that one person employs a construction of experience which is similar to that employed by another his psychological process are similar to those of that other person.
- *Individuality corollary*: persons differ from each other in their construction of events.

Commonality rests on a consensus of meaning, with reference to the dictionary as the final arbiter. The individuality aspect is more complex because it is built up over time and contains within itself associative links with an individual's thoughts, feelings, hopes, fears, aspirations and experiences. Not all of these will necessarily be apparent to individuals themselves (although some hints may be derived from the non-verbal contexts of the spoken word) yet they will colour a person's expectation and influence their actions according to the situation in which they find themselves.

The relative importance granted to these two aspects varies as between individuals and, from time to time, within individuals themselves. Commonality develops out of, and arises from, the child's progressive encounters with the world outside him or herself, first the family, then school and the peer group. Important as the commonality aspect is for the purpose of communication, it is frequently over-valued at the expense of the individuality aspect but, as this paper will show, it is the latter we shall need to have regard to in dealing with problems.

The 'obvious' and the 'ordinary'

Within the context of this brief comment on language the expressions 'obvious' and 'ordinary' take on a special relevance. I give no idiosyncratic meaning to them but rather quote the definition of *'obvious'* in *Chambers English Dictionary* (1988 edition): *'obvious'* *'easily discovered or understood: clearly or plainly visible.'*

By way of comment, this definition points to two separate processes although the language used in the definition obscures the fact. The first is that of understanding as a mental process leading to meaning, the second is that of seeing as a process of discrimination amongst objects. Although the processes are separate they are necessarily linked because there can be no discrimination without some meaning, albeit at the most primitive level.

The same dictionary defines 'ordinary' as: 'according to the common order, usual, of the usual kind: plain, undistinguished, commonplace'.

There is a paradox in relation to the 'ordinary' in that, occasionally, what is seen as 'ordinary' progressively becomes taken for granted and, in the process, ceases to be 'plainly visible'. When this happens, therefore, to illuminate the 'ordinary' is to rediscover the 'obvious' and thereby reinvest it with meaning.

An example will illustrate this. At a consultation with three of the staff in a residential school for 17-to-18-year-old boys we had come to a preliminary view that Frank, characteristically, was reducing the extent to which he was willing to experience both the external world and also his own proprioceptive feelings. In order to test this generalization further I asked about his eating habits, whether or not he had fads or preferences. The key worker immediately said that he ate a big meal (from which one might infer that he enjoyed his food). When, however, I asked further about the manner of his eating I was given a surprising reply.

'He will start at one point on his plate, and, say it's carrots, he will eat all of that before moving on to the next item. When he has eaten that in the same way he moves on to the next. That way he clears the plate. It doesn't matter what's on the plate, that's the way he eats.'

In other words eating has been made into a ritual rather than an occasion either for pleasure in eating or for demonstrating a discriminating palate. Thus, the 'obvious' – the detail of his eating habits – had become relatively invisible until an appropriate question gave it meaning by bringing it into focus.

The essential point in this discussion, however, is of a different order. It is easily forgotten, and sometimes not even recognized, that what is 'obvious' and what is 'ordinary' are so only within the understanding, experience and viewpoint of the individual. Although an assumption of commonality of meaning may work well enough at an everyday level, and between like-minded people, that assumption should always be open to question. At the simplest level an overt agreement on meaning may in reality be a defence against being thought stupid or ignorant, for example 'it's plain as a pikestaff' or 'you couldn't see anything even if it were under your nose.' At a deeper level, and arising from the individuality aspect of a person's language, a too-ready agreement on meaning might obscure a potentiality for serious and apparently unpredictable misunderstandings at some future time.

In essence, when someone engages me in conversation I reconstruct from my own knowledge, experience and associations a set of meanings to attach to the words that person uses. Hopefully there will be sufficient agreement between his or her meanings and those that I have created for meaningful communication to continue between us. (This way of putting things resonates with Kelly's Sociality Corollary to which I shall refer more specifically later in the paper.)

Teachers' problems

The two lines of argument developed in the previous sections can now be brought together in a further consideration of teachers' problems as reflected in their referral of children to a school psychological service. It is the traditional view that such a referral implies that 'something is wrong with the child', that it is the psychologist's job to discover what it is and tell the teacher what to do. In this view the teacher is the channel through which this process is set in motion. By contrast, a personal construct approach puts matters into a somewhat broader perspective by laying much greater importance on the part the teacher plays in setting up a referral.

The idea that 'something is wrong with the child' stems not so much from what the child does or does not do but from the teacher's construction of that behaviour. Moreover, in that whatever is happening represents a breakdown in the teacher's understanding of the situation, that behaviour effectively represents some invalidation of the teacher's own core constructs as a teacher. Typically a teacher will feel anxiety because of an inability to understand what is happening, or inadequacy for failing to be able to make a difference to the situation, or guilt for falling short in his or her construction of self as a 'good' teacher. Placing a referral within a personal construct framework points, therefore, to the requirement, whatever may or may not be 'wrong with the child', to explore the teacher's construction of the situation and to have some awareness of the teacher's personal sense of self.

Inevitably the presentation of the problem in such a referral will rely on the commonality aspect of language for the communication of meaning. A fuller understanding, however, of the situation behind the referral will call for an exploration of the individuality aspect of that same language – to transcend the obviousness that the commonality implies. Out of this deeper exploration a new understanding, and hence a new commonality, may develop that would allow a way forward through the problem.

I can illustrate this through two examples. The first is taken from the same residential school to which I referred earlier. Gary is 17 and shows behaviour that is extremely disturbing because of its unpredictability, its occasional violence and because he is closed to the influence of the staff. After establishing some of the details of what was happening and seeking to move the discussion on, I asked the key worker, a social worker, to give the three descriptions that he felt best characterized Gary. He could in fact give only two: 'loner' and 'strange'. I then asked him to describe boys 'not like that', to which he gave the answers: 'outgoing, joins in willingly' and 'doesn't display strange behaviour'. Bearing in mind the fact that these constructs partly define the basis whereby a social worker expects to operate effectively with a client, I put it to him that Gary makes him feel incompetent. He immediately rejected this but then, after some reflection said 'confused', and with laughter 'inadequate'. Having brought these feelings (which were shared by the other workers, including a teacher) into the open and validated them it was possible to move forward constructively with the interview.

The second example comes from a consultation in an infant school. Miss J was worried about Richard, a 6-year-old boy in her class, whose behaviour she could neither understand nor do anything about. The following information about the boy's background was known. His mother was of West Indian extraction and his father, who had just come out of prison, was white. The parents were deeply antagonistic to each other and each was striving to retain possession of the boy by undermining the other's relationship with him. What follows is part of the discussion with the teacher, presented in the form of an annotated dialogue.

> What does Richard do that troubles you?
> He's noisy.

The key word is noisy. Because this word can cover a wide range of possible activities we need to know just what it is that Richard does in order to establish commonality between the teacher and myself.

> What exactly does he do when he's being noisy?
> He shouts. He draws attention to himself. He's demanding attention.

The teacher gives successively a description, an inference and a diagnosis. 'Demanding attention' is a common formulation given by teachers and usually carried that further implication that a child is not entitled to it. Without challenging the teacher's inference can we explore further in order to draw on the teacher's own individual experiences and creative intelligence?

> Under what circumstances would it make sense for a child to 'demand attention'?
> When he feels 'insecure'.

'Insecure' is another ready-made formulation but one that is pitched at a more sophisticated level than 'demands attention'. It adds little, however, to an understanding of the problem. Can we explore even further?

What would lead a child to feel 'insecure'?
When he doesn't know who he is, he's not sure of his identity.

The teacher has now broken through her previous generalizations (with their implicit commonality) to a recognition of the links between Richard's behaviour in school and his experience at home. This is now a new formulation whereby the central issue to be addressed becomes one of finding ways in which the teacher may validate Richard's sense of personal identity in school in order to ameliorate some of the effects of his divided loyalties at home. (In the ensuing discussion this was in fact successfully achieved.)

Theory and the consultation interview

These matters, under the aegis of personal construct psychology, now provide a framework for discussing the consultation interview. In the approach to such an interview the consultant needs to have in mind the following questions:

* What is the problem for which the consultation is being held?
* What are the underlying bases for that problem?
* What should be the aim of the interview?
* How should that aim be achieved?
* What practical consequences can be envisaged?

Overall the consultation interview may usefully be seen as the working through of a creativity cycle in which the client moves from a 'loosening' process in exploring and elaborating the problem situation to a tightening process in which alternative constructions may be developed and put into operational terms as a basis for future action.

   In order to illuminate the interview further I have abstracted five separated but interrelated aspects of the theory which seem particularly relevant.

1. The underlying epistemological principle of constructive alternativism, i.e. that there are always other ways of making sense of events, the best of which may yet have to be invented.

   In the case of a teacher's referral of a child the importance of this principle is twofold. On the one hand because the teacher is patently stuck in a construction of events that does not pay off, we need to find others that perhaps might. On the other hand when a teacher asks 'why is the child like that?' or 'what is the reason for the child's behaviour?' there is an implicit assumption that there is one correct construction, one 'right' way of seeing things and it is the mark of the 'good' consultant to come up with the 'right' answer. If the teacher is given access to this correct answer then all will be well. The principle of *constructive alternativism* frees us from this implicit demand for truth and allows us to experiment with constructions, not all of which need necessarily be helpful in resolving the problem.

2. The credulous approach, the willingness to accept at face value the 'obviousness' of what the client says not only because, in the words of Kelly, 'his words and symbolic behaviour possess an intrinsic truth which the interviewer should not ignore' but also because it facilitates entry into their personal systems of thought and belief.

This theme provides the basis for the consultant going along with the client in order to establish, if possible, the non-obvious truth behind his language. This is part of the consultant's own internal 'work', not only by listening and matching up from his own understanding and experiences something of the client's own individual meanings, but also by inferring something of the internal logic in the client's communications. In other words, this is one of the ways of transcending the client's 'obvious' in order to illuminate it. The approach does not of course mean uncritical acceptance of what the client says. It does mean seeing his communications as the raw material on which the creative process can work and out of which alternative constructions may spring.

3. Three of the eleven corollaries in the formal presentation of the theory.

- *Individuality corollary:* persons differ from each other in their construction of events.
- *Sociality corollary:* to the extent that one person construes the construction processes of another, he may play a role in the social processes involving the other person.
- *Dichotomy corollary:* a person's construction system is composed of a finite number of dichotomous constructs.

The first two of these two corollaries go together in that they contribute both to an understanding of the problem and to setting at least one aim of the consultation.

Granted a classroom situation out of which a teacher referral has arisen, the teacher and child will each have their own constructions of events. A child's behaviour may be seen as problematic for the teacher in that the teacher's constructions do not enable him or her to cope, either by an understanding of the situation or by some efficacy of action. From the child's point of view, however, the behaviour may well already be a solution to a problem arising out of his or her construction of events rather than being itself a problem, an inference that the teacher has perhaps drawn.

Mahrer (1978), writing from within a different orientation, puts this issue very trenchantly:

> When the little boy in the back row is fidgeting and the teacher experiences the bad feelings of frustrated anger, the little boy is part of the appropriate external situation, while the immediate cause of the teacher's bad feelings lie strictly within her. Where is the problem? Within the little boy or within the teacher? . . . From this vantage point what a colossal error it is to seek changes in some other person when I have the bad feelings. When the teacher tells the school psychologist about the little boy's problem, it is the teacher who houses the problem, not the little boy.

Thus what is presented as a problem by the teacher requires that we go behind that obvious construction to explore the grounds on which the construction is laid. If we can work creatively at this level on a least one case it is possible that the teacher will better be able to cope with comparable situations in the future. In this sense the interview can be seen not just as time for dealing with a specific problem but more importantly as an opportunity for personal growth.

Within this same context, the teacher's referral, arising from the teacher's sense of not being able to cope, suggests a breakdown in effective communication and therefore also in the teacher–pupil relationship. The *sociality corollary* here points out the need for the teacher to try to see things the way the child sees them if he or she is to play a meaningful role in that relationship. The process is, of course, exactly the same for the consultant in relation to the teacher. If the consultant makes no attempt to understand the teacher's ways of making sense the communication is likely to be tangential and therefore unrewarding and unproductive.

The relevance of the dichotomy corollary is of a different order. By making the dichotomous construct the unit in the theory it gives contrast a central place in psychological thinking. We cannot fully know the meaning of a client's statement until we know also know what that statement denies – its contrast. This is valid not only in an obvious way at the level of the construct but also in a less obvious way at the level of a client's deeper understandings. We can elaborate this in a slightly different way. A client's statement carries meaning through its commonality aspect. By seeking for its contrast we may then break through into the individuality aspect of their constructions and construct system and this is a much more profound undertaking than the formal process of construct elicitation. Thus the pursuit of contrast is important as a means of arriving at a psychological understanding of the individual.

Just as the exploration of contrast has a specific value at the level of eliciting the constructs and constructions of the individual client, so it has a more general value for the consultant in moving forward the content of the interview. It suggests asking questions about those things that have not been expressed, but which perhaps have been taken for granted. Some of the polarities which amply repay exploration might be: thoughts as opposed to feelings, internal processes as opposed to actions, what is given prominence (figure) as opposed to what is ignored (ground), what is said as opposed to what is not said, what is specific as opposed to what is general. In fact, at any point in a consultation, the principle of contrast can be used both to elaborate individual meaning but also, by opening up areas not previously considered, to entertain different perspectives. In some ways this discussion has anticipated the fourth of the themes abstracted from the theory, which now follows.

4. The active pursuit of personal meanings especially by way of the question, the consultant's basic tool. To quote Kelly: 'If you don't know, ask. You might just be given an answer.' And 'A pat answer is the enemy to a fresh question.' With my own inversion of this: 'A pat question is the enemy to a fresh answer.'

This pursuit provides a major part of the obvious work of the interview – the elicitation of a client's ways of making sense of things. There is a sense of urgency in dealing with teachers' referrals since teachers are in daily confrontation with the problem situation. They seek some speedy alleviation of their anxieties and time does not stretch forward to a long sequence of interviews, as may be the practice in therapy or counselling. A directness, a Kellyan aggressiveness, therefore, may well get to the heart of matters more quickly than say a Rogerian 'non-directive' approach.

Nonetheless, there are two broad questioning strategies. The first takes the form of directly targeting questions in specific directions, typically by asking, in response to a client's observations, for contrasts, implications, values and specific documentation. These are already illustrated in the case studies quoted earlier. As I said above, questions of this nature go behind the obviousness of what the client spontaneously gives and may open up some of the personal and individual aspects of their communications.

A contrasting strategy is to offer a client quite simply the indirect invitation 'Tell me about . . . ' Depending on the willingness of the client to trust the consultant this will often lead to the communication of personal, albeit loosely formulated, meanings around the problem area. This is illustrated by the case of Mrs. F.

The consultation with Mrs. F. was in relation to stress in school. In talking about events she used the word 'frustrated', which, in the context, seemed unusual to me, presumably because her use of it did not fit with my own reconstruction of her meanings. It pointed, therefore, to some personal use, the commonality of which was being taken for granted. In order to explore this I asked her to tell me about 'being frustrated'. In response she spelled out a richness of meanings, values, implications and feelings centred on 'being unable to control situations'. In particular she said that her marriage was breaking down and this had serious implications for her professional career as she was a Roman Catholic teacher in a convent school. She herself could no longer tolerate her husband and his behaviour, nor would she willingly jeopardize her career. Spontaneously she contrasted all of this with her ability to 'hold a difficult year group of girls in the palm of her hand' together with the personal and professional gratification that came from this. Her narrative (which also included important references to her own life as a child in which power and the use of power was crucially important), therefore, documented a construct, the focus of which was control, which had provided one of the major dimensions by which she had been able to make sense out of her life. The clarification that stemmed from the telling enabled her to make some constructive sense out of her present 'frustration'.

Although I have presented the open 'Tell me about . . . ' as opposed to the direct structured strategy, in practice it is useful to employ them in sequence in order first to elicit and then to elaborate a client's constructions. This is parallel to the rhythms of 'loosening' and 'tightening' which also recurs throughout the interview.

5. An adoption of the propositional *nature of truth rather than the* preemptive *with the corollary of seeking answers to the question 'I wonder what would happen if I saw things like that?' or 'I wonder what would happen if I acted as though that were true?'*
This fifth aspect is aptly illustrated by Philip Toynbee in his autobiographical journal *Part of a Journey* (1982) and *End of a Journey* (1988). In the first of these he writes:

> When Jason asked me why I believed, I said that what had begun as a half frivolous hypothesis – let's see how things would be if we think of man as a spiritual being – had become the best illumination of any that I'd tried. In this light the whole of human life becomes – not intelligible, but alive with meaning; many dimensional; vividly coloured. All the problems have changed into a single luminous mystery. (A mystery is not a problem to be solved but a condition of life to be experienced.)'(p. 112)

In the second volume, on the very first day of the journal he writes, as though drawing a general principle from an experience:

> Almost any venture into strange and alien ideas is worthwhile so long as you have the faculty of lending your credulity. 'Let's support . . . what if it were so?' Even if you come back unconvinced, you may have seen things within that space that you'd never seen before; something perhaps, which the propagators of the ideas never meant you to see in them. (p. 1)

The quotations speak for themselves.

This theme becomes especially important in answer to the last of the consultant's questions, i.e. what should happen next? The 'what would happen if . . . ?' approach opens up the future for the teacher who, willy-nilly, has to return to the problem-provoking world. Whatever it is that is happening 'out there' calls for some new imagination or some new action that might change the relationship between teacher and pupil and which might then bring about a possible resolution of the problem. Posing the question 'what would happen if. . . ?' points precisely in that direction.

Three short examples illustrate some of the possibilities. Mrs H was troubled by 9-year-old Ronald's apparent lack of interest in schoolwork and his rather negative attitude to her. My own interview with the boy, and my discussion with the teacher, gave no indication of any reason for her anxiety. In some despair at having nothing constructive to offer I asked her what she thought would happen if she were to stand back from the boy, observe him closely and keep a record of what happened. I would return in four weeks at a specified time to see how things were. She agreed to do this and when I returned to the school she was waiting at the door. To my surprise she said that my visit was no longer necessary. I asked her what she thought had happened to which she replied quite simply: 'Well, I had help from a student which meant that I could stand back and observe. Really I think that I got off his back and then there was no problem.' In effect my invitation, which implicitly challenged the obvious fact that there was a problem, enabled her to change her role in relation to Ronald and, therefore, to interact with him differently. The problem then dissolved away.

The second illustration involves a consultation with a speech therapist who had responsibility for work with a very disturbing 12-year-old boy in a school for children with severe learning difficulties. She was interacting with him in the rather didactic and inquisitorial way in which she felt she had been trained to interact. It was, however, proving completely ineffective. After considerable discussion, during which it became very apparent that she felt she was being rendered incompetent by the boy, I asked her what she thought would happen if, in her communications with him, she could for a while drop the 'speech' part of her role and adopt instead the more open and reflective style of a 'therapist'. She recognized the professional implications of this suggestion but agreed to try it out. To her surprise she found that she was now able to communicate more fruitfully with him and even to operate more skilfully as a speech therapist. Thus by experimentally letting go of her attachment to a rather narrow role she was able to develop a wider range of skills that would then be available in other contexts.

A third illustration is provided by William, another 7-year-old boy, and his teacher Miss Y. She was worried that he behaved in ways much more like those of a younger boy although in all other respects he appeared to be of average development. In discussion we agreed that her description of William was valid and, moreover, was supported by my own observations. We then debated whether we could engage William's intelligence to observe and comment on his own behaviour. In order to translate this into practice I asked the teacher what she thought would happen if, on some occasion when William had behaved in a very babyish way, she asked him to tell her what he thought a 4-year-old boy would have done. This she accepted as a possible line of action. At my return visit the teacher said, with some feeling, that it had not worked (the inference being that she took my invitation not as an experiment, to see what would happen, but as a piece of advice that was supposed to change things). When, however, I asked specifically what had happened she told me that William had said: 'but Miss, I am 4 years old'. As an experiment this was certainly a success because it allowed William to give an answer about himself that might lead the teacher to respond to him differently. William acted like a 4-year-old because that is what he thought he was. Sadly she failed to recognize it until this was pointed out.

In each of these cases there has been the assumption that the teacher can, in reality, do something that will make a difference in the external world. It needs to be recognized, however, that on occasions, despite the greatest skill and maximum goodwill, the workers are unlikely to bring about change. When this happens the central problem is indeed the teacher's own feelings of inadequacy. The proposition 'what would happen if we see this problem as intractable?' can lead to the response 'then I would not feel a failure because I would recognize my own limitations and would be able to carry on to the best of my ability'. In effect this was the outcome in the case of Gary (see above) in that the staff were able to carry on without feeling bad about things. Eventually Gary ran away, which presumably was his solution to an impossible situation, and he ceased, therefore, to be their responsibility. Sometimes a validation of the impossible is the best that a consultant can do.

Before leaving this section of the paper an important point about the interview needs to be made. The interview itself is an event that clients inevitably make sense out of through their own constructs and construct systems, the limitations of which will set constraints on the accessibility (or acceptability) of ideas which may arise. Although some commonality may be reached between consultant and client there will be levels of meaning and construction that will remain personal and undisclosed. In a positive sense, however, it may well be that it is out of this personal and private response that the client's original genius for resolving a problem may manifest itself rather than anything that the consultant has formally put forward. The new commonality may itself be transcended as a result of a client's further reflections or experiences.

The extended presentation of a final case

I am presenting this case for a number of reasons. Firstly, just as with the first case I quoted, the events that took place presented different problems for each of the protagonists; headteacher, parents, child. Secondly it illustrates some aspects of the interview process that I have already described. Thirdly it shows how consultation can, in fact, be a form of family therapy.

The head teacher's request for help

The head teacher of a comprehensive school rang me and asked what he should do. Barbara was a first year pupil at the school. Her parents had come to him saying that their daughter had twice been mugged by boys wearing balaclava helmets. They had believed Barbara and reported the matter to the police but that had got nowhere. They were afraid it might happen again. What protection could there be? 'If we don't take her seriously the girl will feel abandoned.' The head teacher had doubts about the girl's story. Was she imagining things? Was she suffering from delusions? And what should he do in the face of the parents' request?

My first response was to suggest referral to a child psychiatrist but withdrew that immediately because such a course of action might lead the parents and girl to infer that perhaps she was 'mental'. They would, therefore, reject the idea. It is interesting that the parents saw the girl as a 'victim' and the head teacher as a 'sufferer'. These descriptions each construe the girl as in some sort of 'pain' but are opposite in the sense that the pain comes from without in the case of 'victim', from within in the case of 'sufferer'. Beyond each of these possibilities, however, there might at the same time be other constructions but these could only be explored through finding out more about the situation and the individuals in the situation. With that object in mind I offered a family consultation, to take place in school with the head teacher and this proved acceptable.

The consultation

The head teacher sat at his desk, the parents sat opposite me in armchairs and Barbara sat at my right so that I could engage her during the interview if I wished.

The head teacher identified why we were meeting, outlining briefly the story of the muggings as the parents had presented it to him and indicating that I might be able to help. Thereafter he remained as a silent participant but, inevitably, in the process became a party to all that happened. I then invited the parents, using an open, non-directive approach, to tell me what it was all about.

Father took up the story, speaking strongly and aggressively about the attacks on his daughter. The muggers even knew the name of her younger brother and they had said they would get him as well. When father went to the police after the first mugging they had been helpful and had sent someone to make enquiries. When he went after the second he felt that they did not want to know. In this consultation with me and the head teacher he took responsibility for relating events, just as he had with the police, not allowing (or perhaps not inviting) Barbara to speak for herself. Mother added nothing original to father's account except by being the one who said how worried they were and how they wanted to catch the muggers.

While the parents were giving their account I had asked Barbara to draw a picture based on a line which I had drawn on the paper, adding that if she did this it would probably say something about herself which she could not easily put into words (Figure 17.1). This is a means of involving her in the interview in a protected way. She does not have to say anything publicly, nor defend herself over her own actions.

Figure 17.1: Barbara's elaboration of a line

At this point in the interview, if we accept Barbara's story as a true statement of what had happened, we were trapped because any challenge to this might be seen as disputing Barbara's honesty and the parents' credulity. There was, therefore, no easy way forward. Let us suppose, however, that there are other constructions of events but that these can only be envisaged in the light of more information. In this sense the story of the mugging, because of its dramatic nature and forceful presentation, represents the 'figure' in the total situation, but if it is the 'figure' what is the 'ground'? This we do not know since it consists of obvious matters that the parents have taken for granted and for which I have not asked. To this end, and because I was intuitively aware that there was more to the story than had so far been told, I said quite simply, 'there is something missing, what is it?'

This question, in two senses, now provided a key to the situation. As will be seen it gave a context in which it was possible to make sense of

Barbara's *account* of the muggings but also in opening up a recognition that the *account itself* might be the solution to some other problem of her own which had not as yet been recognized and dealt with.

It was now mother who took up the story of which the following is an abbreviated version.

> Barbara was staying off school on odd days saying that she was sick. I said she must keep going because she would be missing school. One day she came back and said that the school was on strike so she had been sent home. I said they shouldn't do that without warning, I would ring them up. Then Barbara said that was not the reason. She was being bullied. She said about the six boys in balaclavas that they hit her in the stomach. They said that they knew about her brother and would hit him.

Significantly father now lost his aggressiveness and tacitly seemed to have acknowledged that perhaps Barbara's account was not necessarily true by saying he knew something was bothering her inside but did not know what it was.

By this time Barbara had completed her picture. It was drawn in red, showing massive shading like tall grass, with three bare trees and in the sky a flock of birds. Whatever inferences might be drawn from this picture, and they need not be invalid, they would not necessarily represent Barbara's own meanings. To that end I told her that I did not know what her picture meant; would she puzzle out her own meaning and then draw for me a picture which would be the opposite? (It will be recognized that this sequence is almost identical in its use of contrast with that pursued with the parents, using pictures as the form of communication rather than words.) Her second picture showed girls on the swings in a park (Figure 17.2).

Figure 17.2: Barbara's contrast. See text for discussion

The quality and style of the two pictures was markedly different: the second looked like a picture as drawn by a much younger child. Consequently I asked her to look at her two pictures and tell me where a skilled art teacher would place these pictures in relation to drawings of children of different ages. She placed the second picture with drawings of 7-to-10-year-old children and the first with drawings of much older children. I then asked her to tell me about the pictures. Of the first she said 'It was a lonely place. You get all lonely. A mess deep inside.' Of the second picture she said 'The children would be happy.'

Let us now suppose that these two pictures represent two contrasting poles, which effectively define a problem area. It would be a reasonable inference that the basic issue is the transition from primary to secondary school, the onset of puberty with its attendant changes in body functioning, the loss of innocence about sex, anxieties and perhaps ignorance about the changes taking place in herself. Since this issue arises as an aspect of normal development it has potential as an alternative construction, not just for the story of the muggings but for the total context in which they appeared.

Out of all this new material I offered two separate constructions each serving a different purpose. Firstly I told her a Chinese story about a man who saw a ghost who he thought was real and who could also read his mind. He was very worried about this and asked for help from a wise man. This man told him to carry a handful of rice in his pocket and when he met the ghost again he should challenge him to say how many grains of rice were in his pocket. When the worried man did this, the ghost disappeared because he himself did not know the answer. The purpose of this story was to give Barbara a way out of the impasse that she might have created for herself by saying that she had been mugged. Secondly, in order to offer her a different way of looking at which might be her current problems I gave a short commentary on growing up using material which she herself had given: 'Girls grow from happy childhood into young girlhood with a change of school, changes in the body, feelings of loneliness, being afraid of boys and being troubled inside. This is part of growing up and young people are able to deal with it, though sometimes with a little help. If she had some problems which she would like to talk about I would be happy to make an appointment to see her' (which offer she accepted).

These then are new constructions, derived not only from the total story given by the parents, but also from the pictorial and verbalized contents of Barbara's drawings and with them I brought the consultation to an end. Although the story and commentary are given directly to Barbara they are in the air to be heard also both by the parents and by the head teacher, enabling them to entertain different constructions about Barbara. To quote an old saying: 'if you want the walls to hear, talk to the door.'

The outcome

On the day of my appointment to interview Barbara I received a phone message to say that she had been admitted to hospital with suspected appendicitis.

Three weeks later when I enquired again I learned that she had been discharged from hospital as there was nothing wrong. She was now attending school satisfactorily and there were no further problems.

One term later the report was equally good. She seemed to be quite happy and was making good progress with her work. Nothing more had been heard from the parents.

A gloss on the case

As I said earlier, behaviour of a child which is problematic for the adults may in fact be the child's solution to some other problem. Barbara told her mother she had been mugged. But this may well have been a solution to the problem that she had told her mother a 'fib' about the school being on strike. This in turn was an excuse for not staying in school when she should. Not staying in school, by this argument, was the solution to some inner problem, which had not as yet been recognized by Barbara herself, her parents or the school. (In psychiatric terms the problem might well have been labelled incipient 'school phobia' or 'school refusal'.)

It is instructive to work from the other end and take account of the language in which the problem was presented and elaborated. Barbara first complained of 'feeling sick', which mother played down (or perhaps even disregarded). She then describes the boys as 'hitting her in the stomach'. Father concedes that he thinks there is 'something troubling her deep inside' and Barbara herself uses the expression 'a mess inside' to describe the feelings of the girl in the picture. Finally, she must have had further complaints of stomach trouble, to which the parents did pay attention, and which justified a hospital admission for 'suspected appendicitis'.

All of these expressions indicate some important internal discomforts but point at one and the same time to two contrasting sources of the discomfort, physical on the one hand and emotional or psychological on the other. For an 11-year-old girl faced with the physical and emotional changes arising from the onset of puberty, either her own (experientially) or her friends' (through what they say), and the implications for growing up attendant on moving to secondary school, it would not be surprising if for Barbara the expressions carried both meanings at the same time.

Perhaps Barbara needed validation both from a psychologist and from a 'proper' doctor for her to resolve these problems for herself.

In summary

By way of a very short summary of the contents of this paper we might put it all in the following way: in the consultation process a problem inhering in the person presenting it, is communicated by the client through the commonality aspect of language. The problem itself will arise out of some interaction between the client and the external world.

The exploration of the problem will need to be through an elaboration of the individuality aspect of the client's language: personal construct psychology provides a powerful theoretical and practical orientation within which this elaboration may be pursued.

Its resolution may become possible out of some new awareness, some new commonality, which then sheds light on these circumstances which previously had been seen as obvious and ordinary and which had provided a situation within which the problem had arisen.

The consultation process itself offers the possibility of a form of psychological and professional growth that shows striking similarities at an adult level to the processes described by Piaget when children progressively acquire new and broader perspectives whereby they better understand the phenomenal world.

To revert to my opening paragraph, perhaps this too is obvious.

Chapter 18
What would happen if? Personal construct psychology and psychological intervention
(1996)

This paper is also the response to an invitation for an article. The readership of this particular journal might not necessarily be very conversant with PCT, so I give my own construction of the theory, as seen with 'half-closed eyes'. It is a story of an intervention with the care staff of a 15-year-old boy in a residential special school. I was to have re-interviewed him but he had absconded. Instead, I had the opportunity of a consultation with the care staff. The theoretical thrust of the consultation lies in the power of 'contrast' in promoting a reconstruction of the workers' understandings of their particular charge and the consequent revaluing of their own awareness.

The focus of this paper is psychological intervention using a personal construct framework in relation to children who present problems to teachers, care staff and others. Although the work itself is currently carried out in a residential setting for disturbed or 'disturbing' children, it represents something of my own continuing development both in practice and in theory from work in a school psychological service. The sequence I propose to follow is to tell the first part of a story, then to present personal construct theory 'as seen through half-closed eyes' abstracting just two of its themes, which will then be seen to be central in the resumed narration of my story. The themes in question are 'alternative constructions' which stem from the theory's underlying philosophical stance and 'contrasts', a broadening of the notion of bipolar constructs (see below). I shall conclude by making some observations about PCP and the development of imagination in psychological intervention.

The story

I was asked to meet the care staff in one of the houses of a residential school in order to discuss James, now 15 years old, whose behaviour was a serious concern. It had been planned for me to interview James but because of his behaviour at the weekend he had been sent home and had not yet returned. It so happened that I had interviewed James about a year before. At that time he had attended the school on site but had proved too bright and was admitted to a mainstream school, which at that date did not see him as a problem. This report was available and from it I quote the first two and last two paragraphs. As will be seen they say something both of his history and of my observations on the interview itself.

> James has only been at this residential school for a short time and presents something of a conundrum. He has a long chequered history of disturbing behaviour, different schools and different agencies. None of this is apparent here. The one thing that is generally acknowledged is that he is intelligent. An important aspect of his upbringing is a history of splits in the family, rejection by his mother almost from birth, living with a stepmother who did not like him, moving to live with father and a succession of his girlfriends, further rejections.
> Throughout the interview it was my impression that although he responded to my questions it was as though he was psychologically absent but physically present. This was particularly the case when I attempted to go beyond his superficial answers. A full record of the interview would be utterly confusing since the content of his responses effectively defined the context as one of not going beyond the obvious. This, then, implicitly led to his 'self-definition' as intelligent and co-operative but . . . And his definition of me as someone he could string along with pat answers whilst giving away nothing personal.

The final paragraphs read:

> I brought the interview to an end by reminiscing about a farmer sowing his seed in the winter and at first seeing nothing ('of course' said James). Come the spring he looked out and saw sprouts of green coming through the soil. Perhaps some of my questions might be like the farmer's seed and just a few only might sprout.
> I then told him that the interview was finished and that he could go back to his class. He was completely taken aback and did not know how to respond. Somewhat hesitatingly he walked across to the door and left. If I am right that the interview was fundamentally about interactions rather than content it is just possible that he saw it as an event in which his constructions of me and his presentation of his 'sense of self' would receive confirmation. In reality I suspect that I invalidated both and consequently he was 'thrown'.

Personal construct psychology through half-closed eyes

At school, when the art lesson was 'object drawing', the teacher gave a very useful suggestion. 'Look at the object with half-closed eyes,' he would say, 'then you will see the essential form'. Confronted with the task of presenting something of personal construct psychology as simply as possible at various workshops I was reminded of that advice and what follows is my own version, conceding, of course, that others might produce a different account.

(1) Individuals create their own personal meanings of themselves and their worlds
(2) out of their awareness, at different level of consciousness and with affective, cognitive and conative aspects, of
(3) similarities and differences
(4) arising from the succession of events with which they are confronted.
(5) These discriminations lead to the development of two-ended, i.e. bipolar, constructs
(6) which then become interrelated into various systems
(7) enabling individuals to anticipate, with varying degrees of success,
(8) the likely outcomes of their encounters with the world.
(9) Central to these systems are core constructs whereby individuals define themselves
(10) and these are essential for the maintenance of a 'sense of self'.
(11) Persons' behaviour at any moment stems from their constructions of themselves and their circumstances at that time and
(12) they choose that alternative which seems most apt.
(13) The theory is underpinned by the principle of constructive alternativism, i.e. that there never is an inevitably 'right' view of things, but rather there will always be alternatives, some of which may well not as yet exist.

Some of these statements are already exemplified in the report on James that I have given above, for example, the bipolar construct describing him as 'psychologically absent–physically present' (5), my inferences as to his 'self-definition' (9), together with his implied definition of me and reference to the interview confirming or invalidating his expectations (8).

Psychological intervention

Problems

We become involved when a teacher or care worker makes a referral, i.e. an implicit request for help. When this happens we need to recognize that there is never just one problem. The fact of referral already reflects the likelihood that either the worker's sense of competence in coping or skill in understanding – each of which is probably a core construct at a professional or personal level – is at stake. This will seldom be stated as such, but when pressed the referrer may acknowledge it. The usual complaint will be about a child, often with the assertion that he or she has problems, or special needs, whereas in reality it is the child's behaviour or failures that are problematic for the referrer. Not infrequently the child will deny having problems but instead will make complaints about what the world does to him or her. In either case, referrer or child, there will be invalidations of their respective ways of making sense of the world together with threats to their 'sense of self'. As I see things it is the implicit awareness that core constructs are at risk that creates problems, although failures in understanding as such may certainly lead to difficulties.

I was led to this view by the story of Miss B. She had referred a boy ostensibly for his failing to learn to read. I could find nothing in my interview with him that might help to understand the situation but noted his attitude of 'keep away, hands off'. I discussed this with the teacher but felt completely at a loss as to how I might make a difference. In despair I took my courage in both hands and asked how, deep down, she saw herself. After a long pause she commented on the difficulty of my question and then said, 'I suppose it is that I care'. She then immediately saw that the boy's attitudes were invalidating this core construct. When I visited four weeks later she said very simply that there was no longer a problem. It was now just a difficulty.

Alternative constructions

It follows from my observations in the preceding section that the resolution of problems and difficulties usually calls for a change in the way that they are understood. This includes an understanding of the child's 'sense of self and circumstances'. This is not as simple as it may seem. Alternative understandings are unlikely to be arrived at, let alone be acceptable, without exploring the referrer's existing ways of making sense and awareness of how they see themselves. Eventually ideas may need to be put forward propositionally. For example 'what would happen if?' The response to that question may then indeed open the door to further explorations. It is an added advantage that the very exercise of exploring alternative constructions may lead to a change in the existing attitudes and perceptions that the referrer has of the child. Changes in action may then also follow. But how to arrive at such constructions?

Contrasts – a door to alternative constructions

The classic procedure for eliciting constructs is to ask in relation to three elements – for example, persons, events or situations – in what important way are any two of them alike and different from the third. This leads to a dimension of understanding or appraisal that will be adjectival rather than conceptual. When this elicitation procedure is used as a prelude, for example to completing a grid, the process can become rather mechanical. Not infrequently it leads to the difference, or contrast, pole being given either as a simple negation of the similarity pole or as a dictionary opposite. Since the essence of PCP is the personal nature of constructs, these automatic responses seem to me to be minimally meaningful. There are, however, different 'ways of eliciting constructs'.

Landfield (1971), in what he calls a pyramid procedure, abandons the requirement of three elements. Having elicited a single description of a person he then asks the subject to describe someone who is 'not like that'. In my experience this simple 'how would you describe someone not like that?' demands of the subject a conscious search for language with which to verbalize his contrast. This search, and the further elaboration that it entails, often leads to material that may be very illuminating at a 'critical' level. In this sense it then opens doors for an individual to see his or her reality, including his or her 'sense of self' in different ways. I can illustrate this with an example. A lady in a workshop on the use of drawings started to cry. Not knowing quite why this should be, instead of asking why, I asked instead, 'how would you describe a person who would not cry in these circumstances?' She replied that she would think all this was a waste of time. 'So you did not see it as a waste of time?' 'Oh no', she replied and her tears abated. By way of a comment, to ask 'Why?' has an overtone of invalidating a person's right to their own reality. To ask 'what sort of a person would not' validates that right and the response can be used for further growth and development.

The story continued: the staff meeting

A meeting of this nature is always an adventure in the sense that one never knows what will happen. It is also a challenge to one's professional core constructs – can I cope? Can I make sense of things? Can I intervene in some way to make a difference? My basic tool is the question, underlying which is the thought, sometimes put into words, 'what would happen if?' and, pre-eminently the further thought 'What would arise in response to a request for a contrast?' The account that follows shows these thoughts put into action.

There were five residential social workers present. These included the unit manager and James's key workers. An administrative officer was present as an observer. I am indebted to the unit manager for very skilfully recording what happened, not infrequently verbatim, and making this available to me. Passages in double quotes are taken verbatim from this record. Passages in single quotes are my own re-wording of some of that material in order to make clear the logic of the questions. I have also numbered them in sequence.

I was able to present my earlier report on James as a basis for a comparison with the present. Currently he was suspended because of "appalling behaviour at the weekend and a refusal to attend school". At a psychological level my observation of "not giving more than the obvious" in the previous report was matched by the present statement of "his unwillingness to share any of his real feelings, i.e. not to give anything away".

My opening invitation was to look at things within a context of "our own normative frame of reference for judging behaviour in contrast to how we might imagine James might see things". We know how we see the world, but what about James? Specifically I ask: "What sort of boy would behave in ways consistent with how we imagine James sees his world?" (Question 1).

Clearly, however, there are probably many boys who sees things as James does but do not behave like him. My next question is aimed to pick up this contrast: 'What sort of boy sees things as James does but does not behave like him?' (Question 2).

And it would be an inference that James' behaviour may well be an implicit defence against being that sort of boy. Two descriptions were given for Q.1 – 'deeply hurt' and 'rejected' – each with a description in answer to Q.2. I link the two responses into single propositions.

"The boy who is deeply hurt (Q.1) and does not behave like James"
"would feel weak and vulnerable to others if he appeared hurt." (Q.2)
"The rejected boy (Q.1) who did not behave like James"
"willingly accepts substitute love and care from others in place of those who should have (parents)." (Q.2)

This led to an elaboration by staff members to the effect that James does not wish to be seen as other than normal in the eyes of the world. 'He hates it to be known that he lives at this special residential school', i.e. accepting substitute care.

The thoughts expressed in this sequence, adding to my existing awareness, led me intuitively to pose the question: 'Could James be suicidal?' The outcome was surprising and I quote.

'The staff unanimously agreed that some of James's thoughts, fantasies and deeds would indicate that he is at risk of this. They had recently discussed this but with each other one-to-one, perhaps afraid to share fears openly in group until now.'

A further elaboration followed almost as a formulation arising from this new awareness:

"James needs to perceive himself as having strength, power over others and superior intelligence to maintain his self-regard – if this is threatened or lost he would have nothing left."

I do not recall just how this formulation was reached. I suspect that it came from pooling a number of thoughts from different sources. It certainly seems very apt.

My next question followed psychologically from this and hinged on seeing behaviour as surviving: "what sort of a boy is likely to display behaviour like James' as a way of surviving?" (Q.3) with the follow-up question "What sort of boy would have had such experiences and not behave like James?" (Q.4). Again there were two descriptions 'has been abused (emotionally)' and 'unloved'. Once more I link the responses into single propositions

'A boy who has been abused emotionally (Q.3) and did not behave like James' would be
'a victim, compliant, a doormat.' (Q.4)
'A boy who has been unloved (Q.3) and did not behave like James'
'might be withdrawn or seek love from others rather than hide it, try to be popular, loveable.' (Q.4)

If these two Q.4 responses, taken in juxtaposition, were to be valid alternatives for James it would not perhaps be surprising that he should defend himself against them, against, for example, the possibility of falling into a state of homosexual dependency.

At this point I again raised the issue of potential suicide and the formal action that should be taken, e.g. bringing this to the attention of those in authority. And then more surprise. I quote: "The possible danger to others should be noted regarding the observation that James is always testing his limits (like a small child would). This has implications for his safety, does he believe he is invincible? Links with fantasy – belief in UFOs and aliens – believing the X files to be true."

Sadly I missed making the connection that putting himself at risk, as hinted at above, may also be consistent with a less than adequate concern for staying alive. Yet perhaps their observations reflect the possibility that some of the staff were dimly aware of this.

My next question asks 'what kind of boy would see this behaviour (i.e. pushing the limits) as normal?' (Q.5) with the follow-up 'what sort of boy like that *would not* behave like that?' (Q.6). One response only was given: 'egocentric, extending his boundaries'.

"The sort of boy who would be egocentric in this sense (Q.5) but not behave like James, i.e. extending his boundaries . . . would be a boy with support systems, someone comfortable and confident with their ego." (Q.6).

Perhaps this description is that of normal, healthy development in a young person, manifestly not seen to be true for James.

As a way of attempting an integration of all this material in relation to staff anxieties about James, and bearing in mind the implications for their professional and personal core constructs, I put the following key questions:

"James has had an enormous investment (over 10 years) in preventing people from 'getting through' or 'helping'. What would happen if someone broke through his barriers? What are the risks?"

There was a profound silence.

In a sense this was a challenge to social workers' core constructs of themselves as 'helping', 'understanding', and 'relating' with their charges, in particular with James. I think this was tacitly recognized. Hence the silence. I put my understanding of this silence into words, commenting on how hard it was not to try to help because 'helping' in that sense was an important aspect of how they see themselves. But there might be a danger to James and others if the negativities they had recognized underlying James's presentation of himself were to be released.

In retrospect a parallel can be recognized between the situation of James on the one hand and the staff on the other. If we were to succeed in 'breaking through' to him what would he have left? If we were to take away the traditional view of a social worker's professional 'sense of self' as 'helping and understanding' what would she or he have left?

Clearly there was a need for some alternative way of understanding people and situations in order to make good the apparent threat to their role. The communication model of how people interact as described by Watzlawick et al. (1967) seemed very appropriate. They demonstrate how interpersonal communication always calls for a recognition of three components: content (both verbal and non-verbal), an awareness of relationships (how I see you and how I see myself) and the context in which the interaction takes place. Communication automatically involves validation, invalidation or ignoring each or any of these three components. The implications of this model were beautifully captured by the unit manager, who wrote in her record her understanding of what I had suggested: 'Should the aim not be to break through or release trapped feelings or try to change his reality, but try to communicate with him as he is? Accept what he says whilst asking questions to check his reality – raise an eyebrow – cast a seed of doubt to make him question his own perceptions?'

By now I was not surprised that new suggestions from me should immediately be followed by the introduction of new material from the staff. This time it was to the effect that sometimes, just sometimes, he had shown feelings. On one occasion, while telephoning his father, tears had been seen rolling down his cheeks. He was also beginning to acknowledge female members of the staff by calling them by their names. An incident was recalled in which he had 'participated spontaneously in three-way discussions with staff and peers – this was surprising and is positive'. On another occasion he had recently supported a female staff member when verbally attacked by another pupil.

This particular incident was a godsend in providing an opportunity to illustrate the use of the communication model I had just described. James's action could be acknowledged by simply saying, 'thank you for helping me'. This, at one and the same time, validates him as a person and his valuing of the staff member and the appropriateness of the context within which the event had happened.

Perhaps, after all that had been shared in the discussion, these final contributions reflected an incipient reconstruction of James and his problematic behaviour.

Final observations

Quite fortuitously my eye spotted two sentences in succeeding papers of George Kelly (see Maher 1969: 8, 51). They read: 'To ask a question is to invite the unexpected.' And 'Beware of the obvious.' In retrospect it can be seen that taken together they describe the essence of this paper. I asked questions and I did not know what to expect. I guarded against the obvious by seeking contrasts. The aim of this form of enquiry was to promote the possibility that some, if not all, members of the group could begin to see things differently.

I made the point much earlier that to ask for a contrast, in the form I had used in this staff discussion, is usually to require that a person makes a conscious search for an answer. It seldom arises automatically and is seldom obvious. Moreover it is an interesting observation that the search often brings to light material long since known and long since forgotten. Or it may lead to the making of new links and connections between old and new material. The search itself may be seen as the exercise of imagination, in the same way that it requires an act of imagination on the part of the interviewer to invent questions that will promote that end. And, arising from the joint imaginations, alternative constructions of people and events may develop. There can, however, be no guarantee of success.

If my memory serves me correctly I am led to believe that this imaginative process is also the beginnings of the scientific enterprise.

Epilogue: an answer to a 'lifer's' three questions

(1997)

This very short contribution is, in my view, at a different level and with a different focus from what has gone before. Just as the closing paragraph of the prologue looked forward prophetically to future developments in my own progress, so the final paragraph here points to a much wider frame of reference, to life itself and coping with life's vicissitudes. In this sense, perhaps paradoxically, it draws on theory to point to that reality which is beyond theory.

The origins of this short article lie in the International PCP Conference in Seattle in July 1997. It was perhaps a matter of chance that I attended an afternoon session, the second presentation of which was given by Joady Brennan. She described aspects of her research project with 'lifers' serving 'life sentences'. I have to say that it was a thoughtful and moving presentation and it was especially important that she had discussed with some of them what she was proposing to do. Part of the outcome was that they posed three questions, which they would like to have put to those attending the presentation. I had an interesting discussion with Joady after her talk and subsequently she wrote me an appreciative letter. But in the letter she gave three questions the 'lifers' had put. I had not written them down at the time and indeed had not even remembered them, so reading them in her letter came as quite a surprise In particular Question 2 (see below) with its reference to 'frightened' and 'frightening', almost as terms that might be used in an equivalent fashion, immediately struck a familiar chord that I felt, certainly within a PCP framework, called for some elaboration. What now follows is my own way of dealing with the three questions with very special attention to Question 2. It then became clear that my answer to Question 3 would inevitably bear a relationship to what had already gone before.

Quite clearly I am writing to a 'lifer' of my own creation, one who I am assuming might have posed the three questions and who might perhaps be able to make something out of my answers. At the same time, of course, I am also sending the same message to the researcher, Joady, and would like to feel that the contents would be found to have relevance to her own work.

Here now is my letter.

Dear 'Lifer',

Your 'research' worker has passed on to me three questions you have asked and to which you would like some response. I shall delay this in order to make preliminary observations. Your questions are serious and posed in a serious manner. I propose to respond to them seriously. I have to say that they are a challenge in the sense that they call for deep thinking from myself in the light of the circumstances in which you are currently placed. For you 'life', and being a 'lifer', is no academic issue yet, sadly, there is the occupational risk for the 'researcher' to see it as just that. Although I must confess to being a professional psychologist I am neither 'academic' nor a 'researcher' except in the sense that it is an often unrecognized aspect of being human that experiencing may also be seen as some less than conscious research process in the pursuit of meaning and pattern. I am writing this letter to you as though you are a real person rather than an abstraction and my answers to your questions need to be read against the background of these self-revelatory observations.

Question 1. Why did you come to a talk on this kind of subject?

I did not deliberately choose to attend this paper. I did choose to attend the afternoon session in which it was the second presentation. There was a similarity to attending the cinema in my young days when there were usually two feature films and you stayed to see them both. Although this reasoning may not be complimentary to the speaker I can now say that this was one of the two most human and most moving presentations of the whole conference. In a way the letter I am now writing is a tribute to that speaker's offering.

That was a relatively easy, if perhaps, embarrassing, question to answer. The next is much more demanding and has required a great deal of careful thought on my part. I have to say that this has been most illuminating for me, and I hope will be illuminating for you.

Question 2. What do you think made a difference for you, so that you were able to grow up as a man without having to be frightened or frightening?

I am making the assumption that when you use these two expressions 'frightened' and 'frightening' you see them as having reference to yourself in relation to your own life. Hence I need to turn your question round and look at the expressions themselves and your use of them.

On the face of things it looks as though the two questions can be asked, at a personal level, in identical ways. But that is not really true as you will see.

'Frightening', in the first instance, is a description one does not use of oneself but is used by others as a description of a person. It is an index of the effect a person has on the user of the term. For example when you behave in such and such a way maybe I am 'frightened'. In my eyes, then, you become a 'frightening' person. But the label belongs to the user, i.e. to me, and not to the one to whom it is attributed, i.e. to you. You may in time take on the label as having some truth in relation to yourself, but to do so may involve a serious reassessment of yourself in relation to the rest of the world. To admit 'I am a "frightening" person' might indeed have important implications for one's future behaviour.

There is another way, however, in which you may give the label to yourself, but this time stemming from self-knowledge rather than other people's descriptions. Having observed the effect of one's actions on others one might come to the conclusion that if this is how they react to me I must indeed be a 'frightening person'. Such a discovery again might have important implications for one's future development.

By contrast, to describe oneself as 'frightened' is to put a label on one's actual experiencing of events at first hand and the expression then carries the commonly accepted meaning of being, for example, 'scared, terrorized' (*Chambers English Dictionary*, 1988). Thus, the two labels 'frightening' and 'frightened', although sharing the same root, serve different purposes, point in different directions and have radically different personal implications. It is a matter of considerable interest, however, and this is common knowledge, that some persons, who habitually act in a 'frightening' way will, under threat of serious personal harm, collapse into a state of absolute terror. Thus your two expressions can be related as 'I am frightening to other people so they are frightened of me; other people are frightening to me so I am frightened of them'. But it is the same 'I' and the same 'them' in each part of the formulation.

Having thus illuminated that issue I need to turn to another. It is perfectly normal for any person to be 'frightened' or seen by others as 'frightening' according to the circumstances. I could certainly point to occasions when either expression could have real relevance to me. The essential point to make, however, is whether or not the labels become chronically valid as 'self' or other's descriptions of oneself'. In relation to your question it now becomes a matter of how such a chronicity might have arisen

There is the view, and I go along with it, than one tends to see the world as being generally benevolent to one's 'sense of self' and one's interests or that it is generally malevolent or – and this potentially is most devastating – that it is generally capricious. This third view is most devastating because whereas with the first two there is a confirmation that 'I exist', the third is effectively a denial of one's 'sense of self', almost as though my ongoing existence meant nothing to anyone. Again, any of us may feel about the world in any of these three ways according to current circumstances, but, and this is crucially important, we are usually able to tolerate the negative constructions until things change for the better.

I suspect that your use of the two words 'frightened' and 'frightening' is connected to the actual experiencing of the world of people and things and to the perception and toleration of the world as not benevolent, but predominantly malevolent or capricious. Certainly, in the light of such perceptions, one's actions in defence of a profound 'sense of self' might well justify the labels.

I think you may now realize that, without this rather long excursion into language and meaning, had I given 'run of the mill' answers to your question we would probably have failed to achieve any mutual understanding. My answer now is simple but its meaning rests on all that has gone before.

There is no doubt that at times I have indeed seen the world as capricious, and sometimes hostile, in relation to me and my interests. Likewise, at those times I may indeed have been 'frightened' and acted in ways that have appeared 'frightening'. Such occasions, however, will have been transitory rather than permanent and I suspect that I had sufficient trust in my own sense of personal worth and the overall benevolence of the world to transcend both being 'frightening' to others and being 'frightened' in myself.

After all these years, however, in trying to answer a question never before put to me, what I have said may indeed be a self-defensive rationalization. Perhaps, however, just perhaps, the arguments I have put forward may shed a little light on your own concerns.

Question 3 What question do you think should be asked of 'lifers'?

Let me say that for me, even in a research project, the question should be far more than information seeking. Just as your questions led me to some deep thinking so I would like my question to open a door to your own self-awareness. In the process you would at the same time give me information which might promote, to some extent, my understanding of you. My question follows on from all that I have written above. The form in which I give it, i.e. the use of a contrast, may be a surprise to you, but experience tells me that it will probably open doors about yourself that otherwise you might not have opened. As you will recognize, the question and its elaboration go behind 'frightened' and 'frightening' to an underlying alternative potential 'sense of self' – one that may entertain possibilities for the future.

The question

What sort of person, granted very similar life circumstances to your own, would not have acted in ways which lead him to being a 'lifer'?

The elaboration

How might he have got that way?
How would his parents and/or relatives describe him?
How would other men describe him?
How would he describe himself?
What would it have cost him to be such a person?

As I said in my opening remarks, perhaps we are all incipient researchers, albeit unaware of the fact, and these questions might provide a structure for pursuing your own enquiries in a more systematic way. Should you choose to carry out this little personal exploration I wish you an interesting outcome.

Sincerely

The Writer

FINIS

Published and unpublished works by Tom Ravenette

A drawing and its opposite: an application of the notion of the 'construct' in the elicitation of children's drawings. In AT Ravenette (1980) Tom Ravenette: Selected Papers. Farnborough: EPCA Publications. (Reproduced in this book with the consent of EPCA Publications.)

A preliminary experiment in paranoid delusions. Shapiro MB and Ravenette AT (1959) J Ment Sci 429(5): 259–312.

An answer to a 'lifer's' three questions. (1997) EPCA Newsletter 6(3): 4, 22–4. (Reproduced in this book with the consent of EPCA Newsletter.)

An empirical approach to the assessment of reading retardation (1961) Brit J Ed Psychol 31(1): 96–103.

An exploration of personal meanings through the use of drawings: a brief introduction to an experiential workshop (1996). In Walker BM, Costigan J, Viney LL, Warren B (eds) Personal Construct Theory: A Psychology for Future Beings. Sydney: Australian Psychology Society Ltd.

An Extension to the Situation Grid. (Unpublished and undated).

Asking questions within a personal construct framework (1992) The reconstruction of a talk given to teachers at the Institute of Education, London University. In AT Ravenette, Tom Ravenette: Selected Papers. Farnborough: EPCA Publications. (Reproduced in this book with the consent of EPCA Publications.)

Cognitive assessment of culturally handicapped children (1978) In Mittler P (ed.) Psychological Assessment. London: Methuen.

Dimensions of Reading Difficulty (1968) Oxford: Pergamon Press.

Everyone his own scientist. Or behaviour is an experiment (1968) AEP Journal 1(10): 5–9 (reproduced in this book).

Exploring Alternative Identities: An Essay in Personal Construct Theory and Therapy (1977) Paper given to students at the Institute of Child Development, London.

Grid techniques for children. An annotation (1978) J Child Psychol Psychiat 16: 79–82.

Grid Techniques with Children. (Unpublished and undated.)

Intellectual ability of disturbed children in a working class area (1962) Ravenette AT, Kahn JH (1962) J Soc and Clin Psychol 1: 208–12.

Intelligence and intelligence testing: a contribution from a practising educational psychologist (1975)

Kelly on questions (1998) EPCA Newsletter 7(2): 10–11.

Method for Administering Grids with Children (1969). (Unpublished.)

Motivation, emotional blocking and reading failure: a unifying point of view (1974) Therapeutic Education 22(2): 15–22. (Reproduced in this book.)

'Never, never, never give advice.' An essay in professional practice (1980) In AT Ravenette (1997) Tom Ravenette: Selected Papers. Farnborough: EPCA Publications. (Reproduced in this book with the consent of EPCA Publications.)

Open Letter to Educational Psychologists in Training at Southampton University (1985). In AT Ravenette (1997) Tom Ravenette: Selected Papers, Farnborough: EPCA Publications.

Open letter to Wisconsin school psychologists. In memoriam Robin Brewer (1985) In AT Ravenette (1997) Tom Ravenette: Selected Papers, Farnborough: EPCA Publications.

Personal construct psychology and the assessment of young people. The one-off interview (1992) In Maitland P, Brennan D (eds) (1988) Personal Construct Theory. Deviancy and Social Work. (revised second edition). London: Inner London Probationary Service. Originally presented at the first PCT Social Work and Deviancy Conference held at the Kings Fund Centre, London, in February. (Reproduced in this book.)

Personal construct psychology and practitioners who work with children (1985). In AT Ravenette (1985) Tom Ravenette: Selected Papers. Farnborough: EPCA Publications. (Reproduced in this book with the consent of EPCA Publications.)

Personal construct psychology in the practice of an educational psychologist (1988). In Dunnett G (ed.) (1988) Working with People: Clinical Uses of Personal Construct Psychology. London: Routledge, pp 101–21. (Reproduced in this book with the consent of Routledge.)

Personal construct theory: an approach to the psychological investigation of children and young people (1977). In Bannister D (ed.) New Perspectives in Personal Construct Theory. London: Academic Press, pp 251–80. (Reproduced in this book by permission of the publisher Academic Press.)

Planning treatment programmes for school age children (1971). In P Mittler (ed.) CLBA Foundation and ITMR Study Group, No 5. London: Churchill.

Projective psychology and personal construct theory (1972). Proj Psychol J 18(1): 3–10.

Psychologists, teachers, children, how many ways to understand? (1972) AEP Journal 3(2): 41–7. (Reproduced in this book.)

Psychotherapy, 'Psychotherapy' and Therapeutic Interventions: Issue or Non-issue for Psychologists (1975). (Unpublished)

Reading difficulties – and what else? (1970) Paper given to the UK Reading Association, Nottingham, July. (Reproduced in this book.)

Self-description Grids for Children: Theme and Variations. (1977) Paper presented at the Second International PCP Conference, Oxford.

Self-description Grids for Children: Three Versions. Procedures and Analysis (1977) Papers presented at the Second International PCP Conference, Oxford.

Some attempt at developing the use of the repertory grid technique in a child guidance clinic. In Warren N (ed.) (1964) Proceedings of Brunel Symposium.

Specific developmental dyslexia: answer to Critchley (1972) AEP Journal 2(8): 24–31.

Specific reading difficulties: appearance and reality (1978) Presented at a Department of Education and Science Course No 290. Severe Specific Learning Difficulties. Coventry, September 1979 and subsequently published in AEP Newsletter (1979) 4(10): 1–13. (Reproduced in this book.)

Ravenette AT, Hersov LJ (1963) Speed and function in educational retardation. Child. Psychol Psychiat 4, 17–32.

Structured interviewing for exploring a sense of self. Three techniques (1980) (Reproduced in this book as an appendix to Chapter 15.)

The concept of dyslexia: some reservations (1971/2) Acta PaedoPsychiat 38: 105–10.

The exploration of consciousness: personal construct intervention with children (1980) In Landfield AW, Leitner LM (eds) Personal Construct Psychology: Psychotherapy and Personality. New York: Wiley.

The Psychologist in Child Guidance – What is his Role? (1964b) Proceedings of NAMH InterClinic Conference, London.

The recycling of maladjustment (1984) AEP Journal 6(3): 18–31. (Reproduced in this book.)

The Situations Grid. (1968) (Unpublished.)

The Two Way Analysis of an 8 x 8 Grid (Unpublished and undated).

Three Methods of Grid Analysis (1968) (Unpublished.)

Tom Ravenette: Selected Papers. Personal Construct Psychology and the Practice of an Educational Psychologist. (1997) Farnborough: EPCA Publications.

To tell a story, to invent a character to make a difference (1979). In AT Ravenette (1997) Tom Ravenette: Selected Papers. Farnborough: EPCA Publications. (Reproduced in this book with the consent of EPCA Publications.)

Transcending the obvious and illuminating the ordinary: PCP and consultation in the practice of an educational psychologist (1993). In Leitner LM, Dunnett G (eds) Critical Issues in Personal Construct Psychotherapy. Malibar, Florida: Krieger, pp. 217–37. (Reproduced in its original form in this book with the consent of the publishers Krieger.)

Triadic elicitation: academic exercise or key to experiencing? (1992) EPCA Newsletter 2(2): 13–14. (Reproduced in this book with the consent of EPCA Newsletter.)

What's in a name? What's in a grid? A back to basic quest in the rediscovery of meaning (1994) EPCA Newsletter 3(2): 11–12.

What would happen if? Personal Construct Psychology and Psychological Intervention (1996) J Ed Ch Psychol 13(4): 13–20. (Reproduced in this book.)

Who are you? A structure for exploring a 'sense of self' (1989). In AT Ravenette. Tom Ravenette: Selected Papers. Farnborough: EPCA Publications. (Reproduced in this book with the consent of EPCA Publications.)

Who do they think I am? The self-description grid revisited (1995) Paper presented at the International Personal Construct Conference, Barcelona.

References and Further Reading

Bandler R, Grinder J (1979) Frogs Into Princes: Neuro-linguistic Programming. Moab, Utah: Real People Press.

Bandler R, Grinder J (1982) Reframing: Neuro-linguistic Programming and the Transformation of Meaning. Moab, Utah: Real People Press.

Bateson G (1979) Mind and Nature. London: Wildwood House.

Bannister D (ed.) (1970) Perspectives in Personal Construct Theory. London: Academic Press.

Bannister D, Mair JMM (1968) The Evaluation of Personal Constructs. London: Academic Press.

Bannister D, Fransella F (1971) Inquiring Man. Harmondsworth: Penguin.

Brace di Leo Joseph H (1973) Children's Drawings as Diagnostic Aids. New York: Brunner/Mazell.

Bruner J, Haste H (eds) (1987) Making Sense. London: Methuen.

Bugental JFT (1964) Investigations into the self concept: instructions for the WAY method. Psychol Rep 15: 634–50.

Burns RC, Kaufman SH (1970) Kinetic Family Drawings (KFD). New York: Brunner/Mazell.

Burns RC, Kaufman SH (1972) Actions, Styles and Symbols in Kinetic Family Drawings (KFD) New York: Brunner/Mazell.

Burr V, Butt T (1992) Invitation to Personal Construct Psychology. London: Whurr Publishers.

Deikman, Arthur J (1973) The meaning of everything. In Ornstein RE (ed.) The Nature of Human Consciousness. New York: Viking Press.

Di Leo, JH (1973) Children's Drawings as Diagnostic Aids. New York: Brunner/Mazell.

Denicolo PM, Pope M (1997) Sharing Understanding and Practice. Farnborough: EPCA Publications.

Eliot TS (1944) 'Little Gidding' from Four Quartets. Collected Poems 1909–1962. London: Faber & Faber.

Fransella F (1972) Personal Change and Reconstruction. London: Academic Press.

Fransella F (1995) George Kelly. London, Thousand Oaks, New Delhi: Sage.

Fransella F, Dalton P (1990) Personal Construct Counselling in Action. London, Newbury Park, New Delhi: Sage.

Gardner, Richard A (1971) The Mutual Story-telling Technique. New York: Science House.

Goodenough FL (1926) Measurement of Intelligence by Drawings. New York: Harcourt.

Govinda, Lama Anagarika (1977) Creative Meditation and Multi-Dimensional Consciousness. London: Unwin Paperbacks.

Grinder J, Bandler R (1976) The Structure of Magic (2 vols.) Palo Alto, Cal: Science and Behavior Books.

Haley J (1963) Strategies of Psychotherapy. New York: Grune & Stratton.

Haley J (1981) Reflections Therapy and Other Essays. Washington DC: Family Therapy Institute.

Hinkle DN (1965) The Change of Personal Constructs From the Viewpoint of A Theory of Implications. Unpublished PhD. Dissertation, Ohio State University.

Holt J (1970) What do I do Monday? New York: Dutton.

Ichheiser G (1970) Appearances and Realities. San Francisco: Jossey-Bass.

Kahn JH (1978) Recollected grief. J Adolescence 1: 61–79.

Kelly GA (1955) The Psychology of Personal Constructs. New York: Norton.

Kelly GA (1957) Hostility. In Maher B (1969) Clinical Psychology and Personality: The Selected Papers of George Kelly. New York: Wiley.

Kelly GA (1964) The language of hypothesis. In Maher, B (1969) Clinical Psychology and Personality: the Selected Papers of George Kelly. New York: Wiley.

Kelly GA (1966) Ontological acceleration. In Maher, B (1969) Clinical Psychology and Personality: The Selected Papers of George Kelly. New York: Wiley.

Kelly GA (1991) The Psychology of Personal Constructs. Routledge: London. (Republication of 1955 volumes.)

Koestler A (1967) The Ghost in the Machine. New York: Macmillan

Koppitz EM (1968) Psychological Evaluation of Children's Human Figure Drawing. New York: Grune & Stratton.

Kursh CO (1971) The benefits of poor communication. The Psychoanalytic Rev 58(2): 189–208.

Landfield AW (1971) Personal Construct Systems in Psychotherapy. Chicago: Rand, McNally.

Landfield A, Leitner L (eds) (1980) Personal construct psychology: psychotherapy and personality. New York: Wiley.

Lankton S (1980) Practical Magic. California: Meta Publications.

Lawrence D (1971) The effects of counselling on retarded readers. Educational Research 13: 119–124.

Leman G (1970) Words and worlds. In Bannister D (1970) Perspectives in Personal Construct Theory. London: Academic Press.

Lovell K, Gorton A (1968) A study of some differences between backward and normal readers of average intelligence. Brit. J. Educ. Psychol., 38(III), 240–248.

Maher B (1969) Clinical Psychology and Personality: The Selected Papers of George Kelly. New York: Wiley.

Mahoney MJ (1991) Human Change Processes: the Scientific Foundations of Psychotherapy. New York: Basic Books.

Mahrer AR (1978) Experiencing: A Humanist Theory of Psychology and Psychiatry. New York. Brunner/Mazell.

Maxwell AE (1960) Discrepancies in the variances of test results of normal and neurotic children. Brit J. Math Statist Psychol 13: 165–72.

Maxwell AE (1972) The WPPSI: a marked discrepancy in the correlations of the subtests for good and poor readers. Brit J Math Statist Psychol 25: 283–91.

Mehrabian A (1968) An Analysis of Personality Theories. Englewood Cliffs, New Jersey: Prentice Hall.

Mindell A (1987) The Dreambody in Relationships. London: Routledge & Kegan Paul.

Neimeyer G (ed.) (1993) Constructivist Assessment. London: Sage.

Ornstein R (1986) Multi-mind: A New Way of Looking at Human Behaviour. London: Macmillan

Piaget J (1951) Play, Dreams and Imitation in Childhood. London: Heinemann.

Raimy V (1975) Misunderstanding of the Self. San Francisco: Jossey Bass.

Ravenette AT (1964a) Some attempt at developing the use of repertory grid techniques in a child guidance clinic. In Warren N (ed.), Proc. Brunel Symposium.

Ravenette AT (1964b) The psychologist in child guidance: what is his role? In Proceedings of the Inter-Clinic Conference. London: NAMH.

Ravenette AT (1968) Dimensions of Reading Difficulty. Oxford: Pergamon.

Ravenette AT (1969) Child guidance: ideology and institution, or ideal? Mind (autumn), 13–16.

Ravenette AT (1972a) Projective psychology and personal construct theory. J Proj Psychol 18(1): 3–10.

Ravenette AT (1972b) Psychologists, teachers, children – how many ways to understand? AEP Journal.

Ravenette AT (1978) Grid techniques for children, J. Child. Psychol. Psychiat. 16, 79–83.

Ravenette AT (1977a) Exploring Alternative Identities: An Essay in Personal Construct Theory and Therapy with Children. Paper given to the Institute of Child Psychiatry, London.

Ravenette AT (1977b) Personal construct theory: an approach to the psychological investigation of children. In Bannister D (ed.) New Perspectives in Personal Construct Theory. London: Academic Press, pp 251–80.

Ravenette AT (1977c) Self-description Grids for Children: Theme and Variations. Papers given at the Second International Congress of Personal Construct Psychology.

Ravenette AT (1977d) Self-description Grids for Children: Three Versions. Procedures and analyses. Paper given at the Second International Congress of Personal Construct Psychology.

Ravenette AT (1988) Personal construct psychology in the practice of an educational psychologist. In Dunnett NGM (ed) Working with People. London: Routledge.

Ravenette AT (1992) Personal construct psychology and the assessment of young people: the one-off interview. In Maitland P Brennan D (eds) Personal Construct Theory. Deviancy and Social Work (Rev. 2nd ed) London: Inner London Probationary Service.

Ravenette AT (1993) Transcending the obvious and illuminating the ordinary. In Leitner Larry M. and Dunnett, NGM (eds) Critical Issues in Personal Construct Psychotherapy. Malibar, Florida: Krieger (Reproduced in this book.)

Scheer J, Catina A (eds) (1996) Empirical Constructivism in Europe. The Personal Construct Approach. Giessen: Psychosocial Verlag.

Schildkrout MS, Shenker IR, Sonnenblick M (1972) Human Figure Drawings in Adolescence. New York: Brunner/Mazell.

Singer E (1973) Hypocrisy and Learning Disability. In EG Witenberg (ed), Interpersonal Explorations in Psychoanalysis. New York: Basic Books.

Shah, Idries (1969) Reflections. London: Zenith Books.

Siu RGH (1957) The Tao of Science. Massachusetts: MIT.

Skinner, Beavin and Jackson (1967) (see p 25).

Swann J (1962) Toehold on Zen. London: Allen & Unwin.

Thomson A, Cummins P (1992) European Perspectives in Personal Construct Psychology. Lincoln: EPCA.

Toynbee P (1982) Part of a Journey: an Autobiographical Journey. London: Collins.

Toynbee P (1988) End of a Journey: an Autobiographical Journal. London. Hamish.

Tschudi F (1977) Loaded and honest questions. In Bannister D (ed.) New Perspectives in Personal Construct Theory. London: Academic Press.

Vygotsky LS (1962) Thought and Language. Cambridge MA: MIT.

Vygotsky LS (1978) Mind in Society: the Development of Higher Psychological Processes. London: Harvard Univ Press.

Walker BM, Costigan J, Viney LL, Warren B (eds) (1996) Personal Construct Theory: A Psychology for Future Beings. Sidney: Australian Psychological Society.

Watzlawick P, Beavin JH, Jackson DD (1967) The Pragmatics of Human Communication. New York: Norton.

Index